Developing Mental Toughness

Developing Mental Toughness

Coaching strategies to improve performance, resilience and wellbeing

Doug Strycharczyk
and
Peter Clough

KoganPage

LONDON PHILADELPHIA NEW DELHI

First published in Great Britain and the United States in 2015 by Kogan Page Limited

2nd Floor, 45 Gee Street	1518 Walnut Street, Suite 1100	4737/23 Ansari Road
London	Philadelphia PA 19102	Daryaganj
EC1V 3RS	USA	New Delhi 110002
United Kingdom		India

© Doug Strycharczyk and Peter Clough, 2015

ISBN   978 0 7494 7380 8
E-ISBN 978 0 7494 7381 5

British Library Cataloguing-in-Publication Data

A CIP record for this book is available from the British Library.

Library of Congress Cataloging-in-Publication Data

Clough, Peter (Psychologist)
    Developing mental toughness : coaching strategies to improve performance, resilience and wellbeing / Doug Strycharczyk, Peter Clough. – Second edition.
        pages cm
        ISBN 978-0-7494-7380-8 (paperback) – ISBN 978-0-7494-7381-5 (ebook) 1. Performance–Psychological aspects. 2. Stress (Psychology) 3. Toughness (Personality trait) I. Strycharczyk, Doug. II. Title.
    BF481.C57 2015
    155.2'4--dc23
                                                                                        2015021102

Typeset by Graphicraft Limited, Hong Kong
Print production managed by Jellyfish
Printed and bound in Great Britain by 4edge Limited

CONTENTS

ABOUT THE CONTRIBUTORS

Editors and authors

Doug Strycharczyk is the CEO of AQR Ltd which he founded in 1989 – now recognized as one of the most innovative (and fast-growing) test publishers in the world.

Doug's expertise includes development of psychometric tests and programmes – playing a key role in developing MTQ48, organizational development, top team assessment, senior management/leadership development and talent management. Doug has pioneered the application of the mental toughness concept to any sector where individuals face challenge or stressors. He is now recognized as one of the leading authorities worldwide on the application of the model. Doug works in the occupational world, education, social work, sports and health.

Doug has co-authored with Peter Clough chapters in the following leading books: *Psychometrics in Coaching* (Kogan Page/Association for Coaching, 2009), *Leadership Coaching* (Kogan Page/Association for Coaching, 2010) and *Coaching in Education* (2011).

With Charles Elvin CEO ILM Doug has co-authored *Developing Resilient Organizations* (Kogan Page, 2014).

Doug holds a first class honours degree in economics. He has established the AQR Foundation which supports individuals in their development who are otherwise held back for economic, social or family reasons. All Doug's royalties go to the Foundation. E-mail Doug at **doug@aqr.co.uk**.

Professor Peter Clough is Professor of Applied Psychology at Manchester Metropolitan University. His main research interests are in performance in high-pressure environments. He is co-developer, with Keith Earle, of the mental toughness model and of the MTQ48, the mental toughness questionnaire. Working closely with Doug Strycharczyk Peter has researched and demonstrated the application of mental toughness in a wide variety of settings, and is now regarded as one of the leading global authorities on mental toughness and related areas.

Peter's consultancy experience in the world of work embraces a wide variety of projects with major organizations in the UK and elsewhere including the design and implementation of assessment and development centres, work place counselling, employee and culture surveys, leadership development and psychometric testing and training.

Peter's first degree is in psychology and his Masters degree (awarded by Sheffield University) is in occupational psychology. Peter earned his PhD at Aberdeen University. He has co-authored with Doug Strycharczyk *Developing Mental Toughness in Young People* (Karnac, 2014). Peter can be contacted at **p.clough@mmu.ac.uk**.

Contributors

The following have contributed their expertise and their experience of working with the mental toughness model.

Dr Angela Clough is a chartered physiotherapist. Her main applied work is in orthopaedic medicine and sports injuries. Her research focus is on the psychosocial aspects of whiplash. She has extensive experience as a practitioner, a manager and researcher in the UK National Health Service.

Dr Lee Crust is a senior lecturer in sport and exercise psychology at the University of Lincoln. Lee is a chartered psychologist, a chartered scientist and Fellow of the Higher Education Academy. He has published research using qualitative and quantitative methods and has used the MTQ48 in much of his work. His recent research has examined relationships between mental toughness and psychological wellbeing.

Monika Czwerenko is Operations Director for AQR. With Claudine Rowlands, she has organized research and development activity all over the world. Monika is responsible to the application of technology to mental toughness assessment and development. E-mail **monika@aqr.co.uk**.

Dr Neil Dagnall is a principal lecturer in the Department of Psychology at Manchester Metropolitan University. He is a cognition researcher with a particular interest in reality biases and paranormal beliefs.

Dr Fiona Earle is a chartered occupational psychologist working in the field of work and wellbeing. Fiona specializes in stress, workload and fatigue. With significant consultancy experience, she has expertise in the design of assessment centres, development of bespoke psychometric instruments and management development.

Dr Keith Earle is a chartered sport and exercise psychologist working as a senior lecturer at the University of Hull. He is both an active researcher and an applied sport psychologist, working with athletes from a wide range of sports. Keith is the co-developer with Dr Peter Clough of the mental toughness model. Contact Keith at **k.earle@hull.ac.uk**.

Kieran Gordon is the Chief Executive of Career Connect. He has 30 years' experience of working with people of all ages as a professionally trained careers adviser. Kieran is also a past president of the Institute of Career Guidance (ICG), and was a member of the UK Career Council.

Dr Kirsten Jack is a senior lecturer in the Department of Nursing at Manchester Metropolitan University. Her research interests include the use and management of emotion in nursing work, the role of the nurse in public health work and the development of phenomenological research methodologies.

Katarzyna Kloskowska-Kustosz is President of 4Business & People, one of Poland's leading coaching and training organizations. Kasia has worked with MTQ48 for almost 10 years and has introduced it to many international business companies as well as sport clubs eg Legia Warsaw. She has widened her interests to embrace social applications.

Dr David Marchant is a reader in sport and exercise psychology at Edge Hill University. David has worked closely with Peter Clough on a number of projects around mental toughness. David continues to carry out and publish research which embraces mental toughness.

Dr Christian van Nieuwerburgh is an executive coach, academic and consultant. An international authority in the field of coaching, he regularly speaks at conferences in the UK, the USA and Australia. He is Managing Director of Growth Coaching Online, a leading provider of coaching-related online professional development for educators.

Dr John Perry is a lecturer in sport performance and coaching at University of Hull. John is a chartered psychologist and an accredited sport and exercise scientist. John has been instrumental in carrying out psychometric analyses for much of the published research work on MTQ48. His published research includes the development of a new model of sports-personship and examining coping in sport.

Claudine Rowlands is Commercial Director for AQR and works closely with Doug in taking the mental toughness model into more than 80 countries worldwide and into new sectors. Working with the concept since 2002, Claudine has been instrumental in ongoing product development, and is a level 7 coach which provides her with the opportunity to work hands-on with the mental toughness model. She can be contacted at **Claudine@aqr.co.uk**.

Zoe Sweet is Director of Organisational Development for Academi Wales which is the Welsh Assembly Government body responsible for developing and raising standards of leadership development in Welsh public service. Zoe is completing a doctorate where her dissertation is on applications for mental toughness.

ACKNOWLEDGEMENTS

The development of the mental toughness model with its universal application and the MTQ48 has been a long and often complex piece of work. We could not have done it without the support of a lot of people – coaches, development practitioners, leaders, managers and academics – many of whom have given their ideas, their time and their resources freely to enable us to explore new areas and fresh applications.

Some have contributed their experience and knowledge to this book. There are now too many to acknowledge by name. We thank everyone and hope that they are not offended that we haven't singled them out for special mention.

As we develop around the world and into new sectors we can single out one or two people who have encouraged and supported us in spreading the message. Dr Suzy Green in Australia, Aisha Al Suwaidi, CEO of the HR Policies Sector in the UAE, and Bethia McNeill and Graeme Duncan in the world of education and social work in the UK have been amazingly supportive.

Internally at AQR, the whole team has provided support 'above and beyond the call of duty'. Monika Czwerenko has proved to be a proactive collaborator.

We are especially grateful to Doug's co-director Claudine Rowlands – for many years she really has been the hidden cornerstone in all of this work. If you want to see what mental toughness means in practice, look no further.

Finally, Peter offers his dedication to Angela, his wife, and Emily, his daughter – both are tough and sensitive.

Doug offers his to his grandchildren Jay, Charlie, Bella and Axel. They have helped him to find his sensitive side.

Introduction

*Success is not final, failure is not fatal:
it is the courage to continue that counts.* WINSTON CHURCHILL

The mental toughness concept has provided both of us with a truly remarkable journey and experience. What started as a small-scale academic exercise has blossomed into a truly global phenomenon. More about that a little later in this chapter.

Since publication of the first edition, we have seen a significant groundswell of interest in mental toughness as a reasonably complete concept which has a ready application in almost every sphere where individuals, groups and organization have a need to do something of value. It links closely to other concepts which are growing in importance – positive psychology, resilience, character, grit and mindset. Our model and our measure are widely used in the world of work, education, health, sports and, most recently, in social applications.

One pleasing aspect of almost all of this work is that it builds on what practitioners and academics already know and do. It doesn't require anyone to throw away what they know. Our ideas are increasingly being acknowledged as adding ideas, rigour and explanation to the important work that many do. The measure is emerging as a key for more effective diagnosis and, crucially, for more robust evaluation and research.

What has emerged is the identification of a personality trait which appears to be extremely important in considering individual and organizational performance, wellbeing and the development of positive behaviours. All crucially important in enabling people to deal with the pressures and challenge of modern day life.

The first question to answer is: 'What is mental toughness?'

The 4 Cs model

Our work is based on a scientific investigation of mental toughness. Science is all about data and evidence. Reassuringly, the vast majority of the data is supportive, some might appear less so. This is the nature of applied psychology; individuals are complex and no model can encapsulate everything. We define mental toughness as:

> The personality trait which determines in large part how people deal effectively with challenge, stressors and pressure ... irrespective of circumstances.

In the 4 Cs model the overall mental toughness is a product of four pillars:

1 *Challenge*: seeing challenge as an opportunity.

2 *Confidence*: having high levels of self-belief.

3 *Commitment*: being able to stick to tasks.

4 *Control*: believing that you control your destiny.

The model is described in great detail later in this book.

It is useful to understand how we arrived at this model. We adopted what researchers should recognize as a four-step science modelling process: read, create, test, develop and evaluate.

1. Read, read and read some more

Initial work, mostly carried out with Dr Keith Earle, identified a major gap in the literature on mental toughness. Mental toughness was often referred to but rarely operationalized. It became a rather meaningless and empty truism. This type of 'need analysis' is the starting point of most research and development activity.

However, this earlier work was useful in that it provided an insight into what others had imagined mental toughness and similar notions to be. The phrase 'standing on the shoulders of giants' is very apt here. You learn from others and then develop their ideas based on your own knowledge and views. This is what happened here.

2. Create

This is the real joy of science. Creativity has two main strands:

　　a Convergent thinking – the structured approach:

　　Will it work?

　　Can we do it?

　　Have we got the resources?

　　Is the timing right?

　　b Divergent thinking – the intuitive and paradigm-shifting approach:

　　What if?

　　Why not?

　　What assumptions are at work?

Through these two strands a coherent and testable model emerges from the chaos.

3. Test and develop

This is at the heart of scientific research. If something is not directly testable then it does not sit well in the world of science. It should be possible to develop clear and testable hypotheses. These are then actioned and the model developed according to the answers which emerge.

4. Evaluate

When a final model is developed it needs to be evaluated. The key question here is: 'Does it really work?'

Chapters 3 and 4 of this book, substantially written by Dr Keith Earle, put flesh on the bones of this process. They show the time and care that went into the development of the model. It is neither a whim nor an existing concept. It is distinct and built upon sound psychological principles.

　　Once we had a concept we could present with confidence to others – practitioners and academics – we found that we would consistently be asked the same four key questions. In a way they are the obvious questions to ask. There are many questions that can legitimately be asked about our work. We learned to call them the 'four big questions'. Providing an answer to these largely determines the structure of this book:

　　The four big questions are:

1 Does mental toughness really exist?

2 Can it be measured?

3   Is it useful?

4   Can mental toughness be developed?

1 and 2. Does mental toughness exist and can it be measured?

The early part of the book is devoted to these vital questions. The short answer is – we believe mental toughness exists and we have solid evidence to back up that view. Moreover, we have developed the capability to measure mental toughness is a useful way.

Too much popular psychology is merely predicated on an individual's subjective point of view – often emerging as some sort of 'guru'. There is a great deal of 'cod psychology' out there. Much of it faith-based – practitioners adopt these 'models' and 'approaches' on the basis of the flimsiest of evidence – and sometimes no evidence at all. Whilst our views have certainly created many of the hypotheses central to our work and have directed the research, it is important that they have been intertwined with the views and research findings of many others. We are committed to an evidence-based approach.

A longer and more thoughtful answer to these questions is provided in the early chapters in this book. The first two chapters deal with the work's fundamental theoretical beginnings and the design and development of the MTQ48 measure. The following four chapters go into more detail about the 4 Cs, relating them to relevant psychological models. The 4 Cs model does not in any way negate these, it simply builds upon them.

3. Is it useful?

Doug trained as an economist and found his calling in the world of business and Peter as an applied psychologist. What binds our philosophies together is the belief that things we do can and should impact on performance. It is therefore a driving mission that we show that knowing about and measuring mental toughness is more than simply an academic exercise. When answering the question of whether or not it works there are two main approaches.

First, there are the technical aspects. Is it reliable, valid and robust? Information about these aspects is included in the first two chapters. Another way of looking at this question is to think about how the measure and model have been used and whether or not this has helped us understand why some people perform better than others.

Secondly, an equally important consideration has been whether using the instrument has been effective in applied settings. A number of diverse case studies have been included in the book to provide an answer to some of these points. We hope you find these interesting and useful. They include a review of research findings in peer-reviewed journals. The peer-review process is the bedrock of true research. Papers accepted are published solely on their merits, not by grace and favour.

Other case studies focus on education and learning. They raise an important point. Our offering of mental toughness is a developmental concept. It is there to help people progress. The evidence overwhelmingly suggests that it does just that.

4. Can mental toughness be developed?

We believe it can. A good deal of practice in the sports world suggests that this is the case.

Is it nature or nurture? Evidence in this book shows that there is a clear genetic link in mental toughness. As everybody suspects: some people are born tough. This nature element is supported by recent findings relating to brain structure. Again this cutting-edge research is described here. Nevertheless, mental toughness levels can be changed. A case study is included in the occupational section of this book showing an organizational case study that demonstrates that formal mental toughness training can work.

The majority of the final third of the book is given over to techniques that can aid in mental toughness development. They are drawn from many areas of applied psychology and we have asked experts in areas such as relaxation, attention control and fatigue to provide chapters that help explain the processes involved.

Four fallacies about mental toughness

In our many contacts with people, we find we are regularly asked many more questions than the big four addressed earlier. These too are all good questions and must have an answer if the questioner is to be confident about mental toughness. We will attempt to address some of the more popular directly in this chapter. They all address what seem to us to be emerging fallacies. However, we cannot answer every question that has ever been raised, or will be raised, in this book.

We have sought to provide enough information throughout this book for readers to make their own informed choice. When teaching first-year undergraduate psychology students at the University of Hull, Peter continually stresses the importance of a questioning approach to psychological models. Just because someone says it with conviction does not mean it is true. They need to provide evidence that is verifiable. We are confident we can do this for this concept.

Fallacy 1: Implicit in the model is the suggestion that everyone should be mentally tough

It is obvious that some people are tougher than others. We would also argue that mentally tough individuals are better able to deal with high-pressure environments. Consequently they tend to do better at school, at work, at competitive sports etc, and are likely to excel in work assessment systems.

However, it should be clearly noted that the opposite of mental toughness is mental sensitivity *not* mental weakness. A mentally tough person will deal with stress, pressure and challenge by not letting it 'get to them'. Colloquially it is 'water off a duck's back'. A mentally sensitive person will feel the impact of stress, pressure and challenge and it will 'get to them' and they will feel some consequent response. They will be uncomfortable in some way.

A balanced society needs a mix of the sensitive and the tough. It is quite difficult to identify a highly successful yet sensitive elite sports-person just as it can be equally hard to identify a tough-minded artist.

Please note that this does not mean that the mentally tough are not emotionally intelligent, whatever that may mean. Emotional intelligence (EI) describes a different kind of sensitivity – EI people are sensitive to what is happening around them and how others are responding to what they do. Emerging evidence suggests that mental toughness and emotional intelligence can, and often do, go hand in hand!

Whereas it might be generally true that the mentally tough seem to get a better deal in life – for instance, they often earn more, they are more likely to get promoted, they are more likely to be materially successful – all we are saying here is that sensitive people find it harder to cope with the stressors and pressures of life. They are more likely to show some of the negative consequences of not being able to deal with life's changes and will often suffer from conditions such as depression and anxiety.

But it is also clear to us that the techniques in this book can be helpful for everyone – the mentally sensitive as well as the mentally tough – in dealing with the world as they find it. Some people want to be tough. Others want to stay as they are, but they would also like to have a toolkit of skills to deal with some situations which prove difficult for them. And there are also many people who are successful in life on their own terms but who are mentally sensitive and not mentally tough.

In education mental toughness does provide an advantage – but it's certainly not the only, or even necessarily the most important thing for everyone. Measuring mental toughness allows teaching staff to provide the appropriate support for different types of individuals.

What is wrong in being sensitive? Our short answer is 'Nothing at all', but being mentally sensitive does make life a bit harder. At the same time we know that mentally tough people are far from perfect – there are potential downsides to being mentally tough too. These are covered in the chapters describing the 4 Cs (Chapters 6, 7, 8 and 9). Everyone has development needs.

A mentally tough individual may accidentally bruise others by not fully recognizing the needs of a more sensitive individual and, through that, may adversely affect their own performance if that relies in part on the co-operation of others. Knowledge of what you are will always allow people to make better choices.

As ever, there are many ways of looking at this issue. In economics there is an interesting approach that sometimes enables us to ask the same question and get two different but helpful answers. Economists will talk about macro-economics (the big picture) and microeconomics (the specific). So we can ask a global question: 'Should we have a more mentally tough society?' We might conclude that, as stated above, we would prefer a balanced society but we might argue for a small shift generally in one direction or another to secure a desirable benefit.

A more specific question might be about our children or our work colleagues. Would I like them to be more mentally tough? We might, because we know they are likely to get a better deal in life and they are likely to achieve more. However, we also know that they can lead a satisfactory and fulfilling life whilst remaining comparatively mentally sensitive and we know that we can support them in this.

Fallacy 2: We are only interested in success at work or in sports

We are both drawn to performance enhancement and it can be easy to believe this is only related to things like output, sales, promotions, salaries and qualifications. In many situations these are very important but we are concerned with a much broader understanding of performance.

When an economist talks about creating and distributing wealth, they generally talk about wealth in its widest sense. Wealth is the sum of everything that adds up to wellbeing and contentment. In our mental toughness training programmes one emphasis is on the importance of goal setting. This could relate equally well to being the best parent or the happiest person in your town.

Mental toughness does, of course, relate to achievement orientation, meaning that many mentally tough people are driven to rise to the top of their careers. However, this is not for everyone. As an example, Peter was working with an elite swimmer on the fringes of international success. They worked together to develop her mental toughness with a good deal of success. The outcome? She decided to stop swimming and do something she wanted to do more instead! Just because you are good at something does not mean you want to do it. Through developing her mental toughness she was able to make better life choices for herself!

Fallacy 3: Mental toughness is a macho, male-dominated concept

At first sight this might appear to be true. However, when you consider this statement in the light of fallacy 2 it seems less true.

Mental toughness is all about being all you can be. Whilst competitive by nature, mentally tough individuals are often simply competitive with themselves. They are internally referenced. There is very clear evidence from the many studies we have carried out that men and women are equally tough. There may be some differences in the coping systems adopted and the willingness to express their feelings but the underlying core toughness emerges from study after study as being identical.

Fallacy 4: Mentally tough people are uncaring and individualistic

This obviously relates to some extent to fallacy 3. Mentally tough individuals can function well in teams. Many elite sports-people play in very cohesive team settings and they are undoubtedly mentally tough.

The idea that tough individuals are always domineering and unsupportive is simply not the case. Much bullying behaviour and petty sniping is a result of low self-esteem and insecurity. If you are tough, secure in your own skin, there is little need to prove your superiority by 'proving' the inferiority of others.

Defining and describing mental toughness

The first step is to begin the process of defining and describing mental toughness. In our work we now run hundreds of workshops around mental toughness and, between us, make at least 80 major presentations each year at conferences around the world. Quite often we will open a discussion about mental toughness without explaining to anyone precisely what we mean by the term. This is deliberate. We do it to make a point.

What we consistently find is that you can actually have a sensible discussion about mental toughness without a pre-agreed definition. The term is reasonably accessible and self-explanatory. Most people guess correctly that it is to do with mindset and on that basis can usefully contribute to a discussion. However, there will nearly always come a point where the participants recognize that they may also be describing slightly different ideas. It will emerge that some will in fact be speaking about resilience. Others will be talking about commitment and tenacity. Yet others will be describing confidence in some form.

It is ultimately important to have a clear definition of mental toughness around which everyone can examine the concept from their own standpoint. One of the earliest steps in the development of the model and presenting it to the outside world was the development of a clear, accessible and sensible definition of mental toughness. From that solid base most of the rest can follow.

Incidentally, there are still some who do not like the term 'mental toughness' although as the term becomes better understood and used more frequently this is beginning to diminish. For better or for worse, for the present time, psychologists and practitioners in the various fields in which we work have accepted that mental toughness is the correct and proper term for what we are about to describe.

The remainder of this chapter provides another perspective to the mental toughness story. It explains how we came to work on the concept and what provoked our interest. If you are impatient to get into the meat of the matter, skip these sections and move straight on to Chapter 2. You can return to this later.

The remainder of the book explains and brings up to date everything that has emerged through research and application of the model and the measure. It is written with two audiences in mind. One consists of students of psychology who want to know about the concept, how it works, the evidence, and how it relates to the rest of psychological thinking. The other consists of practitioners who are concerned with understanding it well enough to be able to use it effectively in their work. As far as we can we have written it to be accessible to both audiences.

How and why we became engaged with mental toughness

In September 1996 we were running, at a hotel in Newport in South Wales, the first of a series of development centres designed for Her Majesty's Customs & Excise which will eventually embrace over 700 senior managers.

In the evening, when relaxing before reflecting on their day's work, Peter began to describe enthusiastically some work he had been carrying out in sports psychology. It revolved around a concept he calls 'mental toughness' and it seemed to provide an explanation for a number of interesting things.

For instance, he suggested that this is why, often, very talented athletes, sports-people and teams lose out to less able but apparently more successful opponents. This is not that uncommon. It is one of the elements that make sporting contests so interesting – it's not always the favourite who wins. There seemed to be factors involved in success and performance other than talent and raw ability. Peter spoke about confidence, challenge, emotional control and commitment and how these too play a part in sports success.

He and a colleague, Keith Earle, had developed a simple 18-item questionnaire to measure some of this, which had delivered some promising results. Later that evening they got down to the business of the day and began to analyse what they had observed with the dozen or so managers who had participated in the development centre exercises. Amongst those observations were things like:

- some of the managers were clearly very able and exceptionally well qualified but didn't achieve as much as others;
- some who were less knowledgeable were able to be surprisingly effective;
- some appeared happy to be on the programme and were using every minute for their own benefit, whilst others were reluctant attendees;
- some approached the events in the programme with real determination to achieve something, whilst others seemed to be fearful about their attendance.

As the review proceeded, both of us experienced a sense of déjà-vu. A great deal of the observations about managerial behaviour echoed what had been described for the behaviour of athletes earlier. And they appeared to have similar implications.

One immediate consequence was that Doug approached the organizers of the development centre programme with an idea. They agreed that we could introduce, into the battery of tests already being used in the centre, a short 'mental toughness' questionnaire purely for research purposes. Thus began a remarkable journey which has since taken a concept which was 'trapped' in one domain and steadily developed it into a concept which has universal application and real significance for the performance, wellbeing and behaviour of most people in all walks of life.

By 2002 research had enabled Peter and Keith to pin down a robust definition of mental toughness and in 2003 Doug and AQR took the concept to the occupational market. In 2008 it was being used in the educational market at secondary, further and higher education levels in Switzerland and the UK and by 2015 it was being used in more than 80 countries worldwide. In 2010 the first pilots in health and social applications had begun. And of course the sports sector had consistently shown an interest – mostly supportive, sometimes challenging.

Doug has described it as the 'penicillin of the people development business.' Like Fleming's work, the discovery was almost accidental, the impact enormous.

We have both found ourselves 'making a genuine difference' for a lot of people and organizations. We now work regularly in areas that we would never have guessed we would, or could. This includes working with the disadvantaged and the underprivileged as well as the more usual applications in the worlds of work, education and sports.

The mental toughness model we have developed and its associated measure (the MTQ48) are nowadays discussed globally and hardly a week passes without us receiving comments and ideas about our work from around the world. We have had the genuine privilege of being involved with outstanding researchers, business people, educators, sports-people and many others. This constant interaction has both consolidated and developed the model.

We have welcomed enquiry, comment and criticism – it has helped us to develop a better concept. We are especially interested to hear from readers who are interested in using the concept and the measure in some way.

Mental toughness provides an answer and solutions to many issues, but obviously not all. It is simply another tool to help enhance our understanding of behaviour and performance.

The importance of stress 02

To fully understand the concept of mental toughness some background into the broader theoretical underpinnings of the stress literature is required, as these are closely related constructs. One could argue that a central component of mental toughness is how effectively one deals with potentially stressful situations.

Within modern psychology the concept of stress remains a major focus of interest, with significant research efforts across a range of disciplines including work psychology, sports psychology, clinical psychology and health psychology.

Selye (1936, 1950) proposed what he labelled the 'general adaptation syndrome' (GAS), which has its foundation in the activation of the adrenal cortex in response to stress. Where Selye furthered the stress literature was in his idea that changes in homeostasis were not just a response to alterations in the environment, but that an animal's physiological systems could be trained to maintain adaptive defences against potential exposure to stress. This idea of 'toughening' is still relevant today.

Whilst there has been much debate about the exact definition of stress, there has been some broad agreement about the physiological and psychological correlates. Typical physiological changes include increased blood pressure, sweating, increased heart rate and dry mouth, and psychological behaviours may range from aggression to social withdrawal (Tenenbaum, 1984). These symptoms and behaviours can either occur independently or together with stress emotions. In summary, it is generally accepted that stress is associated with physiological changes, a range of psychological behaviours and changes at the subjective/emotional level.

Situational moderators of stress

Research carried out by Frankenhaeuser (1971) was particularly significant in exploring the physiological responses to a range of task-related variables. She found that responses in the adrenal glands were at their greatest when individuals were required to carry out tasks which are multifaceted, require quick decisions and when the individual has little control over the event in question. This highlighted three of the most widely considered stress-inducing factors in the occupational setting – aspects of workload, time pressure and control.

With regard to workload, Wickens (1986) has provided a framework for considering those tasks which are more likely to be stressful when combined. He based his model on the principle that we have a series of 'pools' of resources upon which we can draw to carry out information processing tasks. Essentially, the model proposes that we will be less able to cope effectively with multiple tasks which draw on the same resources: eg two tasks which require auditory processing will clearly be more demanding (and therefore potentially stressful) than tasks which combine aspects of verbal and auditory processing.

Time pressure is a further factor that has been broadly accepted as an occupational stressor (Hackman and Oldham, 1976). This is clearly intuitive, as it is not difficult to imagine the increased subjective pressure associated with having too many things to do in not enough time.

With regard to the factor of control, this construct is a fundamental aspect of the occupational stress literature. The influential job design model of Hackman and Oldham (1976) and the demands-control model of Karasek (1979) both highlight the importance of control as a moderator of the work–stress relationship. The issue of control will be returned to throughout this book, as this construct is an important component of mental toughness.

Stress and performance

A good deal of the research in stress and performance looks at situational moderators and considers stress from the response perspective – as an out-come of environmental conditions. Our work on mental toughness looks at the individual's perspective of stress as a causal factor. Stressors exist but they don't always give rise to stressed people. Stressed people often perform less well; but sometimes they perform better. It depends on the individual.

The following is a brief summary of the most important theoretical explanations regarding the impact of stress on performance.

Drive Theory

Early researchers in the field of performance psychology suggested that there was a direct and linear relationship between arousal and performance. This view was embodied in the work of Hull (1943, 1951). Hull proposed a Drive Theory. In simple terms, this theory states that as an individual's arousal level increases, so does the performance of that individual.

This somewhat simplistic explanation of the relationship between arousal and performance clearly does not fully explain the complex nature of the relationship. However, Drive Theory did highlight the important role of physiological arousal in performance and the theory obviously has implications for training and learning environments.

The Inverted-U Theory

Extremely influential work in this field was undertaken by Yerkes and Dodson (1908) who developed the basic premise on which Drive Theory was based and examined the relationship between arousal and task difficulty and their effect on performance. This is perhaps the best known theory linking stress and performance.

Initial findings were formulated into the Yerkes–Dodson law, which, in its simplest terms, proposed that, as the complexity of a skill required to carry out an action increase(s), the amount of arousal required for peak performance decreases. We see this in all walks of life. Irrespective of the type of skill involved, it was argued that performance always conforms to the inverted-U principle.

Building on this work Easterbrook (1959) attempted to explain this stress–performance relationship and theorized that, as arousal increases, attention narrows and it is a consequence of attentional narrowing that results in information (cues) being missed. It is argued that, at first, the cues missed are irrelevant ones but as arousal increases, relevant cues are likely to be missed.

Therefore, when arousal is low the presence of irrelevant cues is a distracting element and causes performance to diminish. At the optimal level of arousal only the irrelevant cues are removed and performance is subsequently high. When arousal is too high, attentional focus is narrow, and this results in both relevant and irrelevant cues being discarded. It is not difficult to see how this could lead to reduction in performance, as proposed by the Inverted-U Theory, and this clearly provides some explanation to the process which may underlie the stress–performance relationship.

Catastrophe Theory

Since the development of the Inverted-U Theory, a number of researchers and practitioners have criticized this simplistic explanation of the relationship between strain-related variables (stress, arousal and anxiety) and performance.

The basic tenets of the theory propose that relatively small increases in arousal have a proportionate effect on performance, either negatively or positively, and that optimal performance is obtained when arousal is moderate.

However, the Catastrophe Theory, proposed by Fazey and Hardy (1988) brought a new perspective to bear and challenged both of these assumptions. They proposed that when athletes are faced with debilitating stress, they encounter more dramatic decrements in performance (hence catastrophic in nature). They further suggested that small reductions in arousal do not bring the athletes back to their previous level of performance when under a similar amount of stress. This model clearly proposes a more complex relationship between stress and performance than accounted for in earlier models.

Individualized Zones of Optimal Functioning (IZOF)

Yuri Hanin (1980, 1986, 1997) proposed that an individual has their own zone of optimal state anxiety within which they perform at their peak. This theory differs in two ways to the Inverted-U Theory. It states that the optimal level of state anxiety differs from individual to individual and does not always occur on the mid-point of the continuum. Secondly, the optimal level of state anxiety is considered to be a bandwidth rather than a single point. With regard to the issue of individual differences, this has real relevance in the field of applied psychology. If this optimum level of anxiety (stress level) can be determined, it is then possible to manipulate, through psychological interventions, the level of anxiety which has been shown to correlate with optimal performance.

Flow Theory

This theory proposed by Csikszentmihalyi (1990) is closely related to the IZOF model, in that it attempts to identify the optimal performance state for an individual (known as the 'flow' state). This state is one in which the performance of the task undertaken is done in an effortless and almost mystical manner. This theory supports anecdotal evidence from athletes and has been subject to research scrutiny for the past 15 years.

Jackson (1992, 1995, 1996) defines flow as '... a state of optimal experiencing involving total absorption in a task, and creating a state of consciousness where optimal levels of functioning often occur' (1995, p 138).

A further definition proposed by Csikszentmihalyi himself includes a loss of self-awareness (becoming one with the activity) and a loss of time-awareness. While these models clearly have value in the way they describe an important subjective state, they perhaps fall short of providing an explanation of the broader stress process.

Individual moderators of the stress process

Recent models of stress have placed the individual at the centre of the process, providing an active interaction with the situation (Lazarus, 1993). In light of the importance such researchers place on the individual, a major goal within this field has been the identification of potential individual differences which can moderate the stress process.

Many factors have been considered including high trait anxiety and low self-esteem. Trait anxiety is a personality factor that predisposes an individual to view certain situations as more or less anxiety-provoking (Spielberger, 1983). Individuals with high trait anxiety will perceive events as being more threatening than individuals with lower trait anxiety.

Mental toughness is potentially the most important individual difference in the stressor–strain relationship.

An applied perspective on mental toughness, stress management and peak performance

Stress is a complex phenomenon that has a number of definitions. We have adopted the following:

> Stress is an adaptive response, mediated by individual characteristics and/or a psychological process, which is a consequence of any external action, situation or event that places special physical and/or psychological demands on a person.

The main themes encompassed by this definition are that:

● stress is not necessarily bad and is unavoidable;

● individuals react differently to the same stressors;

● stress can be physically and psychologically damaging.

There is a bewildering array of stress models but we find the work of Karasek provides the best understanding of organizational stress. This model concentrates on two components: 1) job demands (these cause stress) – psychological stressors such as the requirement to work fast, having lots to do, working to targets, conflicting demands; 2) job decision latitude (these help individuals deal with stress) – workers authority to make decisions, variety of skills they use. An ideal job for most people will therefore involve high demands but will also give the employee high degrees of operational freedom and a wide variety of activities that will allow them to use all their skills.

However, it is also the case that, as already noted, in many occupations stress is unavoidable – and is a feature of a culture or of the environment in which the organization operates. The challenge here is to identify stressors and to enable the organization and its staff to develop and implement coping strategies and mechanisms which enable them to handle their work without damage.

The stress definition and the following model developed by AQR provide the starting point for much of our work in this area.

The AQR stress model

Stress is most often a result of the combination of the impact of some stressor and the way that the individual responds to that stressor. It is how we respond that leads us either to feeling stressed or alternatively to achieving peak performance.

Stressors exist. They come from many sources. We will be the source of many in our own right. Some will arise from the close relationships we have in our work groups, family groups, social groups etc. Others will come from the environment in which we work, learn, play etc. Finally, stressors can arise from the general world in which we live and operate.

It is important to note here that one important group of stressors which can be self-imposed or imposed by others is the requirement to do well at something. It can be work performance (hitting a challenging sales target), academic performance (a piece of coursework), sports (achieving a personal best) etc. If we succeed in dealing with that particular stressor we find that we achieve peak performance.

FIGURE 2.1   AQR stress model

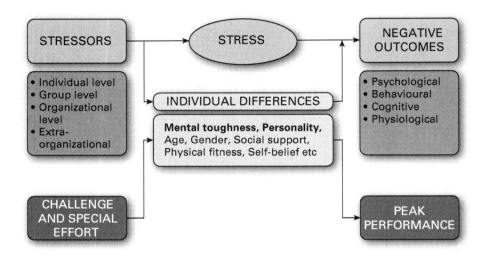

Key factors that influence how we respond to stressors include:

- *Personality.*

- *Age* – it seems there is a U-shaped curve here: the young and the old are better at dealing with stressors than the middle-aged.

- *Gender* – females appear better able to deal with stressors: they are more likely to talk about them and this helps.

- *Social support* – family, friends, carers etc all help you to deal with stressors.

- *Fitness* – fitness and exercise are effective moderators.

- *Mental toughness.*

Examples of sources of stress include:

- *Individual (from within).* Conflict with others – especially role conflict; uncertainty and ambiguity – not knowing what is expected from you; your role overlaps with another's role; the extent to which you have control over your situation and you can make decisions; boredom and repetitive tasks; goals and targets – performance measures; your relationships with key people.

- *Group level.* The behaviour of the group leader; the extent to which there is team cohesion; conflict and dissent within the group.

- *Organizational.* The prevailing culture; structure and processes – the extent to which these exist and the manner in which they are enforced; technology and the pace at which it is introduced; change; commercial and competitive pressures; values.

- *Extra-organizational.* The interface between life–work–family–leisure etc; the state of the economy – one of the key influences on wellbeing; travel – time spent travelling especially to and from work; what is happening in society generally – crime, unemployment etc.

Whether we are talking about education, the world of work, or health etc, all of these areas will have sources of stressors which emerge from those four broad headings.

If we are less effective at dealing with those stressors then there is potential for unwanted consequences of varying severity and impact. These too can be grouped under four broad headings:

- *Psychological.* Low satisfaction and contentment; poor self-esteem; burnout; depression, etc.

- *Behavioural.* These are important – they commonly translate into measurable unwanted consequences which are damaging to the individual and to those around them. They can include absenteeism – poor attendance at work and study; staff turnover and programme drop-out; poor performance; increased propensity for accidents; increased incidence of alcohol and substance abuse etc.

- *Cognitive.* Equally these can be very observable, and include: poor decision making; poor concentration; increased forgetfulness; development of mental health problems etc.

- *Physiological.* These include deterioration of the immune system; high blood pressure; serious illness etc.

However, if you are effective at dealing with and coping with stressors then you may achieve an entirely different outcome – optimizing your performance. Sometimes this is referred to as achieving peak performance.

Principles of peak performance

Evidence shows that high-performing individuals and teams demonstrate the same key characteristics time and time again. Note that many correspond closely with the mental toughness scales, which are set out in Table 2.1.

TABLE 2.1   Key characteristics of high-performing individuals and teams

Passion	A high level of interest in their job, task etc
High self-confidence	A high level of confidence in their own abilities and their ability to deal with others
Controlling the things you can	And not worrying unnecessarily about that which cannot be controlled
Resilience – dealing with setbacks	The ability to bounce back
Seeing the challenge not the threat	Finding opportunities for self-development within each new challenge
Focus	The ability to clear the mind of unnecessary thoughts and clutter
The ability to relax	And can recognize when they need to relax

Peak performance is the ability to efficiently function at your best, enabling you to express your full potential.

And as we see from the above, peak performance is the flip side of effective stress management. The two are inextricably linked. Optimizing performance generally means responding positively to challenge, to pressures to achieve significant goals and targets. It will also usually involve dealing with some form of adversity or difficulty that would deter a lesser motivated individual.

Developing mental toughness is an important ingredient in enabling us to perform to the best of our abilities.

Why does our performance vary?

Our performance does vary. Sometimes we can be highly productive. At other times we can be remarkably ineffective. Research shows that variations in our performance can be attributed to the attributes shown in Table 2.2.

TABLE 2.2   Attributes affecting performance

Your abilities	What you bring to the task?
Your approach	How you approach the task – your motivation and your interests?
Your reward	What you will get if you get involved?
Your colleagues	How you interact with those around you?
Your state of mind	What is happening inside your head? Are you in a state to rise to the challenge?

It has been variously estimated that our state of mind accounts for at least 50 per cent of the variation in an individual's performance but on average we often only spend around 5 per cent of our time in optimizing our performance through mental training.

It is within this notion of stress management that the concepts of performance and wellbeing are connected. When we are more consistent at performing to our optimum we also tend to feel better. When we are more content we perform better. The two notions can connect to give rise to a virtuous cycle of development and growth. Developing mental toughness has an important role in this. Of course, the absence of mental training can lead to the opposite. A vicious cycle of stress and unwanted consequences.

A brief history of mental toughness

03

Since the pioneering work of Loehr in the mid-1980s, the term 'mental toughness' has become synonymous with sporting greatness. Following Loehr's regular interactions with elite US athletes, he identified a highly relevant construct which has become a frequently-used layman's term for individual tolerance to stress and performance maximization. While the work of Loehr was important for bringing the term 'mental toughness' into modern-day parlance, the work was limited in its development of the construct and it could be argued that the anecdotally-based work generally lacked the rigours of a scientific approach.

Resilience and hardiness

These two important concepts have a clear synergy with mental toughness. They have helped us formulate our thinking. It therefore seems appropriate to briefly explore them here.

Resilience

In layman's terms, resilience can be described as the process by which people are able to bounce back from adversity. This ability to bounce back ('reboundability') is an essential tool for humans in everyday life, and this is intensified in the sporting arena and high-powered business. The majority of research in this area has examined resilience in the context of general health, and indeed it has been defined as the way in which a person acts to modify their responses to situations incorporating elements of psychosocial risk (Rutter, 1985).

Resilience is described as a dynamic process in which a number of elements, known as protective factors, are either available or unavailable for a particular person to utilize. These factors consist of specific competencies, or abilities, that an individual can access. These factors obviously have relevance to mental toughness as the resulting effects of the act of resilience lead to psychological toughening of the individual. This 'stickability' represents the amount of effort and perseverance that an individual is prepared to expend in completing a particular task or reaching a specific goal. It can be said that a resilient person is not afraid of dealing with the adversities that are commonplace both in everyday and sporting life.

Jackson and Watkin (2004), using an occupational psychology context, suggested that the following items were key in the way individuals deal with difficult situations:

- the accuracy of analysing events;
- the number of alternative scenarios envisaged;
- flexibility;
- internal drive to face new challenges.

Jackson and Watkin posited that our internal thinking processes can both moderate the impact of these adversities and provide a valuable resource in moving forward from them, focusing on the things we can control rather than those we cannot. They further proposed that the key to resilience is the ability to recognize one's own thoughts and structures of belief and harness the power of flexibility of thinking to manage the emotional and behavioural consequences more effectively. Most interestingly, they stated that this ability can be measured, taught and improved and they further proposed a resilience development programme that is outlined below (Jackson and Watkin, 2004).

Seven factors of resilience

1 *Emotion regulation* – the ability to manage our internal world in order to stay effective under pressure. Resilient people use a well-developed set of skills that helps them to control their emotions, attention and behaviour.

2 *Impulse control* – the ability to manage the behavioural expression of thoughts and emotional impulses, including the ability to delay gratification as explored in the work of Daniel Goleman (1996) on emotional intelligence. Impulse control is correlated with emotion regulation.

3 *Causal analysis* – the ability to identify accurately the causes of adversity. Resilient people are able to get outside their habitual

thinking styles to identify more possible causes and thus more potential solutions.

4 *Self-efficacy* – the sense that we are effective in the world, and the belief that we can solve problems and succeed. Resilient people believe in themselves and as a result, build others' confidence in them – placing them in line for more success and more opportunity.

5 *Realistic optimism* – the ability to stay positive about the future yet be realistic in our planning for it. It is linked to self-esteem but a more causal relationship exists with self-efficacy and involves accuracy and realism – not Pollyanna-style optimism.

6 *Empathy* – the ability to read others' behavioural cues to understand their psychological and emotional states and thus build better relationships. Resilient people are able to read others' non-verbal cues to help build deeper relationships, and tend to be more in tune with their own emotional states.

7 *Reaching out* – the ability to enhance the positive aspects of life and take on new challenges and opportunities. Reaching-out behaviours are hampered by embarrassment, perfectionism and self-handicapping.

Hardiness

Another concept, similar to resilience, is that of hardiness (Kobasa, 1979). This construct also has its roots in the health psychology area, and more particularly in the stress–illness relationship. There has been a plethora of research investigating the concept of hardiness or 'hardy personality' (Funk, 1992).

Kobasa proposed that hardiness consists of three interrelated concepts: control, challenge and commitment. This concept of hardiness is considered to have a buffering effect between stressful life events and illness. Earlier work by Lazarus (1966) suggested that this buffering effect is influenced by the type of coping strategies which are used by the individual, which are in turn dependent on the personality dispositions of that individual.

Kobasa considers that hardiness is an important factor in the way individuals perceive situations and the way in which they decide to undertake an appropriate set of actions. This can best be done by transforming the event so it can be perceived as less threatening, helping to avoid 'illness-provoking' biological states such as adaptational exhaustion (Selye, 1976) or depressed immunological surveillance (Schwarz, 1975; Kobasa, Maddi and Kahn, 1982). It was suggested that the qualities possessed by 'hardy' individuals activated the transformation process so that the event, no matter how stress-inducing, became congruous with the individual's self-view.

If this view is correct, this leads us to a number of implications, one of which is the identification of the less 'hardy' individuals and providing these individuals with appropriate psychological interventions or coping strategies. We have built upon this idea and it is at the core of our development philosophy.

As mentioned earlier, Kobasa proposed three components of hardiness: control, challenge and commitment. These components are briefly summarized below.

Control is 'expressed as a tendency to feel and act as if one is influential (rather than helpful) in the face of the varied contingencies of life' (Averill, 1973; Seligman, 1975; Kobasa, Maddi and Kahn, 1982). As discussed above, this is a complex concept, which operates on a number of levels. Within this context it is argued that control gives the cognitive ability to incorporate stressful events into 'an ongoing life plan' (Kobasa, 1979), using knowledge, skill and choice, thus influencing how situations are appraised. Control is further said to allow an individual to choose the most appropriate course of action when facing a potentially stressful situation. This in turn is likely to transform the situation into something more congruous for that individual.

Commitment is the 'tendency to involve oneself in (rather than experience alienation from) whatever one is doing or encounters' (Maddi, Hoover and Kobasa, 1982). Commitment is relevant to cognitive appraisal as it helps identify and give meaning to new situations in the individual's environment. At the action level it makes the person take the initiative in the environment rather than passively accept it. Moss (1973) proposed that failure to feel involved in an environment that provides accurate and congruent information can leave an individual vulnerable to disease.

The final component of hardiness is *Challenge*, which is expressed as the belief that change rather than stability is normal in life and that the anticipation of change provides incentives to grow rather than threats to security (Kobasa *et al*, 1982). Seeing potentially stressful occurrences as challenging has the effect of mitigating the stressfulness of the situation. In relation to the coping strategies used, the challenge disposition empowers the individual to develop and grow instead of protecting what the individual has already.

What is mental toughness?

The term 'mental toughness' is commonly used in all manner of sporting contexts, whether it is when Michael Atherton bats for 10 hours saving a test match, or when the German football team win another trophy with an apparently 'untalented' side. Vincent Lombardi, former Green Bay Packers' coach stated:

> Mental toughness is many things and rather difficult to explain. Its qualities are sacrifice and self-denial. In addition, most importantly, it is combined with a perfectly disciplined will that refuses to give in. It's a state of mind – you could call it character in action.
>
> Curtis Management Group, 1998, p 20

There are obviously common elements in the range of conceptualizations employed, and, in essence, what this commonly means is an individual's ability to resist the stressors that would normally cause decrements in performance. Within the context of applied experience, mental toughness has been described as follows:

> It's the ability to handle situations. It's somebody who doesn't choke, doesn't go into shock, and who can stand up for what he believes. It's what someone has who handles pressures, distractions, and people trying to break their concentration. It involves focusing, discipline, self-confidence, patience, persistence, accepting responsibility without whining or excuses, visualizing, tolerating pain, and a positive approach.
>
> Brennan, 1998, p 2

Therefore, mental toughness would appear to incorporate aspects of both commonly recognized sports psychology interventions, such as focusing and visualization, and a number of personality characteristics which include persistence, resilience, confidence and discipline. The importance of both these elements needs to be considered to formulate a definitive explanation of what mental toughness is. The concept as it currently stands could be argued to contain both the theoretical underpinnings of personality constructs as well as the practical implications involved with sports psychology interventions. This mixture of application and theory is the key to the comprehensive development of the construct.

The beginnings of mental toughness research

Within the context of the psychology literature, the usage of this term can be traced back to the work of Loehr (1982) who was a sports psychologist working with athletes with the principal goal of improving sporting performance. In this capacity he found that athletes and coaches were beginning to use the term mental toughness to describe a desired trait. This led Loehr to investigate the construct and attempt to identify what this 'mental toughness' actually is. In his book *The New Toughness Training for Sports* (1995), he defined mental toughness as 'the ability to consistently perform toward the upper range of your talent and skill regardless of competitive circumstances', and from his interactions with athletes Loehr expanded upon this definition by identifying four key markers in respect of toughness:

- *Emotional flexibility* – 'the ability to absorb unexpected emotional turns and remain supple, non-defensive, and balanced, able to summon a wide range of positive emotions to the competitive battle. Inflexible athletes are rigid and defensive in emotional crisis and therefore are easily broken.'

- *Emotional responsiveness* – 'the ability to remain emotionally alive, engaged, and connected under pressure. Responsive competitiveness is not calloused, withdrawn, or lifeless as the battle rages.'

- *Emotional strength* – 'the ability to exert and resist great force emotionally under pressure, to sustain a powerful fighting spirit against impossible odds.'

- *Emotional resiliency* – 'the ability to take a punch emotionally and bounce back quickly, to recover quickly from disappointments, mistakes, and missed opportunities and jump back into battle fully ready to resume the fight.'

On the basis of this model, he prepared a 42-item questionnaire consisting of seven scales, which he called the Psychological Performance Inventory (PPI). This questionnaire has been used in a number of studies, and will be discussed in detail later in this chapter. However, it should be noted that Loehr's model of mental toughness and the resulting questionnaire were both generated from informal interactions with athletes and Loehr made no attempt to test the model scientifically or develop his questionnaire into a psychometric instrument.

Following the work of Loehr, a number of further researchers offered alternative conceptualizations of the mental toughness concept. For example, in their review, Williams and Krane (1993) suggested that mentally tough athletes possess a greater ability to concentrate, higher levels of self-confidence, less anxiety before and during competition, and the ability to rebound from mistakes. However, Williams and Krane also recognized that the majority of recent research in sports psychology has focused on the psychological skills and strategies that are used by successful athletes rather than profiling their personality characteristics. This clearly highlights the practical importance of sports psychology interventions; however, if one of the goals of applied sports psychologists is to enhance mental toughness, then the concept must be soundly developed first. Once there is some agreement about what mental toughness is, then attention can be turned to considering if this is something that can be developed, and what should constitute effective training programmes. The following two sections outline the qualitative and quantitative work that has been carried out thus far.

The qualitative approach

As can be seen from the previous section, Loehr uses very emotive language when describing the key markers of mental toughness. These have no doubt been obtained from his many years' experience working with elite athletes. However, no matter how valid this approach is in providing grounded preliminary work, it only represents the beginnings of scientific conceptual development.

In more recent years, research into the concept of mental toughness has become more scientifically rigorous (eg Jones, Hanton and Connaughton, 2002; Golby, Sheard and Lavallee, 2003; Golby and Sheard, 2004; Middleton *et al*, 2004). This body of research has mostly used a qualitative approach to examine a range of issues, using mainly interviews and focus group techniques.

This work has further contributed to the wide variety of mental toughness definitions, and the research of Jones *et al* (2002) reiterates the fact that the concept is well used in terms of both applied sports psychology and in the wider arena of professional sport. However, the wide-ranging definitions of mental toughness have served to confuse the area and inhibited the development of an operational concept.

It would seem that many, if not all, positive psychological characteristics have at some time been linked with the attributes of a mentally tough performer, and this work was summarized by Jones *et al* (2002) who stated that this range of characteristics implies that a mentally tough athlete is generally someone who has an 'ability to cope with stress and resultant anxiety associated with high pressure competitive situations' (p 206).

The most notable qualitative study is arguably that of Jones *et al*, who actively aimed to provide a degree of rigour in their investigation of the mental toughness concept that was previously lacking. Their aim was to define and identify key attributes in the concept of mental toughness and they selected qualitative methods because they, among others, argued that this would provide the opportunity to probe people's responses and establish detailed information, especially with regard to new research questions. The study incorporated both interviews and focus groups, and focused on the views of elite athletes, in order to generate data for a profile of a mentally tough athlete. This approach, described in more detail below, can be considered to have by-passed the 'pop' sports psychology approaches which 'emphasize macro-components such as confidence and coping with adversity as under-pinning the construct and to identify the micro-components of mental toughness' (Jones *et al*, 2002, p 207).

Conversely, Jones *et al* were able to elicit from the athletes their complex construction of what constitutes a mentally tough performer, a process which has been effectively undertaken in a number of specific sports areas such as athletics, cycling, rowing and modern pentathlon among others (Butler, 1989; Butler and Hardy, 1992; Dale and Wrisberg, 1996; Jones, 1993). Their resulting definition of mental toughness was as follows:

> Mental toughness is having the natural or developed psychological edge that enables you to: generally, cope better than your opponents with the many demands (competition, training, and lifestyle) that sport places on a performer; specifically, be more consistent and better than your opponents in remaining determined, focused, confident, and in control under pressure.

The attributes developed by Jones *et al* were as follows (ranked in order of importance):

1 Having an unshakable self-belief in your ability to achieve your competition goals.

2 Bouncing back from performance setbacks as a result of increased determination to succeed.

3 Having an unshakable self-belief that you possess unique qualities and abilities that make you better than your opponents.

4 Having an insatiable desire and internalized motives to succeed.

5 Remaining fully focused on the task at hand in the face of competition-specific distractions.

6 Regaining psychological control following unexpected, uncontrollable events.

7 Pushing back the boundaries of physical and emotional pain, while still maintaining technique and effort under distress in training and competition.

8 Accepting that competition anxiety is inevitable and knowing that you can cope with it.

9 Not being adversely affected by others' good and bad performances.

10 Thriving on the pressure of competition.

11 Remaining fully focused in the face of personal life distractions.

12 Switching a sport focus on and off as required.

This is clearly a broad conceptualization with a focus on the key characteristics to be found within the mentally tough athlete; however, this research does potentially provide fertile ground for further investigation.

An interesting point is made within this definition of mental toughness in that it is considered to be a natural phenomenon as well as being a trait that can be developed with the appropriate psychological interventions. A further point of interest is the fact that the participants acknowledged the complex interaction of the life/sport domains (the importance of dealing with life situations outside of the sporting context), and that this aspect plays an important part in the development of mental toughness. Situations considered include time-management skills, social and personal demands, and balancing their training regime.

The psychometric approach

The use of psychometric instruments in research is commonplace. For example, psychometric methods can be used with the aim of developing psychometric instruments which are capable of reliably and validly assessing a given construct; questionnaires can be devised with the different, but obviously closely-related, aim of examining the underlying structure of a construct, by assessing the nature of relationships between different items; and psychometric instruments can be used to address research questions relating to the extent to which different populations possess given traits.

Such approaches are obviously common in psychology, and within the field of mental toughness there are a number of existing studies which can provide some further insight, and support the development of the construct.

Golby *et al* (2003) used psychometric methods to compare mental toughness across a number of cultures and across different playing standards (ie first division, second division). The driving force for this research was the apparent performance gulf between northern and southern hemisphere rugby league teams. Previous research had not found any significant differences in the tactical or physical attributes of the players (Brewer and Davis, 1995) which has led to questions about the psychological profiles of the athletes as an explanation for performance differences.

In brief, Golby and his colleagues examined the potential cultural differences in both mental toughness and hardiness between rugby nations (Wales, France, Ireland and England) competing in the World Cup of 2000. This work utilized two measures. One was Loehr's PPI, 'designed' in 1986, which claims to assess the mental toughness of an athlete by asking questions in the following categories: self-confidence, negative emotion, attention control, visualization and imagery control, motivation, positive energy and attitude control.

In addition to the PPI, the second instrument used in this study was the Personal Views Survey (PVS) III-R (Maddi and Khoshaba, 2001). This instrument aims to measure hardiness, and possesses three sub-scales of control, commitment and challenge. The psychometric properties of this instrument have been soundly validated with acceptable internal consistency of between.60 and.84 for the sub-scales and.88 for total hardiness.

In summary, the results showed that the Welsh team reported higher levels of commitment and control (hardiness scale) in comparison with the French team. These results were interpreted as the Welsh team demonstrating a more active involvement in progressing in the tournament, as well as feeling that their efforts on the pitch would influence the outcome of a match. Further analysis indicated a strong relationship between the PPI and the PVS III-R.

It was suggested by Golby *et al* that both of the inventories used in the study were probably measuring related but distinct attributes of psychological skills. However, no firm conclusions could be reached from the analysis undertaken, although one interesting issue highlighted in the study was the fact that the majority of athletes scored well above the average scores for both mental toughness and hardiness. This was explained by the fact that there is a 'natural filtering' that takes place, whereby only athletes who possess high levels of both hardiness and mental toughness would reach a position where they could be selected to represent their country.

Two explanations for this are given by Golby *et al:* first, different psychological factors have a highly significant (and maybe undervalued) impact on performance; and secondly, the measures used possess insufficient discriminative power. Finally, it was highlighted that significant differences were only found with the hardiness scale, giving support for the robust psychometrics properties of the PVS III-R.

A similar study was undertaken by Golby and Sheard (2004) which again aimed to compare athletes' measures of mental toughness and hardiness across differing standards of rugby league (international, Super League and Division One). The results again highlighted a very significant difference in both mental toughness (PPI) and hardiness (PVS III-R) across playing standards. In respect of the hardiness measure, it was found that the international players scored significantly higher in the areas of commitment and challenge compared to both Super League and Division One players, as well as scoring significantly higher than Division One players in the control scale. On the other hand, with regard to the measure of mental toughness, the international players scored significantly higher on the areas of negative energy control and attentional control compared to Super League and Division One players. There were found to be no significant differences between Super League and Division One players.

Mental toughness in the 21st century

There has been an explosion of interest in mental toughness this century. We hope we have contributed to this. We developed the 4 Cs model after reviewing the extant literature and feel that it represents a more complete definition of the mental toughness concept. But the debate continues!

The areas of disagreement between the various researchers in this area are:

1 Does mental toughness exist as a separate concept?

2 Is it a unitary concept?

3 What is the opposite of toughness?

4 How can it be effectively measured?

5 Can it be developed?

We will let other researchers and academics speak for themselves – there is room for all. It has always been the case that theories and models are tested and developed from active and open-minded debates. We have certainly thought deeply for many years about the concept and specifically the five questions posed above.

Our thoughts on the five questions

1. Does it exist?

Clearly it does – but is it something unique? There are a number of related constructs, including the following:

- *Resilience* is described as a dynamic process in which a number of elements, known as protective factors, are either available or unavailable for a particular person to utilize.

- *Hardiness* (Kobasa, 1979) consists of three interrelated concepts: control, challenge and commitment. This concept of hardiness is considered to have a buffering effect between stressful life events and illness.

- *Physiological toughness* (Dienstbier, 1989) is the relationship between arousal and physiological toughness, by examining individuals' confrontations with stress that evoke both central and peripheral physiological arousal.

Narrower, but very relevant, constructs include: conscientiousness (eg McCrae and Costa, 1987); goal setting (Locke, 1968); achievement orientation (Murray, 1938); learned helplessness (Seligman, 1972); self-efficacy (Bandura, 1977); and grit and self-esteem.

We believe that mental toughness does exist and is different to these apparently similar concepts. In a later chapter we will explore in more detail the cross-overs with other popular modes. We describe mental toughness as a narrow plastic personality trait which explains in large part how individuals respond differently to the same or similar stressors, pressures and challenges irrespective of prevailing circumstances. It is about prospering under pressure, not just surviving.

We feel that mental toughness is a universal quality. It is present to some extent in everyone and is a factor which determines how we respond, irrespective of what that is – whether that is at work, at rest, at play, at home etc.

2. Is it a unitary concept?

We have developed a model that consists of four main pillars, which are themselves sub-divided. Others, for example Daniel Guccardi, have argued it is in fact a unitary concept. Whilst it is possible to produce an overall mental toughness score which can be in some cases quite useful, it reduces the ability to really understand what is happening and, perhaps more importantly, how to change it. It is therefore a matter of interpretation. We have always had a shorter questionnaire, the MTQ18, which is a measure of unitary mental toughness. We have found it to be less useful in both our applied and research work, but it can be useful when a very short scale is needed.

In summary, we believe mental toughness is a combination of four distinct but related concepts: commitment, challenge, control and confidence. The 4 Cs.

What is the opposite of mental toughness

The opposite of toughness is *not* weakness – it is sensitivity. Whilst the sensitive may have some problems dealing effectively with pressure they have clear strengths and a clear identity. Other modes tend to be rather less respectful implying, or stating, that the less tough are in fact weak and have 'something missing'. After 30 years as a psychologist I am clear that it is never black and white. It is always 'messy' and it this greyness that brings the area to life. For example, we are becoming more focused on areas such as the performing arts where toughness and sensitivity are needed to work in tandem and how this synergy works.

3. How can mental toughness be effectively measured?

This debate about measurement issues has created much smoke, a lot of heat and little light. It is beyond the scope of this chapter to explore the area in depth but recent work is presented in Chapter 4. We firmly believe that the MTQ48 (and its variations) is a reliable and valid measure and we can demonstrate this. There are other questionnaires and other methodologies that offer different perspectives; that is how it should be and would be expected. We have not got *the* answer but we have a solid, research-built and operationally effective answer.

4. Can it be developed?

Yes. We view it as a narrow personality trait but recent research, including epigenetics, has shown that traits can be changed. In addition to this potential fundamental change, improved mental skills can help the 'less tough' perform like the 'more tough'. We used to describe this as providing a 'psychological ladder'. If you are reaching for the top shelf we can provide something to stand on – rather than making you taller. However, recent work on genetics raises the intriguing possibility that you might indeed be able to grow!

In Chapter 4 the way the model came into being is described. It was once suggested that we simply created a model. I guess we did – but based on an understanding of the literature and on research. This is how science works. You establish the facts and then think about what you have in a rational and systematic way. Good science can be very creative – bad science can be very mechanistic.

Developing the model and the MTQ48

04

Early in our work there emerged the need to develop the mental toughness construct in the sense that there was a need to pull together what had been developed by others and add what we had identified. There have been countless attempts to identify the different facets of mental toughness, including: 'the ability to perform toward the upper range of your talent' (Loehr, 1995); 'ability to cope with intense pressure' (Williams, 1988); 'ability to cope better than your opponents with the demands of competitive sport' (Jones, Hanton and Connaughton, 2002). You could say that we made sense out of the chaos that was mental toughness thinking until that point.

Although there are clearly some common elements to these ideas and models, our presentation of mental toughness seeks to clarify this medley of definitions and to offer a model of the construct based on scientific research. This research-based approach has not always been adopted by others who delve into this field. Many users appear to have relatively little interest in the research context and pedigree of tools and techniques, preferring to take a far more pragmatic approach.

Given that our joint interest in mental toughness, initially at least, was very much in its application in the workplace and in sports, it was important that anything that emerged was practical and accessible. It also had to make sense in terms of what the potential practitioners already knew and used. Pragmatism was important to us too.

However, there is already too much practice in people development and organization development which is 'faith'-based and has little real evidence to support it. It was important to all those involved in developing this concept and measure that we adopt an evidence-based approach. Although this approach has its critics and carries risk, not least that you cannot find evidence to support what you are doing, we are happy that we took this course of action. We now have something which we can explain, can develop on and, if needed, defend.

Once we had a sound and research-based definition of mental toughness, it became possible to develop an accurate measure. This involves a basis of theory, followed by item and reliability analysis, factor analysis, tests of convergent and divergent validity, validation in relation to external criteria, and application in research and practice. It is this process which will be briefly described in this chapter.

Preliminary field research

The previous research into mental toughness and related constructs clearly provided a significant volume of information on which to base a further investigation into the nature and breadth of mental toughness. However, past research and existing questionnaires had been beset with inconsistencies and psychometric anomalies.

Considering this, it was decided that a grounded approach should be used (Glaser and Strauss, 1967). This method focuses on the emergence of theory from unstructured data collection, rather than relying wholly on pre-existing theory with its inherent problem of restriction of data collection. It was intended that this approach would ensure that the new model of mental toughness was developed from the bottom up, rather than poten-tially perpetuating a limited framework.

To this end, an exploratory study was undertaken which investigated the extensive range of personal experiences of situations with relevance to mental toughness. This also allowed the researcher to consider the way individuals utilized the terms relating to the different aspects of this construct. Twelve in-depth interviews were then carried out with sports-people. They included three rugby coaches, one rugby chief executive, two rugby players, two golfers, two footballers and two squash players. The interviews lasted for an average of 45 minutes, with the shortest being 25 minutes, with one of the rugby coaches and the longest lasting 90 minutes, which was held with one of the squash players. All interviewees were either professional or playing at an elite level. The aims of the process were twofold: first, to identify notions of mental toughness; and secondly, to identify circumstances and events which necessitated mental toughness.

Although the interviews raised many questions, they also met their broad goal, which was to provide a grounded basis for the development of the construct. The most striking aspect of the interviews was the importance all interviewees placed on having a high level of mental toughness. All interviewees stated that they thought this was a vital ingredient in the profile of a successful athlete. When asked to state what they thought this 'mental toughness' was, however, all interviewees found it difficult to define. Some of the descriptions offered in these interviews are shown in Table 4.1.

TABLE 4.1   Interviewees' descriptions of mental toughness

1   The ability to carry on when the world seems to have turned against you, and keep your 'troubles' in proper perspective.

2   Capacity to face all pressures and deal with them internally, delivering the same level of performance outwardly regardless of what pressures one feels internally.

3   The ability to keep going when the world seems to be against you and keep a true sense of perspective on your situation.

4   Resistance under pressure (and including when working in new areas).

5   The ability to maintain effective personal control over your own stress levels and effective working relationships whilst handling a whole range of complex and sensitive issues/problems.

6   The ability to change when necessary, to be flexible when necessary and to resist when necessary in order to get the job done.

7   The ability to maintain effective control over the environment by displaying commitment to deliver, confidence in their ability, resilience to negative pressures, ability to see change as a positive opportunity and a recognition of their own limits to handle stress.

8   The ability to be reliable, in control, effective and composed under pressure.

9   The ability to handle events, planned and unplanned, and any conflict, emotional or otherwise, which arises from those events.

10   The ability to remain emotionally stable and make rational decisions under pressure.

11   The ability to appear calm and in control when everything is going wrong.

TABLE 4.1 *continued*

12	Ability to withstand the unexpected diverse challenges of i) management, ii) the pressures of legal work, and iii) personal and professional disappointments in a pressured working environment.
13	The ability to be able to continue to focus on long-term outcomes and deliver an effective performance in the face of real or potential obstacles, maintaining perspective and a balanced, objective view.
14	Resilience – not easily balked in the face of opposition/adversity.
15	Ability to think clearly under pressure together with determination to achieve a solution.
16	Intellectual resilience, ability to deal with difficult situations, taking forward ideas which may be subject to resistance. Flexibility and adaptability responding to changing circumstances are competencies (stubbornness to be actively discouraged).
17	Ability to remain objective and complete the task, irrespective of impact on feelings and emotions.
18	Doing what hurts because you know it to be right.
19	Ability to cope and perform under a variety of situations and circumstances.
20	Ability to accept change, resist unacceptable change, be flexible enough to get the job done.
21	Ability to defend arguments and reason situations intellectually.
22	Being resilient to pressures, changes and feedback.
23	A person who is able to stay focussed on important issues when change is rampant and is able to make difficult decisions affecting others, even when they don't like it themselves.
24	The ability to produce quality work, remaining evenly tempered, without changing own attitudes and standards.
25	Ability to absorb pressure without impacting upon performance.

TABLE 4.1 *continued*

26 The ability to react positively to setbacks, whether personal or physical, that affect your thought processes. Not to have fear of failure.

27 Determination to see tasks through in all circumstances whether under internal or external pressure.

28 Resistance to pressure, forcefulness, ability to deal with problems.

29 Ability to deal effectively with stressful situations.

Interestingly, what emerged were two recurrent themes covering new aspects of mental toughness. First, most of the interviewees considered confidence as playing a large part in dealing successfully with the immense problems and setbacks that are faced by professional athletes. Secondly, the ability to suppress emotions during play was also considered to be a key factor for athletes to perform at the top of their ability range.

Development of the four-factor model

Two sources of data now existed on which to begin to develop a model of mental toughness: the existing published research on mental toughness and related constructs; and the interviews with 12 sports-people.

Broadly speaking, all the data pointed to a four-factor model – the model of hardiness put forward by Kobasa seems to incorporate most of the elements generated by the literature. Most of the elements can be summarized under the broad headings of control, commitment and challenge. Secondly, the interviews provided support for all of these elements and provided support for a fourth element of confidence. At that point, none of the research in this field had incorporated this aspect of personality in mental toughness. However, confidence was mentioned by half of the interviewees and it is an intuitively comfortable aspect of mental toughness.

Ultimately, therefore, these two sources of data enabled the emergence of a four-factor model of mental toughness.

There was more. The interviews provided evidence to support the subdivision of two of these factors into four further sub-scales. Two distinct aspects of confidence were generated, ie interpersonal confidence and confidence in one's ability, and two distinct aspects of control were also proposed, ie emotional control in addition to the well-recognized element of locus of control. This work led on to a comprehensive definition of the concept of mental toughness:

> Mentally tough individuals tend to be sociable and outgoing as they are able to remain calm and relaxed, they are competitive in many situations and have lower anxiety levels than others. With a high sense of self-belief and an unshakeable faith that they control their own destiny, these individuals can remain relatively unaffected by competition or adversity.
>
> Clough, Earle and Sewell, 2002, p 38

Preliminary scale development

On the basis of this model, a broad range of items were generated (via a panel of experts). The aim was to develop items which could encapsulate each of the four components of the model (challenge, commitment, confidence and control). Data from the interviews and existing questionnaires were considered in an attempt to sample the full breadth of the construct and different aspects of each factor were incorporated in an attempt to be as comprehensive as possible. Each item consisted of a statement followed by a 5-point Likert scale with verbal anchors ranging from (1) strongly disagree to (5) strongly agree.

The initial questionnaire consisted of 66 items. They were written to en-sure that all items were understandable, unequivocal and specific. The items were piloted with 20 participants who examined every item to ensure each was unambiguous and clear. All the items examined were thought to be suitable to be understood by the general population.

Questionnaires were then completed by the sample of 215 students, professional athletes and administration/managerial staff. The data were analysed using complex statistical techniques such as factor analysis. A six-factor mental toughness model emerged on the basis of the following: related theoretical perspectives; existing questionnaires relating to mental toughness; qualitative data from the interviews; and the analysis of the various factor solutions of the questionnaire.

To investigate the factor structure further, a second development sample was obtained and subjected to analysis. In total, 963 questionnaires were completed, the sample consisting of students, administrators/managers, engineers and athletes.

A preliminary analysis of the gender data revealed statistically significant differences in total mental toughness as well as all the sub-scales. However, in order to ascertain the practical significance of these findings, effect calcu-lations were carried out using the guidelines provided by Cohen (1988). Even the largest differences produced small effect sizes eg MT: eta squared = 0.001. Expressed as a percentage, only 0.1 per cent of the variance of mental toughness is explained by gender. It should be noted that when the MTQ48 is used for non-research purposes the scores produced for the scales are converted to stens; these stens are clustered into three broad groupings (low = 1, 2, 3; medium= 4, 5, 6, 7; high = 8, 9, 10). None of the gender dif-ferences noted would impact in any significant way on the reported score. This sample was subjected to the same approach as the first sample. The same model emerged from the forest of data.

How can you judge the quality of a test? There are two main benchmarks to judging the quality of tests: reliability and validity.

Reliability

Reliability is basically concerned with consistency. It relates to the test's ability to measure in the same way. If a test reported that you were mentally tough one week and then the next week it reported you were very sensitive it would raise concerns, particularly if there had been no events or interventions which might explain such a shift.

Obviously mental toughness could change. Much of this book is given over to mental toughness development using targeted interventions – so it can change. However, for most people, most of the time, it won't change on its own. Reliability is usually estimated using two methods: internal consistency and test–retest.

Internal consistency looks at the way the items cluster. So, for example, items written to measure confidence should co-vary together. Score high on one item and you would normally score highly on the others in that category. Cronbach's alpha was calculated for each sub-scale as a measure of internal consistency (Table 4.2).

All sub-scales reached the minimum acceptable level. This supports the homogeneity of each sub-scale and the MTQ48 as a whole.

Test–retest reliability is basically doing the questionnaire twice, after a suitable gap. The relationship will never be perfect, but it should be substantial. The test–retest reliability measured by Pearson's correlation coefficient was high for all scales, with a range from .80 for challenge to .87 for emotional control. The sample consisted of 108 psychology undergraduates tested at a six-week interval.

TABLE 4.2 Scale reliability of the Mental Toughness Questionnaire 48 (MTQ48)

MTQ48 sub-scales	No of items	Cronbach's alpha
Challenge	8	.71
Commitment	11	.80
Control	14	.74
Emotional control	7	.70
Life control	7	.72
Confidence	15	.81
Confidence in abilities	9	.75
Interpersonal confidence	6	.76
Whole scale	**48**	**.91**

Validity

Basically, validity answers the question: does it work? There are many types of validity. We will focus on four of them here:

- face;
- content;
- construct;
- criterion-related.

Face validity refers to how the instrument is accepted by its target population. Too simple or too complex questions quickly lead to non-acceptance of the questionnaires. Likewise if questions appear odd or inappropriate people will not answer them. For example, you might find that a question about toilet habits relates to anxiety. From a technical point of view this would probably work – there is a relationship – but it would create a degree of defensiveness and suspicion on the part of the respondent! The MTQ48 is acceptable to a wide range of people and there are seldom any issues about its applicability.

Content validity refers to the instrument's ability to cover the full domain of the underlying concept. So, for example, if you wanted to test somebody's geographical knowledge you ask them to name the capitals of various countries. You would get very different results if you restricted this to Western Europe or opened it up to the rest of the world. The former would in fact be a very poor measure as it clearly lacks content validity.

Construct validity can be a very complex thing indeed. However, at its simplest it is very easy to describe. Basically it signifies the test's relationship with other similar tests. For the MTQ48 to be said to be valid in this domain it has to relate to other closely-related constructs. Much work has been done on this and the results are both supportive and encouraging. An example of this type of approach is shown below and in Table 4.3.

An example of construct validation

A sample of 106 individuals completed both the MTQ48 and a variety of personality measures. The sample consisted entirely of undergraduate students, who completed the battery of measures during a research methods lecture.

Significant correlations were found with the MTQ48 and all of the five scales investigated. Interestingly, the highest correlations were found with the self-efficacy scale. This is an expected finding as the concept of self-efficacy has strong associations with that of confidence which is a sub-scale of the MTQ48. Indeed the correlation with the sub-scale confidence in abilities was even higher. Another relevant finding was the correlation with the State Trait Anxiety Indicator (STAI), with the strongest correlation of the sub-scales being control. Again, this finding was expected as the control sub-scale does include the element involving the ability to control oneself in stressful experiences.

Finally there is *criterion-related validity*. We feel this is the both the core and the key to the MTQ48. It is a measure of whether or not a score on the MTQ48 is associated with an external measure. For many this is the acid test for a psychometric measure: 'Can it predict what it claims to predict?' Chapter 26 dealing with research presents a range of studies that show the predictive power of the model and measure. In addition, a number of case studies are included to provide a real-world perspective.

TABLE 4.3 Correlations table for MTQ48 and various personality scales

	Life orientation test	Satisfaction with life scale	Self-esteem scale	Self-efficacy scale	State trait anxiety inventory
Overall MT	0.48**	0.56**	0.42*	0.68**	−0.57**
Challenge	0.39*	0.59**	0.45*	0.66**	−0.54**
Commitment	0.45*	0.52**	0.40*	0.69**	−0.59**
Control	0.49**	0.55**	0.41*	0.64**	−0.61**
Control: life	0.53**	0.59**	0.49**	0.66**	−0.63**
Control: emotions	0.46*	0.56**	0.34*	0.59**	−0.61**
Confidence	0.47*	0.50**	0.39*	0.70**	−0.58**
Confidence: in abilities	0.49**	0.49**	0.45*	0.74**	−0.60**
Confidence: interpersonal	0.41*	0.56**	0.37*	0.69**	−0.61**

NOTE: *n p<0.05 **p<0.01

Post-development 'testing' of the MTQ48

Since its development in 2002 (as described in this chapter), thousands of people have completed the MTQ48, which has allowed the questionnaire to be further evaluated. Establishing validity and reliability is considered to be an important ongoing process. One of the most important aspects of any questionnaire is referred to as 'internal consistency' or how well the items on the questionnaire relate to each other. The overall internal consistency of the MTQ48 has in general been found to be excellent (eg Kaiseler, Polman and Nicholls, 2009).

In developing the MTQ48, Clough *et al* (2002) found that mental toughness consisted of six components or factors. Since the initial identification of these factors, independent researchers have tested the factor structure of the MTQ48 using a statistical procedure called confirmatory factor analysis (CFA). With a large sample of participants, Horsburgh *et al* (2009) provided support for the factor structure proposed by Clough *et al* (2002).

In order to further validate the 4 Cs model, and to answer criticism made by another research group, a very large-scale study was carried out (Perry *et al*, 2013). In total, 8,207 participants completed the MTQ48. The model fit was assessed using CFA and exploratory structural equation modelling. The results supported the factorial validity of the 4 Cs model showing that the MTQ48 is a robust psychometric measure of mental toughness. This will not end the academic debate – that is after all what academics do! – but we are fully confident that the MTQ48 is a sound, robust and user-friendly measure that has made a major impact in the world of mental toughness.

Much of our work has concentrated on performance measures. Many of these studies are liberally sprinkled throughout this text. The rest of the book is mostly devoted to examples of using the test in the 'real world', research findings, and tools and techniques for developing this vital trait.

Mental toughness and the MTQ48 measure

05

The MTQ48 was originally created to meet a very tangible need in the occupational world. It sought to respond to four questions increasingly at the front of the minds of most coaches, trainers, teachers and managers:

- Why do some people handle stressors, pressure and challenge well and others don't?
- Can we measure where people have strengths and weaknesses in these matters?
- Can we do something to improve 'mental toughness' in people which improves their performance and wellbeing?
- Can we evaluate the effectiveness of interventions which are all claimed to be effective?

In 2002, more than eight years of careful and innovative research enabled Professor Peter Clough and Dr Keith Earle to emerge with a tool that allowed these questions, and many others, to be answered positively and effectively. The MTQ48 questionnaire has now developed into a significant resource which is used by an astonishing range of people who are concerned with issues around three core themes which appear to matter everywhere:

- performance;
- wellbeing;
- positive behaviour.

Initially, the concept and the measure were applied mainly in the occupational world – looking at developing employees and managers to perform effectively, especially in challenging environments (eg emergency services) and in adverse circumstances (eg the 2008/9 economic downturn). These are obvious applications for mental toughness and MTQ48.

Since then, additional versions of the MTQ48 measure have emerged where the items and the expert report text database use language more appropriate to the needs of young people and sports-people. They are all based on the original.

The MTQ48 is a 48-item questionnaire which takes about 10 minutes to complete. It is most commonly completed in online format. It features the ability to generate expert reports for each individual's scores almost instantly on completion of the measure. There is a 'paper and pencil' version which uses the online facility to process data and create reports.

At the time of writing, there are two basic versions: the Standard Version which generates up to five different reports (described below) and which meets the needs of most users; and the Young Person's Version which produces a reduced range of reports. This version is most widely used with young persons (typically up to secondary school level – age 17–18 in most environments) where it is much more appropriate to provide feedback in oral rather than written form.

There are now major applications in education, health, social work, sports and care as well as in occupational settings. As of 2015, the model and measure are in use in more than 80 countries around the globe and are already available in 12 major languages with a programme to extend that significantly as demand arises.

A great deal of thought has been put into the development of the measure to enable it to be used properly and with confidence by the widest range of users. It is rarely described as a psychometric measure although this is, at heart, what it is. The MTQ48 is more commonly described as a people development tool. It is:

- Extremely easy to administer. The questionnaire uses a five-point Likert scale to capture responses. The test is available in online or paper and pencil format. Online instructions are intuitive and easy to follow.

- Accessible. The reading age for the item databank in the original UK English version is 9+ years of age. Language in the reports is such that the reports can be read and understood by those who are not trained psychologists. This principle is applied to all versions including versions in other languages.

- Quick. Test results are processed immediately online and expert reports are available within seconds of test completion.

- User-friendly in its reports. Several expert reports are available to the test user (see below).

- Reliable. A technical term to indicate whether MTQ48 measures mental toughness consistently. The reliability score for MTQ48 overall is 0.91 which is generally acknowledged as a high or acceptable score.

- Valid. Another key technical term which indicates whether it measures what it claims to measure. The concurrent validity score for MTQ48 overall and its scales ranges from 0.25 to 0.42 which again is generally acknowledged as a high or acceptable score. The MTQ48 measure is generally recognized as a valid and reliable measure. It is increasingly used by other independent researchers, and academic journals accept studies for publication which are based on the use of MTQ48.

- Normative. This means that test results for an individual are compared to test results for a relevant norm group which represents the population at large. It is designed to operate in a normative sense. This provides significant additional value for the user. This means that the measure can be used for:

  - diagnosis: to identify what may be the issues for attention for individuals and groups in each situation;

  - evaluation: to measure progress consistently and assess the impact of interventions on mindset; this is now an important requirement in many development programmes – especially where they are funded;

  - research: for instance, to assess which interventions are most effective and with which people, whether there are differences in development between different groups etc.

The MTQ48 Technical Manual provides a significant amount of information about the technical characteristics of the MTQ48 measure, particularly in terms of reliability, validity and the norm group composition. The technical manual is downloadable from the AQR website on **www.aqr.co.uk/ Downloads/MTQ48%20Technical%20Manual%20Jan%202007.pdf**.

The MTQ48 test platform

This was upgraded in 2015 to provide additional functionality to users, whether they are coaches, trainers, managers or researchers – and increasingly often users are both practitioners and researchers.

The test platform is supported by a very secure database where data captured through completion of the MTQ48 measure is stored together with any additional data captured at the time of completion. This is retrievable in two ways: 1) Sten score data can be retrieved by registered users, which enables them to carry out straightforward analyses of data they have gathered and to measure distance travelled for groups and individuals in terms of sten scores; 2) Raw score data (for scales and items) can only be retrieved or accessed through the test publisher, AQR, subject to the usual requirements – compliance with data protection regulations, approval from providers of the data etc. This is obviously of great interest to researchers, particularly in the academic world.

There are two important sets of additional features to the new 2015 platform: customization of additional data and increased flexibility in administration.

Customization of additional data

Originally, the additional data was a default setting which provided the capability to capture data about the individual's age, gender, job level, first language and ethnicity. All of these options remain but there is now an additional option to add department/location.

Users can select which parameters they wish to use. The ethnicity facility can be adapted to suit the specific requirements of the user. There is also the facility for adding telephone number where respondents are interested in over-the-phone feedback. This data can be retrieved by users along with sten score data to enable a wide range of useful analyses.

Flexibility in administration

Previously the platform required users to issue one password at a time. There is now a generic registration link which enables large groups of individuals/candidates to receive invitations for completion with the same log-in. This significantly simplifies test administration for large groups, where e-mail addresses for individuals in large groups are known invitations can be scheduled to go out automatically on a given date. The system can also set up mini-accounts for individuals which they can access at any time (provided they use the same e-mail address). This enables an individual to track their reports over time (this includes other AQR test reports). This is a very useful feature where the emphasis is on personal development.

MTQ48 report types

The Standard Version

MTQ48 generates up to five different reports from the candidate's data using an expert report system. Users and candidates should read the introduction to each report carefully to ensure that they use the report properly.

Development report

This provides the individual's scores and an explanation of what they mean, together with an indication of possible implications. With each of the four component scales, generic development suggestions are offered to enable the candidate to think about modifying behaviour should the situation require this. Figure 5.1 shows an extract from a development report.

FIGURE 5.1 Extract from a development report

Challenge

1   2   3   4   **5**   6   7   8   9   10

You will be able to cope effectively with most of life's challenges, and may use these as a way on enhancing your personal development. However, you might shy away from some of the most daunting opportunities.

You may at times seek "change for change sake", but you are reasonably accepting of a degree of routine. You should generally be comfortable working and living in environments and situations where there is a reasonably significant degree of risk, change and challenge. At times of high stress you may become overly risk avoidant. You will be comfortable in an environment where there is a balance of predictability and flexibility.

Although being happy in comparatively stable and unchanging environments you will usually be able to react quickly to the unexpected when necessary. Sustained exposure to change and challenge can wear people down and you might find that your enthusiasm for change diminishes in these circumstances. You may experience a sense of "burn out" from time to time.

Development suggestions:

- You may benefit by considering that all challenges you face can be used to enhance personal development. Recognise each challenge and carefully consider how each one can be used to help you maximise your potential.
- Consider time management tools and techniques to help organise your time and your resources better.
- Work with someone else to help you to review and prioritise your work – particularly when things are changing quickly.
- Put challenges you face into wider perspectives. If asked to do something which appears daunting, check whether others with similar or lesser abilities than you have achieved it.
- Review your goals and targets to check that they are realistic and achievable. Have you genuinely got the resources you need to achieve? If reliant upon others to what extent are they dependable?
- Develop skills in coaching and delegating – to enable your work to be handled and to appreciate the value of adopting a structured approach to work.
- Review and develop team working – to enable resources and priorities within the group to be better focused.
- Review performance regularly – are your goals still achievable; are you beginning to experience "burn out"; what can you do to refresh yourself.

FIGURE 5.2   Extract from an assessment report

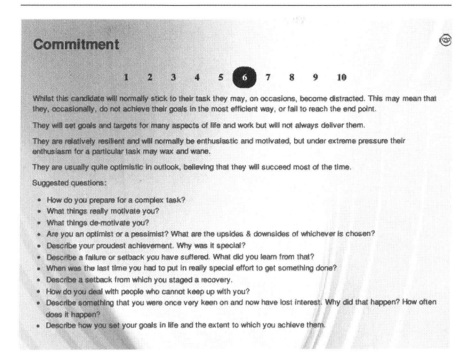

Commitment

1   2   3   4   5   **6**   7   8   9   10

Whilst this candidate will normally stick to their task they may, on occasions, become distracted. This may mean that they, occasionally, do not achieve their goals in the most efficient way, or fail to reach the end point.

They will set goals and targets for many aspects of life and work but will not always deliver them.

They are relatively resilient and will normally be enthusiastic and motivated, but under extreme pressure their enthusiasm for a particular task may wax and wane.

They are usually quite optimistic in outlook, believing that they will succeed most of the time.

Suggested questions:

- How do you prepare for a complex task?
- What things really motivate you?
- What things de-motivate you?
- Are you an optimist or a pessimist? What are the upsides & downsides of whichever is chosen?
- Describe your proudest achievement. Why was it special?
- Describe a failure or setback you have suffered. What did you learn from that?
- When was the last time you had to put in really special effort to get something done?
- Describe a setback from which you staged a recovery.
- How do you deal with people who cannot keep up with you?
- Describe something that you were once very keen on and now have lost interest. Why did that happen? How often does it happen?
- Describe how you set your goals in life and the extent to which you achieve them.

Assessment report

This report provides an interpretation of the individual's scores and identifies some potential implications for the workplace. The narrative is provided for the overall measure and for each of the four component scales. With each narrative, a list of 6–10 suggested questions is provided to enable a user to probe the score. The questions are designed to be open and to be behaviourally orientated to generate the fullest responses. They need adjustment by the manager to ensure that they are appropriate to their specific situation. Figure 5.2 shows an extract from the assessment report.

Coaching report

This report provides an interpretation of the individual's scores and identifies some of the potential implications for the workplace. With each narrative comes a list of suggested coaching or development actions that the user (including manager or coach) can consider for application with the candidate. It is important that the candidate accepts and agrees with any action to be taken. Figure 5.3 shows an extract from a coaching report.

FIGURE 5.3   Extract from a coaching report

Control ◎

| 1 | 2 | 3 | 4 | 5 | 6 | **7** | 8 | 9 | 10 |

This individual is likely to feel in control in most situations, although they may occasionally feel that events are overtaking them. Their control orientation can be split into two distinct areas: Life Control and Emotional Control.

Typically in the workplace these are people who might work steadily for long periods of time with significant success but who will occasionally appear to reach a impasse. For the most part they can cope with work and with life but can be worn down. The solution often lies in rebuilding their feeling of control.

Coaching suggestions include:

- Ensuring the individual understands that this occasional impasse is normal and will happen to most people.
- Identify the cause of the issue and use it as a learning point. Introduce development actions which restore the feeling of control.
- Help them to put into perspective what they can control and what they can't control.
- Give the individual some breathing space to recover – but do it for a finite period by assigning to a less demanding task.
- Help the individual to handle the next set of tasks to a satisfactory conclusion, give them due recognition for this and build up their feeling that they are back in control.

Distance travelled report

This is a comparison report based on a current and a previous assessment for an individual. This will identify areas in which an individual's sten scores have changed or remained the same after a period of time and/or a period of training and development. This report is widely used in training, development and coaching programmes to assess differences arising from the intervention. Hence this is very valuable in ROI (return on investment) studies.

Group report (formerly called the organization development report)

This report is created from data gathered from individuals who form a particular group. The report takes the form of histograms of the patterns of scores for individuals who form the selected group. It also provides tables of data for each group showing (a) spread of sten scores for overall mental toughness and each scale; and (b) means for overall mental toughness and each scale. For example, the group can be a specific team, or it could be the entire management cohort of an organization or a year group in a school or college. The report shows the pattern of results for each scale as a histogram of the total number of people who achieve a particular sten score within that group.

This report is useful in identifying trends and patterns and can be an indicator of cultural issues within an organization. Figure 5.4 shows an extract from this report.

FIGURE 5.4   Extract from a group report

Descriptive Statistics

If the sample is normally distributed the mean will be 5.5. Scores above or below this level may indicate where the selected group's overall mental toughness.

Please note that 5.5 is not necessarily an "ideal" score. It is for each organisation or group to determine what the preferred level of mental toughness could be for its particular situation.

	N	Range	Min	Max	Mean
Total Mental Toughness	4	8	2	10	3.5
Challenge	4	9	1	10	1.75
Commitment	4	6	4	10	5.25
Control	4	6	4	10	4.5
Emotional Control	4	6	4	10	5.0
Life Control	4	7	3	10	4.25
Confidence	4	7	3	10	3.75
Confidence in Abilities	4	7	3	10	4.25
Interpersonal Confidence	4	8	2	10	3.0

Note: On each page there is space provided for you to make notes on your observations on the histogram.

The Young Person's Version

This is the version normally used within secondary education and FE, and generates:

- A coaching report – reporting the scores, what they mean, and offering general coaching suggestions and suggested interview questions to explore.

- A development report – reporting the scores, what they mean, and offering general development suggestions, which can be used in conjunction with the coaching report to encourage the candidate to think about modifying behaviour where required.

- A group analysis report – as the group report described above.

It is generally not recommended to provide copies of reports to young persons. It is more effective to provide oral feedback which is correlated to other information and data.

The future and ongoing development

Users over the world have been immensely helpful in identifying how, where and why the MTQ48 measure can be enhanced or developed further. The following section describes the developments underway at the time of writing.

Additional sub-scales for MTQ48

Currently the control and confidence sub-scales each have two sub-scales. Two sub-scales have been identified for the challenge and commitment scales. Development activity is underway to ensure that their psychometric properties are robust. This will increase the size of the questionnaire to something like 54 items, and is likely to be available by 2016.

Norming

The core version of the MTQ48 measure uses a global norm which is reviewed regularly. The new platform will have two additional capabilities here: 1) the ability to create local norms and use these for report generation and analyses – users will be able to switch between these and use both; 2) the introduction of a perpetually reviewed norm.

A further development will include a feature which will remove long-dated data and replace it with current data enabling the norm to reflect present circumstances.

Customization and white labelling

The new platform will also host other AQR measures (ILM72, Carrus etc). It will be possible to combine the MTQ48 measure with scales and items selected from other measures to create a single 'test' both for easy administration and to enable the assessment of additional attributes in which the user may be interested.

Early years version

The success of MTQ48 in working with students and young persons has led to a significant demand for an early years (typically ages 4–10) version. Educators are increasingly recognizing the value of early interventions to develop young people, and early assessment and diagnosis must play a part in this. The questionnaire design is completed. At the time of writing, studies to establish validity and reliability are underway, and the version is likely to be available in 2016.

Development of a shorter version: MTQ18 or MTQ24

This will produce outputs in terms of the 4 Cs but not sub-scales.

Development of a platform for interventions and linking report outputs to that platform

An important development is taking place with partners who specialize in online delivery of training and development programmes. This development is key to scalability and enabling the concept and its many features to be available to many at realistic and affordable pricing.

Control

06

Destiny is as destiny does. If you believe you have no control, then you have no control. WESS ROBERTS

The more that an individual feels that they can shape and influence what is happening around them the more likely they are to feel that they can make a difference and achieve what is necessary. This is a reasonably well-understood concept, particularly when it comes to stress management and peak performance. Studies consistently show that the less people feel they are in control, the more likely they are to feel more stressed in a way which leads to negative consequences.

Early work on developing the mental toughness model showed that there were two components to the control scale: life control and emotional control.

Life control represented what many understand to be meant by control generally. This captures the idea that the individual believes that they have sufficient control over the factors that influence their behaviour and their performance for them to believe that they are capable of achieving what they set out to achieve.

Those with high levels of life control will have a sense that success is down to them and their own attitude towards the task and they won't be prevented from achieving it. They will generally not need validation or encouragement or support from others. Their own inner belief is enough. Those with low levels of life control will not possess that inner belief and are much more likely to seek support and encouragement from others which may mean that they are dependent upon others whether they are individuals or groups.

It is not difficult to see examples of both ends of the scale in all walks of life. Those with a strong sense of life control often emerge as better managers of their own time. They are more effective at prioritizing tasks and at planning and organizing these tasks. As a result they are usually effective at handling more than one task at a time. If asked to take on additional tasks, they are likely to do so in the knowledge that they can do it. Unsurprisingly therefore they will typically emerge as more positive than the norm – tending to see the solution and not the problem. They are also more likely to 'do what it takes' to complete the task. They are hard-working.

Those with a low sense of life control tend to be less well-organized and can be messy. They are often only effective when handling one thing at a time. If asked to take on additional tasks, they will feel anxiety and be more prepared to fail. They are much less positive and are more likely to find blame for failure in their environment – something will have prevented them from succeeding. They will often see the problem and not the solution, readily identifying reasons why they might not succeed. Again this is a mindset. They may be the equal in every other respect to the individual with a high sense of life control.

The difference often becomes apparent when an individual is asked to take on an additional task. The response typically can be different. Those with a high level of life control are much more likely to respond by saying 'OK. Leave it with me'. They may not know yet whether they can do it and they may otherwise be already busy. But they will have a sense of 'can-do' and have that inner belief that, even if they don't yet know fully what needs to be done, they will be able to organize their work to, at the very least, accomplish this new addition to their workload. As we will see later this can carry a potential downside in that they might find they can't do it, but mostly they will.

Those with a much lower sense of life control are much more likely to respond more cautiously. They may respond by saying 'Can I think about it?' or 'I'm already tied up' or 'I'm not sure, is there not someone else you can ask?' They may not be busy or they may have the time and the capacity to do what is being asked but their inner thoughts are more likely to be 'I am not sure I can do this'. Of course, this might be a sensible response in some situations but the point here is that whether or not this additional task gets done by the individual will often be determined by their life control mindset. As Henry Ford once famously said: 'Whether you think you can, or you think you can't – you're probably right'.

It is not difficult to see examples of all points on the scale in work, in education, in sport and in society. Current attention on worklessness, where unemployment is institutionalized into several generations of a family or community, provides a good example. The inability to get a job will be substantially down to the belief that they are flotsam on the oceans of life.

The second component is *emotional control*. This describes the extent to which individuals are in control of their emotions and the extent to which they will reveal their emotional state to others. This does not mean they do not experience emotions or that they are not emotionally sensitive (intelligent). This is about their ability to manage those emotions.

Our understanding of this component has developed in recent years. Those with a strong sense of emotional control can choose how much of their emotional state they will reveal to others. This can be relevant and valuable in a number of interpersonal situations. Handling complex negotiations will be one obvious example. Operating in a leadership role where you need to portray a sense of calm in difficult circumstances will be another.

A less obvious example might be bullying or harassment. Quite often the modus operandi for the bully is to provoke the victim. However, if the victim does not appear to respond to that provocation, then the bully is often left unsure as to their impact and may well cease that activity because it is not producing the desired effect. We look at this in more detail elsewhere in the book.

Those with low levels of emotional control will find it difficult not to reveal their emotional states to others. They will respond more readily to provocation or annoyance. They are typically more likely to show their emotions in the sense they will show anger, embarrassment, frustration, etc. As a result they will often deal poorly with criticism, feedback (especially negative feedback) and setbacks. Another response can be to sulk if things don't go their way. Studies show that they are more likely to report bullying, They may see bullying behaviours in others (teachers, managers, coaches etc) when others in their group with stronger emotional control simply shrug them off and see the behaviour as the other person's problem.

There is an emerging understanding that emotional control is closely related to the notion of 'intelligent emotions' being championed by people like Professor Paul Brown. The suggestion is that emotional intelligence is 'less intelligent' than currently supposed and that, for many, the more valuable concept here is that of intelligent emotions.

Emotional intelligence describes the capacity for an individual to be aware of his or her emotional impact on others and of the emotional impact of others on the individual. We'll see later in the book (Chapter xx) that there is growing evidence that mental toughness and emotional intelligence are closely correlated.

The notion of intelligent emotions can be usefully illustrated in the following way. Imagine a very good actor playing a character on stage. The actor and the character are quite different in terms of personality. Nevertheless, a good actor can portray a wide range of types convincingly. Actors are trained not only to say the words but to show characteristics and mannerisms which add meaning to the words. The audience in the theatre is expected to understand what the character is feeling as well as saying. Moreover, everyone in an audience of, say, 500 people is expected to get the message. Now, consider that you are one of those people in the audience. Whose emotions and feelings are you reading – the actor's or the character's? If the actor is doing his or her job well you are reading the character's emotions. The actor is managing their emotions to reveal to you/the audience what they want you to see, know and understand.

It is increasingly argued that this is the truly 'intelligent' bit. Most of us will be able to read what we are shown – that's emotional intelligence. This is what we mean by emotional control in mental toughness. It has important and valuable implications. People who lead, manage, teach etc, know that if their inner emotional state is negative and they show it to others (their staff, students, colleagues etc) then they will impact negatively on them. You might have had a terrible weekend or suffered a personal setback which makes you unhappy. If you let others know, you are likely to spread that to others. A teacher will quickly lose control over students. A mentally tough individual with a strong sense of emotional control is more likely to say 'I know I am not happy but I am going to show my happy face to others when I see them and I won't reveal how I am truly feeling at the present time'.

And generally, providing you present an authentic version of yourself, this works. The mentally tough individual also knows that by lifting the mood of those around them that this will lift his or her mood too. There is growing evidence for this which is provoking the development of innovative interventions ranging from introducing actor skills into leadership and inter-personal skills development programmes through to the development of mood enhancement apps such as Mood Mint.

Managing emotions is very important in leadership roles and many interpersonal settings such as negotiations. Authenticity is important. It's not likely to work if you present a 'happy' version that others won't recognize. People are emotionally intelligent. Of course, this is not suggesting that anyone should bottle up their emotions and feelings and never reveal them to others. In that route madness lies. This is entirely about managing emotions and the emotional signals individuals send to other. It's perfectly OK to show your true emotions to others – coaches, counsellors, friends etc. However, you only have to think of those who constantly reveal their emotional stages – especially negative emotions – to understand how counterproductive and damaging that can be.

Control – defined and applied

Control

Defined

Control is the extent to which people feel they are in control of their life. Some individuals believe that they can exert considerable influence over their working environment, that they can make a difference and change things. In contrast, others feel that the outcome of events is outside their personal control and they are unable to exert any influence over themselves or others.

Applied

This means, for example, that at one end of the scale individuals feel their input really matters and are motivated to make a full contribution. At the other end, they may feel that their contribution is of little importance and hence may not play as full a part as they could. An implication may be that one can handle lots of things at the same time and the other cannot.

Sub-scales

Ongoing development has enabled the identification of two sub-scales to this scale:

- *Controls (Emotion)* – individuals scoring highly on this scale are better able to manage their emotions. They are able to keep anxieties in check and are less likely to reveal their negative emotional state to other people.

- *Controls (Life)* – those scoring highly on this scale are more likely to believe they control their lives. They feel that their plans will not be thwarted and that they can make a difference.

Emotional control

This measures the extent to which we control our anxieties and our emotions and reveal our emotional states to others (Table 6.1).

Life control

This is a measure of self-worth. It indicates the extent to which we believe we shape what happens to us ... or the other way around (Table 6.2).

TABLE 6.1 Emotional control scores

Lower scores	Higher scores
Let everyone know exactly how they are feeling	Reveal only to others emotions and feelings that they want to show
Feel things happen to them	Feel they shape what happens
See issues as 'my problem'	See issues as 'someone else's problem'
See things in terms of guilt and blame	
Internalize problems and the feelings that arise from them	Good at controlling emotions
Show emotions when provoked or challenged	Understand other people's emotions/feeling and know how to manage these
Pick up quickly on others' emotions and are affected by them	Difficult to provoke or annoy
Anxious	Do not appear anxious
Show a reaction when criticized	Impassive when others make comments which could upset or annoy
Show anger or annoyance when things don't go their way	
Show discomfort when others 'have a go at them'	Can be insensitive to others remarks
Deal poorly with provocation	Stay calm in a crisis
Respond poorly to poor marks or the prospect of poor performance	Keep a broader perspective on things
	Believe they make their own luck
Can create a sense of fear and avoidance in others	Better able to articulate their emotions
Will cry or show histrionics and may try to get others to behave in the same way	Use active language
	Direct their energy to their choices
	High level of self-awareness
Sulk when things don't go their way	Better at helping others to manage their emotions
Adopt a fatalist approach	Appear to detach themselves from others' emotions and feelings
Use negative language a great deal	
Use passive language	Have a sense of 'I have earned this' or 'I deserve this'
Feel 'I don't deserve this ...'	

TABLE 6.2   Life control scores

Lower scores	Higher scores
Believe things happen to them	Believe they can make a difference
Often believe 'I can't do this because of my ... beliefs/religion/upbringing etc'	Generally believe 'they can'
	Comfortable when asked to do several things at a time
Will readily find excuses for not getting things done	Happy to take on additional tasks even when already busy
Will adopt the use of cautious language and phrases	Good at planning and time management
Tend to wait for things to happen rather than take an initiative	Good at prioritizing
Their 'cup is half-empty' most of the time	Will use positive language and expressions
Live in chaos which provides a ready excuse	Prepared to work hard to clear blockages
	Their 'cup is half-full' most of the time
Find it hard to do more than one thing at a time	Happy to take on multiple commitments and know how to deal with them
Prone to depression	
Will tend to respond to the last person who pressures them	Tend to see others as problems ... which can be handled
Freezes when overloaded	Will feel they have more choices in life – 'If this doesn't work I'll do something else'
Can feel stretched with modest workloads – poor at time management	Happy to re-organize as they go along – aren't unsettled by errors and mistakes
Will tend to blame outside factors for preventing success	
May panic when given assignments	Believe they can define what needs to be done
Tend to be 'staid or stuck in the sand'	
Comparatively un-resourceful	Break down tasks into manageable chunks
Won't see the opportunities within their own skill set	Able to say 'no' when needed – 'I can do that for you, but I can't do it now'
Have a limiting belief system – 'I can't do this because ...'	See the solution rather than the problem
	Will enjoy working in a positive atmosphere

Are high levels of control always a strength?

Generally, the answer is a resounding 'Yes'. However, as we will see with all of the components of mental toughness, without self-awareness, high levels of mental toughness in each of the areas can carry the seeds of problems and issues. Sometimes these affect the individual directly, eg over-committing. Sometimes they affect others where the individual forgets or is unaware of their impact on others. This, of course, is important when the individual needs to achieve through and with others – especially if the others are mentally sensitive.

This suggests that there will often be learning for everyone, whether they have high or low mental toughness. The key is self-awareness – this applies to everyone. The potential downsides for the mentally sensitive are fairly apparent. We can briefly summarize the most common downsides for the mentally tough below:

TABLE 6.3 Possible downsides for the mentally tough

Potential downsides for those with high ...
Life control
• Can take on too much.
• Can be intolerant of those who aren't as positive.
• Can be micro-managers – take over when others don't step up.
• Can perceived as bullies – 'can-do' behaviour can intimidate.
• Can fail to see own weaknesses.
Emotional control
• Difficult to read.
• Can appear insensitive – may show no emotion at all.
• Unflappability can confuse others.
• Can stress others with whom they work – can appear impassive or unenthusiastic.
• Sometimes have difficulty in communications – sending the right signals.

The psychological context of control

These are:

- learned helplessness;
- attributions;
- luck;
- superstitions;
- neuroticism.

A look at learned helplessness

The control dimension of mental toughness is closely related to that of learned helplessness. This important idea was proposed by Seligman in 1975. At its most basic, when people have learned helplessness they have the generalized perception that things are outside their control. Whilst it is obviously the case that some things are outside an individual's control, in a learned helplessness scenario even things that should be controllable become uncontrollable.

When under pressure learned helplessness individuals tend to underperform. For example, Peterson and Barrett (1987) reported that college students with helplessness beliefs obtained lower marks. They tended to be more passive learners, for example, seeking out less help from their academic advisors. Similarly, work carried out at Hull University by Clough and Earle over the period 2001 to 2013 showed that undergraduates with lower control scores were more likely to drop out of the course, and those that stuck to it tended to obtain lower marks. Again, these students tended to have much less contact with their home departments and were often described as 'invisible'.

> Do not let what you cannot do interfere with what you can do.
>
> John Wooden

Learned helplessness refers to the expectation, based on previous experience, that one's actions cannot possibly lead to success. Much of the early work in helplessness focused on animal studies and was really an accidental finding. Seligman was investigating classical conditioning when he made an interesting discovery. Most people are aware of the work of Pavlov who paired sound with food, resulting in the finding that in the end the sound on its own would produce the desired response from the animal.

Seligman paired the auditory tone with a mild shock to a dog suspended in a hammock. The idea was that the tone itself would induce a fear response. This element worked as predicted. The 'trained' dogs were then put into a box which was split into two areas, separated by small barrier. The researchers expected that the dog would jump the barrier when they sounded the tone – to avoid the shock. However, they just sat there! They had learned (falsely) that there was no point in trying to avoid the pain.

This early animal work has been extended to human behaviour. It is argued that some individuals' life experience has shown them that there is no point in trying – no matter what they do, they cannot change their life experience. So, for example, a small child who constantly finds that when they cry they are ignored will in the end simply stop trying to influence the world in this way. This can have both positive and negative consequences. Some child-care experts suggest that it is important not to run to baby every time they cry and in the end this leads to more independent children (and better sleep for all). However, at the opposite end of the 'care continuum' a small number of children experience serious parental neglect. This often results in mental health and adjustment issues in later life.

It has been argued that it is not simply exposure to uncontrollable events that produces helplessness. Peterson and Barrett (1993) argue that individuals must attribute the lack of controllability to their own inadequacies. Other authors have suggested that it is not simply a disconnect between actions and outcomes; rather it is repeated failure that is the vital ingredient. The evidence is far from clear.

CASE STUDY   The impact of failure on performance

The criterion-related validity of the MTQ48 was investigated by a study which examined the moderating effects that mental toughness has on performance. The study explored the ability for individuals to compartmentalize or show resilience when faced with 'failure'.

The study involved 79 participants (42 males, M age = 22.74 years, SD = 3.43; 37 females, M age = 22.43, SD = 3.85) who were given either positive or negative feedback after completing a number of motor tasks. They then carried out a cognitive task (planning exercise) as an objective measure of performance. The motor tasks and cognitive tasks should have been completely independent, involving very different skills.

Feedback tasks

Task 1

The shooting task entailed shooting a 'laser' gun at targets. The task was initially and successfully demonstrated by the experimenter. For each of the 30 trials, the experimenter switched on the appropriate light bulb for the target and the participants were asked to shoot. Dependent on the feedback categories the participants either scored 20 per cent less than estimated (negative feedback group) or one higher than estimated (positive feedback group). The success rate was manipulated by the experimenter. When all 30 trials had been completed the participants were fed back their actual results.

Task 2

Immediately after the first task the participants were asked to complete a snooker shot task. After rating their snooker ability on a 1–10 scale, participants were asked to complete five practice shots. Participants were then directed to carry out five pre-set shots and each shot was rated as to its success. At the end of this task the participants were given either negative or positive feedback in accordance with their allocated group. Again this feedback did not relate to actual performance.

Planning task

Straight after the snooker task the participants undertook a planning exercise. The exercise required various details and information to be organized into a timetable of sessions for a series of training classes. The main sub-tasks involved arranging appropriate dates for trainers, candidates and availability to hold the training sessions. More than one answer could be found for each sub-task to fit in the appropriate slots on the timetable. However, only one totally correct answer could be found in which all details would fit into the timetable. Participants were provided with all sub-task information at the beginning of the exercise and were able to work through the information in any order they chose. All participants were given 30 minutes to complete the exercise.

The extreme scores of mental toughness (high and low 25 per cent) were examined and they showed that the participants with high mental toughness scored significantly higher on the planning exercise than the low mental toughness group (M = 2.71, SD = 1.10, M = 2.05, SD =.97; t = 2.08, df40, p =.044).

The group that were given negative feedback scored significantly lower than the group that received positive feedback (M = 2.86, SD =.96, M = 2.29, SD = 1.14; t = 2.02, df77, p =.047).

TABLE 6.4   Population scores of mental toughness

	N	Minimum	Maximum	Mean	Std Deviation
Challenge	79	2.50	4.75	3.75	.44
Commitment	79	2.00	4.36	3.47	.44
Control	79	2.36	4.07	3.30	.38
Confidence	79	2.27	4.60	3.47	.47
Mental Toughness	79	2.48	4.17	3.46	.34

TABLE 6.5   Performance scores on planning exercise for participants receiving positive and negative feedback

Mental Toughness Group	N	Negative Feedback		Positive Feedback	
		Mean	Std Deviation	Mean	Std Deviation
Low	9	1.56	.882	2.42	.90
High	12	2.25	1.055	3.33	.87

The results

These results clearly illustrate how failure can loom over an individual, impacting on other aspects of their lives. However, the performance level of high mental toughness participants was not adversely affected by negative feedback. In other words they had not *learned to fail.*

> I am not judged by the number of times I fail, but by the number of times I succeed; and the number of times I succeed is in direct proportion to the number of times I can fail and keep on trying.
>
> Tom Hopkins

The power of attributions

However, one repeated and validated finding is that attributions are central to feelings of control. Two seminal pieces of work have tackled this: Rotter's (1966) work on internal and external locus of control and Heider's/Weiner's work (1944, 1972) on attributions.

People with an internal locus of control believe they make things happen. This is obviously reflected closely in high scores on the MTQ48 control dimension. This clear dichotomy between internal and external loci is also reflected in the work of deCharms and Carpenter (1968). They too believed that there are two types of people: *origins* – these people love to be in control and originate their own behaviours; and *pawns* – these people often feel powerless and disenfranchised, being swept along by external pressures.

Writing about locus of control, Cox (1998) states: 'Research suggests that an internal orientation is more mature than an external orientation' (p 218). He then goes on to argue that childhood attributions should shift towards the internal and that perhaps involvement in sports and exercise may facilitate this shift.

It is perhaps one of the most powerful ideas in psychology that it's not what is happening that is important; rather it is what a person thinks is happening that is the key.

It can be claimed that it was Fritz Heider (1944) who first developed a coherent and useable theory of attributions. He again emphasized the importance of internal and external factors but further sub-divided these. Within the internal category he identified ability and effort. In the external category he described task difficulty and luck. So when an activity is performed the success or otherwise of it can be attributed to ability, hard work, its difficulty or chance. However, it was Weiner (1972), building on this work, who produced the model that is most widely used today (see Table 6.6).

TABLE 6.6   Attributions

	Internal	External
Stable	Ability	Task Difficulty
Unstable	Effort	Luck

In this model, ability and effort are within the person. It is assumed that ability is relatively fixed in nature, but effort is very malleable. An individual who believes they control their destiny will attribute success *and* failure down to the internal factors. In other words, they will succeed because they had talent and worked hard. They fail because they did not have the skills or they simply did not try enough.

One of the core philosophies of mental toughness is just that. Success and failure is down to the individual. We are an intensely blame-ridden society at the moment – but that blame is usually focused on everything but ourselves. The mentally tough individual is willing to accept the consequences of their actions: both good and bad.

Later, Weiner added a third dimension: controllability. This dimension related to the individual's belief that something was under his or her control or not. It is quite hard to identify an external factor that is also controllable. One candidate here is perhaps luck.

Emotional control

Whilst the clear focus of the control component is on individuals controlling their own lives and development, an important sub-component is the control of emotions. It has long been recognized that some individuals are more emotionally reactive than others. This particular personality dimension, usually described as neuroticism, is often seen as one of the 'big five' personality factors that are used to describe humans. The big five dimensions are:

1 *Openness* – inventive/curious vs consistent/cautious.

2 *Conscientiousness* – efficient/organized vs easy-going/careless.

3 *Extraversion* – outgoing/energetic vs shy/reserved.

4 *Agreeableness* – friendly/compassionate vs cold/unkind.

5 *Neuroticism* – sensitive/nervous vs secure/confident.

Research at Hull University has shown that scores on the emotional control sub-scales correlate negatively with both neuroticism and trait anxiety. Individuals with greater emotional control have lower levels of neuroticism. Lower scores on neuroticism are also related to emotional stability and the ability to bounce back quickly from setbacks.

Eysenck, who carried out the initial work on neuroticism, felt that his traits were closely linked to the operating of the central nervous system and also that personality is highly heritable. This 'biological basis' of personality has echoes in the latest work involving brain scanning. This has shown a number of interesting findings. Control of emotion showed a correlation with the precuneus and with the inferior parietal lobule. The inferior parietal lobule has been shown to have a number of links to emotion; for instance, it is involved with perspective taking of social emotions and it has been shown to be involved in the processing of happiness-specific information. These links to the regulation of emotion and recognition of the emotion of happiness, again combined with the feeling of agency provided by the precuneus, could explain why a person with these attributes would feel that they have good control over their emotions.

Commitment

07

"Courage and perseverance have a magical talisman, before which difficulties disappear and obstacles vanish into air.
JOHN QUINCY ADAMS

This scale measures how we see goals and targets. The component reflects the extent to which we make promises, particularly those which are tangible and measurable, and the extent to which we commit to keeping those promises. Those can be promises we make to others and/or promises we make to ourselves. These notions of 'making promises' and 'keeping promises' are emerging as the two sub-scales for the commitment component.

We tend to make promises to others commonly in the workplace. This underpins many appraisal or personal development processes. But it can also include working towards sales or delivery targets, completing projects on time, dealing with a rush job etc. We are often pressed to make similar promises to others in many other ways. For example, promising to visit ailing relatives, to help someone achieve something, to train to be a fit or competent member of a team, to do well in exams, to get a job etc.

We also make many promises to ourselves. New Year resolutions are one obvious example; giving up smoking, trying to lose weight, passing an exam, staying in touch with friends are others.

Fall seven times, stand up eight.

Japanese proverb

Making and keeping promises are important aspects of the way people deal with each other. We can sometimes be judged in terms of our reliability: 'I can trust him/her to do that'. It can be an important aspect of the way that others see us. This can have a big impact on performance, particularly in groups or teams. If you are viewed as unlikely to be committed to something, then others with whom you need to co-operate may take the view that it's not worth the effort of supporting you and will avoid doing just that, negatively affecting your ability to succeed.

Our approach to goals and targets (and indeed the same goal or target) can vary. For some of us the very notion of a target is motivating. In our mind we can see that goal or targets as helping to define what success looks like. Providing it is reasonably achievable we will go for it and do whatever it takes to hit the target. Even if obstacles arise, this won't necessarily dampen our enthusiasm for the target. The driver is there – we want to hit most of or the entire target. It equates broadly to notions of tenacity, persistent determination, perseverance, doggedness, resolve, diligence, application and purpose.

Quite often, for these people all that is needed to get them going is the goal or target. It is sufficiently motivating to them to work out how that target can be achieved. For others, goals and targets are intimidating and will induce fear, anxiety and even mental paralysis. For them, goals and targets are to be avoided or ignored. The notion is one which doesn't describe success – it also indicates what failure might look like. The object of our commitment can appear overwhelming: 'When I fail to achieve this, and it doesn't look achievable, then I and everyone else will know I am a failure'. Indeed the more they think this way the more they believe the goal is not achievable. Again, two people of equal ability, experience and skill can look at the same goals or targets, and one will view them in one way and the other will view them differently. This translates into differences in performance, wellbeing, behaviour etc.

As with all the components of mental toughness, an exceptionally high level of commitment can have its downside. Highly committed people can be obstinate, intransigent, and stubborn. They can persevere with a task past the point where it makes any sense to continue. If in a managerial position or a position of authority this can mean they will drive others with the same level of will. At times this may mean that the individual is being driven out of their comfort zone with all the attendant consequences. Similarly, they will often 'manage by numbers'. Because knowing the goals or target is sufficient for their own need to get going they may not appreciate that others (who may not be as committed) will need a degree of support or guidance in order to deliver a task. Most people need to know not only 'what' is to be achieved but something about the 'how' it is to be achieved. Without that, delegation or tasking others can simply become a stressful exercise.

Commitment – defined and applied

Defined

This sub-scale measures the extent to which an individual is likely to persist with a goal or work task. Individuals differ in the degree to which they remain focused on their goals. Some may be easily distracted or bored, or divert their attention to competing goals, whereas others may be more likely to persist.

Applied

An individual who scores at the high end of the scale will be able to handle and achieve things when faced with tough and unyielding deadlines. An individual at the other end will need to be free from those types of demands to handle work.

Sample descriptors and behaviours which are often associated with extreme positions on the commitment scale are shown in Tables 7.1 and 7.2. These lists are not exclusive or comprehensive.

Are high levels of commitment always a strength?

Generally the answer is again a resounding 'Yes'. As we will see with other components of mental toughness, without self-awareness, high levels of mental toughness in this area can carry the seeds of problems and issues. Sometimes these affect the individual directly, eg over-committing. Sometimes they impact on others where the individual forgets or is unaware of their impact on others. This, of course, is important when the individual needs to achieve through and with others – especially if the others are mentally sensitive.

TABLE 7.1 Setting goals and targets – making promises

Lower scores	Higher scores
Intimidated by goals and measures – they induce paralysis	Like goals and measures – these describe what success looks like
May feel inadequate or 'stupid' when asked to do something	Goals are translated in their heads into something which is achievable
Will include terms such as 'if ...' and 'but ...' into their response to be asked to do something – providing the future reason for non-achievement	Tend to be more objective about things
	Like the repeated opportunity to measure and prove themselves
May lack a sense of purpose – they can think 'win–lose'	Accept responsibility
	Set high standards for self and others
Goals become something which appears overpowering	Like being judged or assessed
	Won't let others down
May resent the imposition of goals and targets	May deliver too quickly at times
May respond emotionally when given tasks	Can inconvenience others with their focus on KPIs
Will avoid targets	Have a sense of purpose – will often think 'win–win'
Will skip meetings or classes	Like ownership, acceptance and responsibility
More likely to be late for things	
May sleep in at times	Like being judged or assessed
Find reasons to miss the target – 'I can't do ... *maths*'	Like the objectivity of goals and measures – avoids being subject to others' opinions about their capability
May try self-sabotage in order to get out of doing something	
Will default to a life experience which provides an excuse to blame someone else for failure – 'I couldn't do this because my parents ...'	
Unlikely to volunteer for things, especially extreme tasks	
Prepared to let others down	
Can be seen as irresponsible	
Not happy about being judged	

TABLE 7.2 Achieving goals and targets – keeping promises

Lower scores	Higher scores
Unwilling to make an effort or give up something less important	Will break things down into manageable chunks
Allow themselves to be easily distracted	Prepared to do what it takes – will work long and hard if needed
Adopt a minimalist approach – will do the absolute minimum	Maintain focus
Will skip meetings or classes	Diligent about projects – delivers on time
More likely to be late for things	Tenacious
Attendance can be poor	Will prioritize effort and activities
Find reasons to miss the target – I can't do ... *maths'*	Will attend meetings/classes even if they don't like the people/topic
May try self-sabotage in order to get out of doing something	(Hyper-)Active
Will default to a life experience which provides an excuse to blame someone else for failure – 'I couldn't do this because my parents ...'	May overachieve (may overwork too)
	May deliver too quickly at times
	Can inconvenience others with their focus on KPIs
Easily bored – won't commit time and effort	Have a sense of purpose – will often think 'win–win'
Can feel unlucky – it's not my day	Have a strong sense of conscientiousness
Find working to a goal stressful	Like celebrating success – own as well as others' successes
	Find working to a goal exhilarating

Once again, the key is self-awareness – this applies to everyone. The potential downsides for the mentally sensitive are fairly apparent. We briefly summarize the most common downsides for those with high levels of commitment in Table 7.3.

> Nothing in this world can take the place of persistence. Talent will not; nothing is more common than unsuccessful people with talent. Genius will not; unrewarded genius is almost a proverb. Education will not; the world is full of educated derelicts. Persistence and determination alone are omnipotent.
>
> Calvin Coolidge

TABLE 7.3   Possible downsides for those with high levels of commitment

Potential downsides for those who like ...
Setting goals and targets – making promises
• Can overcommit!
• Can be perfectionists when realism is a better option.
• Can fail to see that others aren't motivated in the same way.
• Can intimidate others with their goal orientation.
• May 'manage by numbers' – knowing a goal is often enough for them, they can work out what needs to be done. Others may need more support and guidance.
Achieving goals and targets – keeping promises
• May miss doing things that are equally important or more pressing.
• May overachieve in one area and underachieve in another.
• Can be intolerant of those who aren't as committed.
• Can overwork if others don't play their part.
• Can be frustrated if others don't recognize or celebrate their achievement.
• Can be 'taken for granted' – the reliable deliverer.
• Can be anxious until the task is achieved.

The psychological context of commitment

Procrastination

Putting things off, or procrastination, is one of the most common forms of self-handicapping amongst a wide range of people.

> Self-handicaps are anticipatory excuses that are presented to obscure the link between performance and ability. Self-handicaps protect people's images of self-competence in the event of poor performances.
>
> Galluci, 2008, p 217

There have been a number of explanations given as to why people put things off when they know they shouldn't. It can be seen as a coping mechanism to reduce stress. However, whilst it can certainly help in the short term, in the longer term it makes the situation much worse. At best it's an effective passive coping strategy. It has been suggested that trait procrastination comes into being as a result of childhood experiences. It can be suggested that it might be a passive–aggressive way for a child to express their anger at having to achieve all the time. This links closely to learned helplessness. Ferrari and Tice (2000) showed in an experimental study that procrastinators sometimes find it better to risk failure than to look foolish. Galluci (2008) writes:

> ... procrastinators protect their self-esteem at the cost of underachievement, unrealized goals, and wasted potential. Perhaps ruminations about 'what might have been' sustain hope in abilities, but again this comes at the considerable cost of regret regarding lost and squandered opportunities.
>
> Galluci, 2008, p 240

The trait of conscientiousness

Another way of looking at the problem of procrastination is to adopt a trait approach. It has been suggested that human beings only have five predominant personality traits (eg McCrae and Costa, 1987). These are often described as the 'big five' personality traits and are as follows:

1 extraversion;

2 agreeableness;

3 conscientiousness;

4 neuroticism;

5 openness.

Conscientiousness reflects an individual's degree of self-discipline. High scorers plan and are organized, avoiding distractions. Conscientiousness has been clearly linked to academic and business success. Intriguingly, people who are more conscientious – or have a tendency to be self-disciplined, careful and purposeful – appear less likely to develop physical and psychological diseases.

That conscientiousness seems to promote longevity is not surprising. People with this trait tend to practise a number of healthy behaviours such as not smoking, drinking in moderation, exercising regularly, and adhering to medical recommendations. They also tend to get better jobs and earn higher salaries.

It has been shown that out of the big five personality traits only conscientiousness predicts success across *all* categories of work. The other four have specific advantages across specific jobs but conscientiousness has a generally powerful impact across the board. Although it is the case that this trait has a generally positive impact on people, it can have its dark side. Individuals who are high on conscientiousness or commitment can suffer if they are prevented from reaching their goals by outside factors.

For example, Boyce, Wood and Brown (2010) carried out a four-year longitudinal study of 9,570 individuals. They found that the drop in an individual's life satisfaction following unemployment was significantly moderated by their conscientiousness. After three years of unemployment individuals high in conscientiousness experienced a 120 per cent higher decrease in life satisfaction than those at low levels. Individuals who score highly on commitment are more likely to succeed, but are also more likely to suffer if they fail.

> Apply yourself. Get all the education you can, but then, by God, do something. Don't just stand there; make it happen.
>
> Lee Iacocca

Goal setting

Goal setting is a very important psychological technique. Its practical applications will be discussed in some detail in Chapter 25. It was initially developed by Edwin Locke (1968) who conceived it as a cognitive process, with a person's conscious goals and intentions the primary drivers of behaviour. Goal setting has had a major impact on all walks of life, leading Mento, Steel and Karren (1987) to write:

> If there is ever to be a viable candidate from the organizational sciences for elevation to the lofty status of a scientific law of nature, then the relationship between goal difficulty, specificity, commitment and task performance are serious contenders.

However, as is the case with the underlying trait of conscientiousness itself, the story is a little more complex. First, individual differences play a part in the use of goal setting techniques. Individuals low on commitment often find goal setting difficult, and attempting to set goals can create very high levels of anxiety. Whilst these problems can be overcome with appropriate and individualized training it is important to recognize that one size does not fit all.

Similarly, whilst the research evidence into the effectiveness of goal setting in the workplace has been impressive, other areas of life do not seem to show this clear pattern. For example, research within the sporting domain has been equivocal at best. As this world is dominated by the ability to measure almost every aspect of performance, this, at first sight, seems in-explicable. The problem seems to stem from a whole host of methodological inadequacies of the studies that have been undertaken. Where these have been addressed the findings appear to be more consistent with these emanating from the world of work.

It is clear that goal setting works but:

- some individuals, for example those scoring low on the commitment scales, need more help in using this technique;
- the goal setting process is complicated and the goals set say as much about the individual as they do about the task to be performed;
- poor goal setting not only does not work, it has a negative impact on performance.

CASE STUDY Sticking to a boring task

One area of performance required in a number of occupations is sustained attention or vigilance, which involves maintaining focus and awareness for extended periods of time. Nakamura (2001) reported that high mentally tough individuals have higher levels of concentration (of which vigilance is a major dimension) than low mentally tough individuals. This study sought to investigate the relationship between mental toughness (as measured using the MTQ48) and vigilance as a measure of performance under mental stress.

What was done

Twenty-two healthy participants (8 males and 14 females) took part in this study, with a mean age of 21 years. Participants were grouped as either high or low mentally tough in relation to their MTQ48 scores.

Participants carried out a vigilance task under both normal and stressed conditions. The vigilance task consisted of watching a computer screen on which a circle of 20 points would progressively illuminate one by one, similar to the second hand advancing round a clock face. This is widely known as the Mackworth Clock task.

Participants watched for a 'missed' advancement, where the point supposed to illuminate does not, and the next one does. When this event occurred, participants were to respond as quickly as possible. The task lasted 10 minutes, during which each point was highlighted for 0.7 seconds and 40 'misses' would occur. The number of errors (missed responses and incorrect responses) was calculated for comparison.

Following completion of the first experimental 10-minute stage, participants were asked to place their hand into a cold water bath, keeping it open, for three minutes, but were informed that they were free to withdraw their hand at any time if it became too uncomfortable. The second stage of the Mackworth Clock task was identical to the first stage, and was completed immediately after the end of the cold pressor test.

The results

High mentally tough individuals performed significantly better on the Mackworth Clock task, reporting higher levels of vigilance, than did the lower mentally tough individuals. This was apparent in the significantly lower number of errors for high mental toughness participants for normal stage 1 and stressed stage 2 when compared to low mental toughness participants for stage 1 and stage 2 (Figure 7.1).

FIGURE 7.1 Mean number of errors in a vigilance task for low and high mental toughness groups

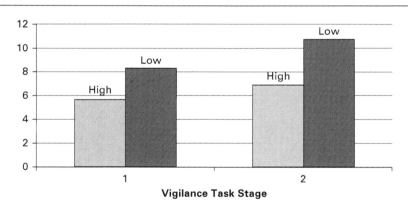

The conclusion

The MTQ48 successfully predicted performance on a standard test of vigilance. High mentally tough individuals were more vigilant under both normal and stressful conditions. It can be argued that they were more committed to an intrinsically dull task. They were less likely to lose focus and concentration, not allowing themselves to become distracted.

Challenge

08

*Accept challenges, so that you may feel
the exhilaration of victory.* **GEORGE S PATTON**

This component of mental toughness addresses how we, as individuals, respond to challenge. A challenge represents any activity or event which we see as out of the ordinary and which involves doing something that is stretching. It is where an important element of 'drive' sits.

Like the other components of mental toughness we have identified two sub-scales for this element. Firstly, there is the attitude towards change and new experiences. Some will see that as threatening – an uncomfortable step into the unknown. Something to be avoided if at all possible. Others will see stretching oneself, seeking out new experiences and taking risks as both exciting and interesting in that they see the opportunity for learning and for personal development in doing this. In our work with coaches, trainers and teachers we are finding many illustrations of how this determines openness to learning. The MTQ48 measure is increasingly used to assess this aspect of mindset before individuals are introduced to training and development activity.

The second sub-scale identifies how individuals handle all outcomes and respond to stretching themselves. Pushing oneself necessarily involves some risk which means that not everything one does will always be successful. The more mentally tough will see learning and development in every outcome – success or setback. They are more likely to think 'That may not have worked but I have learned something valuable from doing it' and their subsequent response might be 'I now know how to do it better next time' or even 'I will give it another go ... I won't let that beat me'. The mentally sensitive are more likely to think 'That didn't work. That was unpleasant. I won't do that again'. One can argue that there is learning going on here but it is negative in direction.

In 2014, researchers at the University of Basle provided an interesting insight here. They carried out a study on c 800 vocational students in their final year on a programme. This was the exam year – for many a source of pressure. No interventions were offered. It was simply an important longitudinal study to see what happened to their mental toughness. The researchers assessed the mental toughness of the students using MTQ48 at the start and at the finish of the year. They found, not surprisingly, that the mentally tough generally achieved better exam results than the mentally sensitive. However, they also found that, over the year, the mentally tough generally improved their mental toughness as they learned to deal with the pressure of the exam year. And the mentally sensitive became generally more mentally sensitive over the same period.

The challenge scale can be seen as an important factor in drive and motivation. It sits very well with Maslow's concept of the hierarchy of needs and the model of motivation more recently described succinctly in Daniel Pink's book *Drive: The surprising truth about what motivates us*.

As we know, Maslow suggested that once some basic needs were met, most people were motivated by attending to what he called the higher-order needs, the most important of which was self-actualization. This is where the idea of contentment sits. The notion here is that we are on a lifetime learning journey and the goal is to be the best that we can be. Openness to learning is a vital aspect of this.

Challenge is where we learn to manage our fears too. For someone in the workplace it might be doing a presentation to senior managers, being put in charge of an important project, representing the organization in a negotiation, or simply delivering some output in an uncomfortably tight timescale. For students, exams and coursework represent challenges. For athletes achieving personal best times and performing in competition (especially in front of a crowd) are good examples. For someone who is unemployed, getting a job can be a challenge. For others it could be giving up smoking, recovering from illness etc. Probably the most important type of challenge everyone faces is the need to deal with change (and in some cases, variety and flexibility).

How we perceive challenge is key to how we cope and deal with challenge. For some a major challenge or a major period of change will be considered exciting, even welcomed. The individual is likely to view the challenge in a positive light. This will be an opportunity to push back the boundaries, to demonstrate to oneself, and perhaps to others, that one can deal with the unknown or the risk entailed in dealing with a significant change. This could be a chance to prove something to yourself.

Others (who might have the same or even higher levels of ability) will see the same situation as threatening and almost certainly not an opportunity for positive self-discovery. Change and facing significant challenge are likely to be considered as negative opportunities: 'this is something that will find me out and will expose me'.

If we look at the example of being asked to do a presentation, the immediate reaction for many will be to be fearful of the experience. They visualize a presentation where things go wrong rather than going well. They visualize a situation where notes are lost or dropped. Slides are in the wrong sequence. They forget what comes next. They stutter in the wrong places and, worst of all, someone asks trick questions that leave them speechless. The biggest fear is that everyone there will know more about the subject than they do. Small wonder then that the prospect of doing a presentation can terrify someone. And it impacts in a negative way that reinforces the fear. As much as they try to prepare, nothing seems to work and it only serves to convince them that they will do a very poor job and will be humiliated by the experience.

On the other hand, a more positive outlook will create an entirely different picture in the mind of the would-be presenter. This time the individual sees it as something that provides an opportunity to impress or to get an important message over to some key people. In their mind's eye they see everything going smoothly. They anticipate most questions, acknowledge the questioner and respond firmly and convincingly. Even if asked an unexpected question, they have the confidence to deal with it. They look forward to the presentation and, for them, even preparing for the event is enjoyable and comes easily. The difference between the two is in the mind.

Challenge – defined and applied

Challenge

Defined

Individuals differ in their approach to challenge. Some consider challenges and problems to be opportunities, whereas others may be more likely to consider a challenging situation as a threat. This sub-scale measures the extent to which an individual is likely to view a challenge as an opportunity. Those scoring highly on this scale may have a tendency actively to seek out such situations for self-development, whereas low scorers may avoid challenging situations for fear of failure or aversion to effort.

> ### Applied
>
> So, for example, at one end of the scale we find those who thrive in continually changing environments. At the other end, we find those who prefer to minimize exposure to change and the problems that come with that – and will strongly prefer to work in stable environments.

This concept of challenge emerges as a significant factor in a wide variety of applications. Essentially it describes how we approach a variety of different situations. The term challenge doesn't mean that the situation itself has to present a big challenge. It can be something that many people might recognize as comparatively insignificant. However, for the individual, and in his or her mind, it does represent something significant. It can explain why, on occasions a perfectly competent individual might underperform and why a moderately competent person might perform better than expected. They will 'punch above their weight'. The situation itself doesn't have to be unduly threatening or stimulating. The individual must see it as such. It is their perception of challenge and change that determines how they behave and how they perform.

We often see this clearly in school years. Those whose challenge scores are low will see examinations, tests and coursework as opportunities to expose how little they know about a topic. Just the thought of this will create anxiety. Studies indicate that language plays a part here too. If the prospect of examinations creates anxiety, then simply the use of the word 'exam' itself can create that anxiety. Alternatively, there are those who see the same situation as exciting ... as an opportunity to show the examiner what they know and to achieve some recognition for their effort.

In the world of sport we see athletes who are excellent technicians but who fail to succeed on the big day. Others of more modest ability will emerge as champions because they are geared up for the big event. The big game player is not a myth. In recent years, we have seen Tiger Woods dominate the golf world. He is certainly the most successful golfer in recent times but there are few who would say he is the most gifted golfer although all would agree he is a very good golfer. That difference – the ability to optimize his talent on the big occasion – can partly be explained by his mindset as he approaches major competitions. His approach to challenge is nothing but positive.

In business there are very many applications for the concept. If we look at commonplace business activities such as meetings and negotiations, success is often not down to innate ability, nor does it even reflect the quality of work done in leading up to the activity. It will just as often be down to entering those activities with the right frame of mind. 'I am going to do a great job... this is my chance to show what I can do... I know enough to deal with it' as opposed to 'This won't go well, I know my stuff but I can see someone will try trip me up... I'll get it over with as fast as possible'. An increasing proportion of white-collar work is project-based. Entering a project on a 'can-do' (not a 'gung-ho') basis is likely to produce better results than a sense of intimidation and seeing the challenge as overwhelming.

As with mental toughness generally and with each of the components, we can be forgiven for thinking that being very mentally tough is always good. It is certainly the case that on the whole, the more mentally tough you are, the better you are able to perform and the more likely you are to enjoy better wellbeing.

However, being strongly orientated towards challenge (typically achieving sten scores 8/9/10 in MTQ48) may also have potential downsides. Someone strongly focused on challenge may like this so much that they will put themselves (and others) forward for challenges that are either extremely difficult to achieve or perhaps, for most people, impossible to achieve. Similarly, if they like change and variety then they are unlikely to be happy in a stable and slowly changing environment. They may provoke change for change's sake and may prove disruptive in a well-regulated environment.

They are also likely to be the type of person who comes into work each morning with a new idea. This may be a positive quality in many situations but in some it can be a problem. If these are managers or leaders (and they often are) then they may be guilty of creating 'initiative overload'. They may take on too many challenges and too much change on behalf of the team and may take on tasks that others simply find intimidating. If others in their team aren't so orientated then they will find this type of behaviour extremely stressful and may find they cannot deal or cope with it. This can produce the paradox where the most creative person on the team does what is required but finds that their own behaviour affects the behaviour of others to the extent that their own performance and the performance of others is adversely affected.

So the challenge for people who score high on any of the scales is to capture the essence of this and play to their strengths whilst understanding the potential impact on the behaviour of others on whom they may depend; and learn to develop tools, techniques and behaviours which mitigate the unwanted responses and encourage positive responses. Sample descriptors and behaviours which are often associated with extreme positions on the challenge scale are presented in Table 8.1. This is not an exclusive or comprehensive list.

TABLE 8.1   Sample descriptors and behaviours

Lower scores	Higher scores
Attitude towards change and new experiences	
Don't like sudden changes	Like challenge
Don't like shocks	Easily bored – will seek change
Fear of failure	Provoke change
Avoid effort	Like problem solving
Intimidated by challenges	Work hard
Dislike being in new situations – new colleagues, new bosses, new premises etc	Happy to commit to projects, studies etc
Prefer routine	Volunteer for projects and tend to commit others?)
Avoid risk (particularly of failure)	Enjoy competition and show it
Uncomfortable with competitive settings	Happy to receive attention
Worry about the views of others	May not always be content with daily life and routines
	'Addicted' to adrenaline
	May have little regard for the impact of their ideas or activities on others
Dealing with all outcomes – positive and negative	
Tend to achieve minimum standards	See the positive in most outcomes
Respond poorly to competitive people	Enjoy learning
See failure and setback as terminal	Motivated to apply what they know to the next challenge
Poor or negative outcomes switch them off learning	Aspirational – would like to have another go and do it better next time
Stressful situations and failure makes them more likely to avoid risk again	
May get things out of perspective	

Are high levels of challenge always a strength?

Generally the answer is again a resounding 'Yes'. As we will see with other components of mental toughness, without self-awareness, high levels of mental toughness in this area can carry the seeds of problems and issues.

Once again, the key is self-awareness – this applies to everyone. The potential downsides for the mentally sensitive are fairly apparent. We can briefly summarize the most common potential downsides for those with high levels of commitment in Table 8.2.

TABLE 8.2   Possible downsides for those with high levels of challenge

Potential downsides for those who ....
Have a positive attitude to change and new experiences
• Can take on too much!
• Can get excited about everything – and may not prioritize
• Will take on too much risk – can sometimes fail
• May not assess risk and opportunity well enough
• Bored – will often create too much change
See all outcomes – positive and negative – as opportunities
• As managers will often create initiative overload
• 'Addicted' to adrenaline
• Can appear arrogant
• May fail to see the significance of an unsuccessful outcome
• Can enjoy the learning more than the application

The psychological context of challenge

Put simply, the challenge component of mental toughness relates to individuals' views about what challenge has to offer them. High scorers see a challenging situation as an opportunity to show off their talents and as a way of developing themselves. A number of psychological models relate to this:

- achievement orientation;
- fear of failure;
- competitiveness;
- the adrenaline junkie.

Achievement motivation

Murray (1938) defined the need to achieve as the desire to 'overcome obstacles, to exercise power, to strive to do something as well as and as quickly as possible.' This obviously has a major resonance with mental toughness. Murray was in many ways a pioneer in performance psychology. This is reflected in his approach to measuring achievement orientation. He devised the radical Thematic Apperception Test (TAT). This is basically a series of pictures, from which respondents have to produce a story. So for example one of the pictures is of an old woman and a much younger one. A very achievement-orientated individual may tell a story about the younger women being held back by having to look after the older one. An individual higher on affiliation may interpret the picture in a different way, for example focusing on a supportive relationship between the two characters.

McClelland's Learned Needs theory

McClelland (1962) suggested that individuals learn needs from their culture. Three of the primary needs in this theory are the need for affiliation, the need for power and the need for achievement. The need for affiliation is a desire to establish social relationships with others. The need for power reflects a desire to control one's environment and influence others. The need for achievement is a desire to take responsibility, set challenging goals and obtain performance feedback.

McClelland's impact has arguably been in the area of achievement motivation. He adopted an experimental approach to his work. The basic paradigm was that during the experiments participants were asked to throw hoops over pegs. No rules or parameters were set by him, but he noted that a small number of highly achievement-orientated people had a particular approach to goal setting. They would set their hoop performance goals in a way that were not too easy but also not too hard. He coined the term 'balanced challenge', which is an excellent way of understanding the challenge component of our mental toughness model. Research looking at people with a high need for achievement has shown that they are more persistent, work harder and are medium risk-takers.

McClelland identified a number of other core characteristics of achievement-orientated individuals. These include the following:

- achievement is more important than material or financial reward;
- financial reward is regarded as a measurement of success, not an end in itself;
- feedback is essential, because it enables measurement of success, not for reasons of praise or recognition (the implication here is that feedback must be reliable, quantifiable and factual);
- achievement-motivated people constantly seek improvements and ways of doing things better.

McClelland's work has been very influential. It is possible to use the theory to generate an action plan for developing a positive challenge-focused orientation, which includes:

- allowing feedback;
- using achievement heroes – publicize the successes of similar types of people;
- working to improve the self-image of individuals – a confident person is a productive one;
- introducing realism – people should think in realistic terms and think positively.

McClelland's theory has one fundamental difference from the other need theories. It suggests that needs can be acquired or taught, and therefore provides a less deterministic view of motivation. An individual who finds an activity challenging but rewarding will seek out more of this type of action. Individuals with a high need for achievement tend to come from families where achievement was positively rewarded. Often individuals within this environment report that their parents were not particularly warm, emphasizing achievement rather than affiliation.

Another important voice in the area of achievement is that of John Atkinson, a student of McClelland. Atkinson was drawn to an expectancy–value approach. Basically he attempted to understand why people do things on the basis of three components:

1 *Valence* – the attraction of psychological objects.

2 *Instrumentality* – relationship between outcome and other outcomes.

3 *Expectancy* – probability estimate of the relationship between action and outcome.

He felt that McClelland's achievement theory was not complete. He emphasized the role of the balanced challenge, focusing particularly on the key balance between the need for achievement and the fear of failure. He was aware that linking achievement orientation to performance is not quite as straightforward as it would seem. People high on achievement orientation are not always drawn to the most difficult tasks. Instead they tend to be drawn to moderately difficult activities; ones in which they have a good chance of succeeding. Motivation to perform an activity is a complex interrelationship between need to achieve and the need to avoid failure.

Fear of failure

The importance of confronting failure was well described by Theodore Roosevelt who stated: 'It is hard to fail, but it is worse never to have tried to succeed.' It is widely understood that you can never succeed or win every time. The old adage that 'you learn more by your mistakes' is undoubtedly true, but perhaps not for every one. The less mentally tough individual may in fact find the experience of failing so traumatic that they simply withdraw from the situation.

> Failure is the opportunity to begin again more intelligently.
>
> Henry Ford

The research evidence suggests that there are significant differences in the levels of fear of failure experienced. It is unclear why this variation occurs, but many authors have relied on a psychoanalytical approach. These tend to suggest that differences in parenting behaviour and other socializations can have a profound effect on this.

A major force in developing the concept of learned helplessness was Martin Seligman. His initial work with animals led him to consider the wider implications of this important concept. He wrote:

> I was stunned by the implications. If, dogs could learn something as complex as the futility of their actions, here was an analogy to human helplessness ... helplessness was all around us – from the urban poor to the despondent patient with his face to the wall.

Learned helpless is obviously highly related to the control component of our model as well as challenge. The 4 Cs are distinct in their own right, but there is a degree of overlap.

What of competiveness?

Competitiveness is certainly an identifiable characteristic. We meet competitive people every day. The challenge component of our model includes an element of competitiveness – the desire, or even need, to win. This particular aspect of the challenge component can obviously be both a positive force for good and a negative. It can be a driver for success but it can also be a disrupting influence, especially when working with other people.

In a study carried out with 200 students at the University of Hull, MTQ48 scores were compared to a measure of personality, the ICES scales in the Prevue Assessment. This is a reliable and validated measure of ability, interests and personality. Within its personality scales there is a measure of trait competitiveness. It has been shown that the challenge component of the MTQ48 is significantly correlated with the competitiveness sub-scale.

> The difference between a successful person and others is not a lack of strength, not a lack of knowledge, but rather a lack of will.
>
> Vince Lombardi

Research has shown gender differences in competitiveness. It is often assumed that males are more competitive than females. These differences helped prompt the development of a rather interesting model of achievement orientation by Spence and Helmreich (1983). They noted that there were not really gender differences in the desire for achievement or challenge but rather that the differences lay in the type of achievement orientation displayed. Their model of achievement had three main strands:

1 Satisfaction with the performance itself. This is basically getting a buzz from a job well done.

2 Sense of completion. This is gaining satisfaction from getting something finished.

3 Sense of competitiveness. This is the enjoyment derived from winning.

Spence and her co-investigators repeatedly identified that males were more competitive, defined by them as 'the enjoyment of interpersonal competition and the desire to win and be better than others', but the two other dimensions did not have any gender variation.

In their research programme it became clear that objective measures of success, for example salaries and academic success, were higher for individuals who had higher levels of performance satisfaction and completion, as long as they were lower in competitiveness. Higher levels of competitiveness led to performance decrements, perhaps because these individuals focused more on winning than on doing a good job.

Our challenge component tries to take a broad perspective, ensuring it incorporates all aspects of achievement. Support for this approach is apparent in the fact that no gender differences exist in the component; nor in mental toughness as a whole.

Mental toughness and risk – the adrenaline junkie

The challenge component certainly has a risk flavour about it. It is clear that individuals high on challenge are drawn to controlled risk, and we discuss this later in the book.

> You'll either step forward into growth or step back into safety.
>
> Abraham Maslow

Crust and Keegan (2010) carried out a study examining risk-taking attitudes and mental toughness (using scores from MTQ48). They concluded that a willingness to take risks was an important attitude that characterizes mentally tough athletes. They also found that overall mental toughness and the sub-scales of challenge and confidence in abilities were significantly and positively related to attitudes to risk. However, these relations were limited to attitudes toward physical risk-taking. Indeed, only the mental toughness sub-scale of interpersonal confidence was found to be significantly related to attitudes towards psychological risk.

Confidence

09

> *It's not who we are that holds us back,*
> *it's who we think we're not.* **MICHAEL NOLAN**

Confidence measures the extent to which we have self-belief to see through to a conclusion a difficult task which can be beset with setbacks and the inner strength to stand your ground when needed – particularly when you might need to persuade others to your point of view. This scale has two component sub-scales.

Overall, it describes how we deal with setbacks or with challenges which might threaten setback. These setbacks can be physical, mental or they can be oral (such as oral challenge or criticism from others). It introduces another positive element into the model linking it to developments in positive psychology.

Those with high levels of overall confidence will accept that setbacks are part and parcel of everyday life. When these occur, a confident person will take them in their stride. A setback or a vigorous challenge from others may stop them in their tracks. But the overall response is likely to be that they will pick themselves up, dust themselves off and continue with even greater determination. The setback may spur them on to try harder to ensure success or to recover lost ground – 'this isn't going to beat me!'

Those with low levels of overall confidence will see the same setback or oral challenge in a different way. They are more likely to feel defeated and accept that what has happened is so significant that it will prevent them from achieving the goal or task. They are more likely to give up and feel that they 'have given it their best shot' and do no more.

Twenty years from now you will be more disappointed by the things that you didn't do than by the ones you did do.

Mark Twain

Confidence – defined and applied

Confidence

Defined

Individuals high in confidence have the self-belief to successfully complete tasks that may be considered too difficult by individuals with similar abilities but lower confidence.

Applied

For example, individuals at one end of the scale will be able to take setbacks (externally or self-generated) in their stride. They keep their heads when things go wrong and it may even strengthen their resolve to do something. At the other end, individuals will be unsettled by setbacks and will feel undermined by these. Their heads are said to 'drop'.

Sub-scales

Continuing research has identified two sub-scales for this component:

1 *Confidence (abilities)* – individuals scoring highly on this scale are more likely to believe that they are truly worthwhile people. They are less dependent on external validation and tend to be more optimistic about life in general.

2 *Confidence (interpersonal)* – individuals scoring highly on this scale tend to be more assertive. They are less likely to be intimidated in social settings and are more likely to promote themselves in groups. They are also better able to handle difficult or awkward people.

When we first started to examine the confidence scale, our first thoughts were that confidence was largely down to the extent to which someone had confidence in their abilities. This has some kind of simple appeal. However, at the same time we were managing and running a major development centre programme for HM Customs and Excise in the UK. This involved assessing around 700 senior managers through a series of observed exercises which required groups of these managers to work together to solve problems and carry out tasks together.

All of the managers were well-educated and well-qualified. Some were exceptionally well-qualified. As time went by, we noticed that the most effective managers weren't always the best qualified. It became apparent that many of these very knowledgeable managers would barely contribute to discussions and take a lead even when they were the acknowledged 'expert' in the matter at hand.

Curiously, at about the same time we were carrying out a similar exercise with several hundred middle and senior managers in a major automotive component manufacturer, AP Lockheed, where we observed exactly the same phenomenon. In both cases we would see individuals playing a major role in a discussion and often being highly influential even though it was apparent that they were not particularly able in the area in question. In both cases the client organization had agreed that we could use the experimental mental toughness questionnaire to gather data on participants. What emerged was an understanding that interpersonal confidence was a significant component of overall confidence. Confidence therefore had two sub-scales:

1 *Confidence in abilities* – the confidence that you have the intellectual toolkit (knowledge, skills, education and experience) to attempt and to complete a particular task or action, even if this task was difficult in some way and had the potential for setbacks or failures along the way to completion.

2 *Interpersonal confidence* – the confidence to deal with oral challenges which might interfere with successful completion of the task. These include dealing with criticism and adverse comment when problems arise as well as having the oral confidence to represent your views and your position compellingly, often in the face of alternative views expressed by others, and the ability to hold your own when you know you are right to do so.

Again we see the relevance of the confidence scale in all walks of life. It is commonly said of the most successful sports teams: 'they expect to win and go out there believing that'. There may be a narrow line between arrogance and confidence but it is difficult to be a successful athlete unless you have that confidence.

Any educationalist will give you hundreds of examples of the ordinary students who 'overachieved' because they believed in themselves and of the impossibly bright students who 'underachieved' because they didn't have the confidence to express themselves. Under-confident students will look at a question in an exam paper and believe they can't provide an answer even when they know everything they need to know. They may even minimize response because providing a full answer carries for them a risk that this might not be what the examiner is looking for. And so the examiner never sees what the students do know.

In the workplace, examples are equally common. In one extreme example a few years ago, whilst involved in a selection interview, we could hear the applicant audibly mutter: 'This is not going well. I am not going to get this job'.

Confidence in abilities

Confidence in abilities is a measure of self-esteem, identifying the extent to which you feel worthwhile and in need of external validation (Table 9.1).

TABLE 9.1   Confidence in abilities scores

Low scores	High scores
Low self-belief Not confident that they know your subject matter even when they do Produce minimal responses when asked Will be reluctant to express a view in discussion or debate Will be reluctant to ask questions 'in case it makes me look stupid' Reluctant to do presentations or oral work Inner belief missing – need others to build that Unsure whether they have grasped a subject or not – feel they are still missing something Will take critical remarks as confirmation of their self-limiting beliefs Can be inhibited by competence or excellence in others – feel they don't measure up May try to bluster or over-talk May be inexperienced and underestimate their own capabilities	Can believe they are right ... even when they are wrong Little or no need for external validation Happy to ask questions Happy to provide full responses to questions and in tests/exams See critical feedback as feedback (no more and no less) See competence and excellence in others as a motivator – 'I can aspire to that' Happy to draw their experiences into what they do

Interpersonal confidence

Interpersonal confidence measures the extent to which we are prepared to assert ourselves and our preparedness to deal with challenge or ridicule (Table 9.2).

TABLE 9.2   Interpersonal confidence scores

Low scores	High scores
Easily intimidated	Will stand their ground
Won't express themselves in class/debate even when they know they are right	Will face down criticism etc
	Will easily engage in class and group activity
Lack the confidence to express what they know in writing – will understate a position	Will use this quality to argue down others more knowledgeable
Won't ask questions – low engagement	Can be aggressive
	Not easily embarrassed
Will accept criticism and ridicule even when not warranted	Comfortable with negative situations – can deal with the fall out
Will back down quickly when challenged	Tend to be more risk-orientated
Will allow others to dominate debates – even when they are more knowledgeable	Comfortable working in a group and making a contribution
Will have difficulty dealing with assertive people	Happy to ask for help and support – won't see this as a shortcoming – it's just something that is needed
Not good with negative situations	More likely to be involved in lots of things
Will minimize communications – 'won't ask for help when needed'	Won't be 'shy coming forward'
May fail to see opportunities as they arise	
Will tend to be less successful	
Can be shy or self-effacing	
Will seek to avoid risk or making mistakes	
Will miss out on opportunities	
A passive team worker – may not contribute as well as they can	

Are high levels of confidence always a strength?

Once again, mostly this will be the case. However, without self-awareness, high levels of mental toughness in this area can create problems for others and for the individual. We briefly summarize the most common potential downsides for those with high levels of confidence in Table 9.3.

TABLE 9.3   Possible downsides for those with high levels of confidence

Potential downsides for those who ...
Have a high level of confidence in their abilities
• May not have the abilities with which they credit themselves
• Can take on too much
• Extreme confidence can intimidate others and cause them to query their own ability
• Can be intolerant of those who aren't as able
• Can appear arrogant
• Can be perceived as bullies
• Can believe they are right – even when they are wrong
• Can persuade others to their point of view even if they are wrong
Have a high level of interpersonal confidence
• Will get their own way – even when others may have a better case or are right
• May appear to be poor at listening
• Won't allow others to contribute to discussions
• Can interrupt a great deal
• Can be seen as 'aggressive' and as 'verbal bullies'
• Can rely on the 'gift of the gab'

The psychological context of confidence

Self-confidence is a very fuzzy term. A number of constructs have been related to it but it is fair to say that the picture is rather messy. In this section we will describe and discuss some of the main constructs that have been related to confidence. Overall mental toughness is clearly related to a number of the constructs that can be, and have been, labelled 'confidence'. For example, in a sample of 200 managers the correlations shown in Table 9.4 were found (all significant at the p<0.001 level).

TABLE 9.4   Correlations between mental toughness and confidence

	Pearson's Correlation	Scale
Optimism	0.48	Life orientation test
Life satisfaction	0.56	Satisfaction with life scale
Self-image	0.42	Self-esteem scale
Self-efficacy	0.68	Self-efficacy scales
Trait anxiety	0.57	State-Trait Anxiety Questionnaire

Self-efficacy

Self-efficacy is perhaps the most influential theoretical idea in the area of confidence. According to Albert Bandura, self-efficacy is 'the belief in one's capabilities to organize and execute the courses of action required to manage prospective situations'. In other words, self-efficacy is a person's belief in his or her ability to succeed in a particular situation. Bandura described these beliefs as determinants of how people think, behave and feel. Many authors use the terms self-confidence and self-efficacy interchangeably and it is not unusual to find the sentence 'For self-efficacy please see self-confidence' in a number of publications. Professor Bandura was very clear about the distinctions between the two:

> It should be noted that the construct of self-efficacy differs from the colloquial term 'confidence.' Confidence is a nondescript term that refers to strength of belief but does not necessarily specify what the certainty is about. I can be supremely confident that I will fail at an endeavour. Perceived self-efficacy refers to belief in one's agentive capabilities that one can produce given levels of attainment.
>
> A self-efficacy assessment, therefore, includes both an affirmation of a capability level and the strength of that belief. Confidence is a catchword rather than a construct embedded in a theoretical system.

> Advances in a field are best achieved by constructs that fully reflect the phenomena of interest and are rooted in a theory that specifies their determinants, mediating processes, and multiple effects. Theory-based constructs pay dividends in understanding and operational guidance. The terms used to characterize personal agency, therefore, represent more than merely lexical preferences.
>
> Bandura, 1977

This clearly reflects a frustration about what can be perceived of the inherent emptiness of the term self-confidence. However, in developing our model of toughness it quickly became apparent that confidence, although poorly operationalized, was a key factor. We conceive it to be a heritable, generic trait. However, it does share many characteristics of self-efficacy, and Table 9.4 shows they are quite clearly related.

Bandura felt that there could be no such thing as general self-efficacy. People are confident about doing some things but not others. This must be true to some extent, but we would suggest that underpinning these variations is a foundation of confidence that permeates across a broad domain of activities. There is a little evidence that self-efficacy might be more generalizable than it is usually represented.

Holloway and her colleagues (1988) found that increased self-efficacy of adolescent girls through strength training generalized to more dispositional attitudes and confidence levels about their bodies and self-esteem. Bandura was convinced that people learn through observing others' behaviour, attitudes, and outcomes of those behaviours (social learning theory). The necessary conditions to learn are:

- *attention* – various factors increase or decrease the amount of attention paid;
- *retention* – remembering what you paid attention to;
- *reproduction* – reproducing the behaviour;
- *motivation* – having the motivation to imitate.

It is argued that levels of self-efficacy within an individual are the product of this social learning process. People with a strong sense of self-efficacy:

- view challenging problems as tasks to be mastered;
- develop deeper interest in the activities in which they participate;
- form a stronger sense of commitment to their interests and activities;
- recover quickly from setbacks and disappointments.

People with a weak sense of self-efficacy:

- avoid challenging tasks;
- believe that difficult tasks and situations are beyond their capabilities;
- focus on personal failings and negative outcomes;
- quickly lose confidence in personal abilities.

Bandura has suggested that people avoid potentially threatening situations not because they experience anxiety and arousal but, rather, they fear they will be unable to cope. This coping relates to the actual behaviour and the underlying cognitive processes. These latter processes are perhaps the key to the impact of low confidence on performance. Individuals fear they will not be able to control perturbing thoughts.

This type of observation is often criticized as lacking scientific rigour. In the case of negative thinking, at least there is a wealth of hard data under-pinning the research findings. For example, there is a strong link between adrenaline and noradrenaline levels and doubt. As doubt increases these two catacholamines increase – both are closely intertwined with the generation of feelings. High self-efficacy is associated with low levels of adrenaline and noradrenaline when put under pressure.

It is clear that higher levels of self-efficacy are an advantage to an individual and the model, based on social learning, clearly identified ways in which learning could take place:

- *Performance accomplishments* – successfully completing a task.
- *Vicarious experiences* – seeing other people succeed. The closer these individuals are to the type of the person the observer is, the more powerful the impact.
- *Verbal persuasion* – this is the basis of many of the cognitive behavioural therapies available and is the bedrock of coaching.
- *Techniques that reduce emotional arousal* – dispersing the emotional fog can allow an individual to develop more rapidly.

These techniques are very valuable and form the core of the mental toughness interventions described later in this book. Bandura also emphasized the reciprocal nature of the mastery–performance link. Feelings of mastery lead to performance improvements which lead to greater feelings of mastery – the virtuous circle.

Confidence and anxiety

These two areas are closely linked. Bandura argued that reducing anxiety increases self-efficacy and this principle has been adopted by many practitioners working in this field. If you are unable to control your anxiety levels you are unable to control yourself.

This linkage has been made even more explicit by Martens *et al* (1990). Martens included a sub-scale within the Competitive State Anxiety Inventory (CSAI and CSAI-2) to measure self-confidence. He suggests that anxiety is on a continuum. At one end of the scale he has high anxiety; at the other he has confidence. This topic is very hotly debated – but it is certainly interesting.

Optimism

> A pessimist sees the difficulty in every opportunity; an optimist sees the opportunity in every difficulty.
>
> Winston Churchill

The trait of optimism has received considerable research effort. Again, it is clear that mental toughness and optimism go hand-in-hand. Greater levels of optimism have been found to be associated with better mental health, a greater striving for personal growth, better moods, academic and job success, popularity and better all-round coping.

Optimistic individuals tend to adopt a problem-based coping style which is also typical of mentally tough individuals. Optimism and pessimism are not two ends of the same continuum. It is clear that pessimism is associated with neuroticism and negative moods whereas optimism is principally linked to extraversion, positive moods and happiness.

Extraversion

Extraversion, one of the big five personality traits, is clearly linked to mental toughness in general and interpersonal confidence in particular. This is shown in Table 9.5.

TABLE 9.5 Correlations between MTQ48 and Prevue Personality Instrument

	Independent	Competitive	Assertive	Conscientious	Conventional	Organized	Extrovert
Overall MT	0.30**	0.11	0.34**	−0.09	−0.16	0.01	0.33**
Challenge	0.38**	0.26**	0.33**	−0.33**	−0.32**	−0.19	0.30**
Commitment	0.20*	0.11	0.22*	0.17	0.04	0.22*	0.22*
Control	0.03	−0.03	0.06	−0.06	−0.15	−0.01	0.08
Control: life	0.11	−0.11	0.21*	−0.05	−0.18*	0.06	0.15
Control: emotions	−0.06	−0.08	−0.05	−0.09	−0.07	0.10	0.15
Confidence	0.39**	0.12	0.51**	−0.06	−0.17	0.03	0.41**
Confidence: in abilities	0.15	0.05	0.19*	−0.03	−0.09	0.03	0.27**
Confidence: interpersonal	0.46**	0.23*	0.50**	−0.16	−0.20*	−0.08	0.28**

** Correlation is significant at the 0.01 level (2-tailed).
* Correlation is significant at the 0.05 level (2-tailed).

Both confidence in abilities and interpersonal confidence relate to extraversion. It can be seen that interpersonal confidence has particularly strong relationships, especially with assertiveness and independence. The core of extraversion is based on how people interact with others.

Eysenk (1967) suggested that the engine behind extraversion was arousal. He suggested that extraverts have a low arousal level whereas introverts have a much higher one. On average extraverts need more external energy, meaning they are much more likely to seek out social contacts. Social interactions are strongly related to positive moods, but the interactions obviously need to be positive themselves. Confident individuals both seek out opportunities to interact with others and maximize the impact of these contacts.

The success of social interactions is closely linked to assertiveness. It is clear that the 'everyone wins' core of most assertiveness techniques maximizes the effectiveness of social interactions.

CASE STUDY   The importance of interpersonal confidence: a case study in a UK police force

The practical implications of interpersonal confidence were demonstrated by Honey Langaster-James in some of her postgraduate studies.

Police performance and behaviour is of continued critical interest. Of particular interest is police officers' willingness to participate in stop and search activities, regardless of the risks involved in such actions. This study assessed police officers' stop and search behaviour whilst on the beat.

Stop and search responsibilities and actions are a key performance criterion for the beat police officer. Such actions are difficult to perform and are often carried out in difficult and dangerous settings. As such, there have been concerns that some officers may be avoiding this activity to reduce their stress levels.

The study gave 110 police officers hypothetical scenarios about stop and search. All completed the MTQ48.

Results

TABLE 9.6 Relationship between the MTQ48 and the desire and usage of 'stop and search'

	Overall desire	Overall use	Overall anxiety
Total mental toughness	0.19*	0.24*	−0.59*
Challenge	0.15	0.21*	−0.53*
Commitment	0.18	0.18	−0.40*
Control	0.15	0.19*	−0.51*
Confidence	0.18	0.26*	−0.60*
Control (emotional)	0.16	0.14	−0.29*
Control (life)	0.10	0.19	−0.59*
Confidence (abilities)	0.11	0.15	−0.61*
Confidence (interpersonal)	0.22*	0.33*	−0.42*
Overall desire		0.81*	−0.15
Overall use	0.811*		
Overall anxiety	−0.11	−0.15	

* Significant correlations

What did this tell us?

First, it is important to note that actual use of stop and search activities was associated with an increased desire to carry them out.

In relation to mental toughness, higher levels of overall mental toughness were associated with an increased desire to carry out and actually use the stop and search activities. Additionally, desire to stop and search was associated with high levels of interpersonal confidence. This can be explained as follows. Officers who had high levels of interpersonal confidence believed that they could defuse potentially volatile situations. They believed that that could control the social situation.

Self-esteem

A final theoretical construct that can be linked to confidence is self-esteem. This is a little bit more removed from the concept, but still pertinent. The key to self-esteem is pride.

This pride is related to oneself and is based on both individuals' strengths and an acceptance of their weaknesses. Pride in young people, like so many things, can be enhanced or destroyed by parents and teachers. If others take credit for an individual's achievement and/or blame them for their short-comings, then the ability to feel pride can be greatly reduced.

Low self-esteem can be easily related to feelings of shame and lack of self-worth. Low self-esteem people believe that they lack skills and have little to offer the world. They will often actively resist attempts to bolster their esteem, for example, failing to acknowledge positive feedback. In addition they set low goals, again perpetuating their feelings of inadequacy.

Self-esteem seems to be a critical component of how people deal with the world. Its pervasive effect on people has been linked to terror management theory. This theory attempts to explain human behaviour by placing it within the context of a deeply-rooted fear of depth. Basically, self-esteem allows us to deal with the inevitable end of life by allowing us to recognize our importance and what we have contributed to the world.

A pursuit of self-esteem is not without its pitfalls. It has been argued that pursuing self-esteem may in fact limit learning. Individuals could avoid challenging situations which threaten their self-image. This sort of self-validation relies on inappropriate behaviours such as making excuses. This type of approach would be clearly linked to low scores on the challenge scale of the MTQ48.

Mental toughness and its relationships with other important models

10

Mindset, positive psychology and emotional intelligence

Although mental toughness is in many senses unique, in that it defines and operationalizes an important personality trait, it is also related to a number of other important ideas old and new which have emerged in the 21st century. Some, like mindfulness, are discussed elsewhere. The purpose of this short section is to acknowledge and celebrate where there is synergy with ideas promulgated by others.

We will start with the work of Dweck on mindset and Seligman on learned optimism.

Mindset

Carol Dweck is a professor at Stanford University in the USA. She carried out some important work around the notion of 'mindset', which is a widely used idea. Through her research she came to the conclusion that mindset – the attitude of mind – was an important determinant of success for many – especially in the world of education.

She defined mindset in terms of character, heart, will etc. Her work led her to the conclusion that there were basically two types of mindset: 'fixed mindset' and a flexible or 'growth mindset'.

The *fixed mindset* had a focus on ability rather than effort. You can achieve things because you possess ability. Those with a fixed mindset typically adopt the position that success should be effortless, perhaps even that effort was somehow disagreeable. Where failure occurs, this can be attributed to others (blame) and to other external factors. In the flexible or *growth mindset*, challenge is a good thing. Mistakes are acceptable because that is where learning occurs. Effort and hard work are important and are encouraged and considered more important than ability alone. Moreover, ability can be developed particularly through practice. People aren't defined by their ability. They can change and for many this is fairly unlimited; what one person can learn, everyone can learn. Her research showed that only the growth mindset delivers sustainable success.

It's not difficult to see that what Dweck describes as the growth mindset, Clough describes as mental toughness. And although a focus on ability doesn't necessarily imply mental sensitivity, there are many connections with the implications of adopting a fixed mindset.

Learned optimism

Seligman is professor of psychology at Pennsylvania University in the USA. Known the world over as the 'father' of positive psychology, like Dweck he divided the world into two types – pessimists and optimists. Pessimists, as you might expect, achieved less than optimists. He believed, as we do, that one can learn to be an optimist. But you could learn one of two things: helplessness or optimism.

Learned helplessness

Essentially this is the result of always being shown what to do and having people do things for you. When difficult situations arise and someone with learned helplessness has to deal with it, they feel out of control. Without their usual sources of support they avoid challenge and lack confidence.

Doing things for people can teach them to be helpless. Seligman is critical of a good deal of modern education and training because of its potential to produce helplessness.

Learned optimism

This involves visualizing a world full of opportunity irrespective of the immediate situation. It is about recognizing that the world is full of opportunities but that a degree of resilience is needed to make something of these.

This, he said, would translate into feelings of control and confidence and ultimately optimism.

Initially he spoke about this process leading to happiness – a theme which has been enthusiastically taken up around the world. His conclusion is similar to Dweck's – optimists achieve more in life. Once again there is a clear synergy with the concept of mental toughness. Arguably mental toughness is more focused on accepting the world as it is (realism) and then visualizing the future, rather than trying to reframe the current situation in a positive envelope.

At its core, mental toughness adopts the idea of 'contentment' rather than 'happiness'. This has a clear synergy with the ground-breaking ideas of Maslow.

Hierarchy of needs

Abraham Maslow, working in the early 1940s, found that people responded to five sets of goals which he called 'basic needs'. These operated at different and progressive levels. There are five levels, which he termed his Hierarchy of Needs:

TABLE 10.1   Maslow's Hierarchy of Needs

1 Self-actualization/Fulfilment
2 Esteem
3 Belonging (to a team)
4 Safety – need for security
5 Physiological – need to eat/keep warm/etc

The most important factor is the highest-order need – self-actualization. This is all about achieving your potential, being the best that you can be and accepting that this is a journey and not necessarily a destination.

This is essentially what mental toughness is about. It is about contentment – and that you are on a journey. This journey will have difficulties and challenges but hard work and ability can surmount these. Satisfaction is at the core of happiness. This satisfaction is derived just as much from being on that journey, and developing these qualities to be able to travel that road, as it is from achieving a particular state.

In many ways, the mentally tough are realists who have as their goal the higher-order factors and derive contentment from meeting their objectives along the challenging road they choose to take.

Mental toughness, emotional intelligence and compassion

It is often thought, and sometimes espoused, that high levels of mental toughness must be related to not understanding or caring about others. It is easy to see why this view might have emerged but the evidence suggests that this is not the case. In this chapter, the links between mental toughness, emotional intelligence and compassion will be explored.

Emotional intelligence and mental toughness

There are clear links between mental toughness and emotional intelligence, and this is perhaps most pertinent in the emotional control scale. High levels of emotional control do not mean that you do not have emotions, or that you do not have empathy. As it 'says on the tin', it means that the emotion is controlled. Whilst this might appear at first sight to suggest a coldness, there is a contrary argument. It is not easy to understand the emotions of others when you are emoting yourself. The behaviours exhibited by those with low control include:

- revealing their emotional state to others;
- dealing poorly with criticism or negative feedback;
- feeling things happen to them;
- getting down when things go wrong;
- losing it when provoked or annoyed.

None of these behaviours are particularly helpful when dealing with others. Again, and at the risk of labouring the point, being emotional is not the same as being emotionally intelligent. In order to show this more clearly it is useful to examine the concept of emotional intelligence more closely.

Emotional intelligence (EQ) can be defined as the ability to identify, use, understand, and manage emotions in positive ways to relieve stress, communicate effectively, empathize with others, overcome challenges, and defuse conflict. If you have high EQ, you are able to recognize and control your own emotional state and the emotional states of others, and engage with people in a productive way. Goleman (1998), who is the central figure in this area, described EQ as having five attributes:

1 *Self-awareness* – the ability to recognize own emotions and how they affect thoughts and behaviour.

2 *Self-regulation* – the ability to control emotions in healthy ways, take initiative, follow through on commitments, and adapt to changing circumstances.

3 *Social skill* – the ability to deal effectively with a range of people.

4 *Empathy* – the ability to understand others, especially when making decisions.

5 *Self-motivation* – being driven to achieve.

One of the reasons why many assume that mentally tough people may be less emotionally literate is a lack of knowledge about emotional literacy itself. The definitions provided by Goleman show that there is in fact a very clear synergy with the 4 Cs model – especially with emotional control, interpersonal confidence and challenge. Support for the notion that mental toughness might be a useful concept when exploring emotional intelligence comes from a recent study. Nicholls *et al* (in Press) reported a strong positive relationship between emotional intelligence and mental toughness.

One fascinating area that is rarely discussed in relation to emotional intelligence is the 'dark triad' of personality variables. The dark triad consists of Machiavellianism, narcissism and psychopathy. Put simply, might a very emotional literate person be manipulative? They would certainly have the skills. Onley *et al* (2013) reported that mentally tough individuals produced lower psychopathy and Machiavellianism scores, suggesting that they were genuinely concerned about the wellbeing of others. This again challenges the stereotype of 'emotional good, non-emotional bad'.

Compassion

Compassion is a fundamental and important concept. Chapter 18 on health and social factors reveals that the link between caring and toughness is indeed a complex one.

An example: mental toughness and compassionate nursing

A key question is: 'Can mentally tough individuals show compassion?' We would argue a clear 'Yes', and suggest that it may in fact be much harder for sensitive individuals to maintain a compassionate stance.

Nursing, and the NHS in general, are wrestling with the problems associated with a perceived lack of compassion. They have developed a 6 Cs model to help focus efforts to improve this area. The 6 Cs are:

- care;

- compassion;

- competence;

- communication;

- courage;

- commitment.

The 4 Cs model of mental toughness clearly has a synergy with these 6 Cs. *Care* is the core business of health services and there is clear evidence that mentally tough individuals are more effective in demanding roles such as nursing.

Commitment is common to both models, and can be described as the ability to remain focused and persist with goals or tasks, even under pressure. Nurses and others require high levels of commitment to maintain a compassionate stance; the ability to be non-judgemental, to acknowledge the suffering of another and to care for them unconditionally can be challenging for the nurse (van der Cingel, 2009).

Compassion is based on empathy, regard and respect for another as a fellow human being (Blum, 1980). The clear links between mental toughness and emotional intelligence show that mentally tough individuals do not lack empathy, but they do not necessarily show this through emotional behaviour. A compassionate response might not be one expressed in terms of outward-facing emotions, but it will still be a caring response (Pask, 2003). In the 4 Cs model control is conceptualized as two sub-scales: emotion and life control. Individuals who have high emotional control do not reveal their emotional state to others, have high levels of self-awareness and are more able to understand and manage others feelings (Clough and Strycharczyk, 2012). Individuals with high life control possess a 'can-do' attitude, are good at planning and prioritizing and see solutions rather than problems. This does not mean that individuals with high levels of emotional control are unfeeling or uncaring.

An intriguing study by Crust (2009) tested the relationship between mental toughness and affect intensity to determine whether mentally tough individuals generally experienced more or less intense emotions. Mental toughness and affect intensity were found to be unrelated. This is an important finding because it suggests participants with high or low levels of mental toughness do not characteristically experience more or less intense emotions. Thus it appears that the ability of mentally tough individuals to remain relatively unaffected by pressure or adversity is not due to them experiencing lower levels of affect intensity.

A grounded theory approach was adopted by Curtis *et al* (2012). When exploring student nurses' socialization in compassionate practice, they found that students experience dissonance between professional ideals and practice reality. Students have to balance between their intention to uphold their ideals and challenge constraints or alternatively, adapt their ideals and accept the constraints on compassionate practice.

Courage has significant links with confidence. Confidence is the way in which we deal with setbacks, physical, mental or oral, such as criticism from others. Those with high levels of confidence accept setbacks in their stride and continue with even greater determination to succeed. Conversely, those with low levels of confidence might feel defeated by setbacks and be more likely to give up. A phenomenological study exploring the use of reflection in professional development found that nurses who felt able to take risks, and had the courage to try new approaches, gained more confidence in their practice for the future (Gustafsson and Fagerberg, 2004). When reflecting, nurses require courage to question and challenge their own behaviours and judgements, and it would seem an important factor for the development of confidence. Courage perhaps epitomizes mental toughness.

Mentally tough individuals are able to stand up to social pressures and do what they believe is right, an important aspect of leadership, particularly in times of change. Challenge describes the ways in which individuals approach different situations. A challenge might be perceived by some as a threat whereas to others, challenges are opportunities. This pillar has particular relevance when dealing with change.

Compassionate care is a fundamental value in contemporary nursing practice and we suggest that mental toughness can support compassionate care delivery. Being able to understand and deal with challenge, stress and pressure is at the heart of compassionate care provision. Nurses need to be able to cope in times of change and care for themselves compassionately first, in order to be able to show compassion to others. Behaviours that are seen as inappropriate may be more a product of stress rather than a lack of empathy or a training deficit. If we do not equip nurses with ways to deal effectively with the stress which can ultimately end in them underperforming or leaving the profession, then a compassion culture is simply not possible as resources become more stretched, leading to a classic vicious circle. Sensitive individuals have a great deal to offer the nursing profession, but are vulnerable to the stresses that the job involves. Mental toughness can be developed and support mechanisms can be introduced to help nurses deal effectively with the intense pressures that impact upon them.

A summary: 6–5–4

There are certainly many models, and numbers, that have been related to emotional intelligence, caring and toughness. There is the UK National Health Services's 6 Cs model of compassion; the 5 elements of emotional intelligence; and, of course, the 4 C s of mental toughness. It is clear to us that you can be tough and emotionally intelligent. You can be tough and caring. And perhaps most importantly, toughness enhances both!

Decision making

11

Decision making is at the very heart of business, sport and most aspects of life. It has long been known that individual differences impact on decision making. This chapter will provide some insights as to how mental toughness may impact the decision-making process. It is important to understand this for a number of reasons:

- to help people make better decisions;
- to identify people who might be at risk of faulty decision making;
- to understand how stress might impact on the decision-making process;
- to help promote creative thinking.

Mental toughness and creativity

Gardner (1989) suggested that creativity is best described as 'the human capacity regularly to solve problems or to fashion products in a domain, in a way that is initially novel but ultimately acceptable to a culture'. Creativity is basically the ability to see relationships where none previously existed. It is clear that problems cannot be solved by thinking within the frameworks in which the problem was created. It is fair to say that: 'Nothing is more dangerous than an idea ... when it's the only idea you have'.

Edward de Bono identified six ways in which people tackle problems, which he called Thinking Hats:

1 White hat – data and information.
2 Red hat – feelings and hunches.
3 Black hat – critical judgement.
4 Yellow hat – optimism, logical positives.
5 Green hat – new ideas.
6 Blue hat – process control.

This important work emphasizes that creativity is not simply about 'Eureka moments'; rather it is a complex interaction of many thinking-based activities. Clearly, there are many ways of being creative ranging from hunches through to a data rational, scientific approach. There are two main ways that mental toughness can be applied to creativity.

First, there is thinking style. Mentally tough individuals tend to be more analytic whilst sensitive individuals tend to be more intuitive. It is quite possible to be sensitive *and* analytical or tough *and* intuitive but it is much less common. Both analysis and intuition are valid creative orientations and we are beginning to explore this and other thinking styles in an ambitious 5-year project at Manchester Metropolitan University (MMU). Some of the initial findings and theoretical musings are reported later in this chapter.

A second and powerful way that mental toughness can influence creativity is its ability to reduce the negative impact of stress. Stress and anxiety are idea killers! Whatever your thinking style there is constant pressure to stick to the status quo. It is the human condition.

There are two basic thinking styles: convergent thinking and divergent thinking. *Convergent thinking* is conservative in nature and revolves around questions such as:

- Will it work?
- Can we do it?
- Do we have the resources?
- Is the timing right?

Divergent thinking is more challenging and revolves around questions such as:

- What if?
- Why not?
- What rules can we break?
- What assumptions are at work?

The pressure to 'converge' can be time-related, performance-related and, perhaps most often, social in nature. Many times we face the 'it will never work' folk or the 'we have tried that before' brigade. It takes real strength to maintain your focus. A number of techniques, for example classic brainstorming, were developed to help combat this pressure to tendency.

We are very interested in performing arts and mental toughness. Performers are subjected to intense pressures and very demanding auditions.

At the same time they are often expected to be sensitive! At first sight, it is difficult to square the circle. However, in other chapters we have shown that mentally tough individuals are not without emotions – they simply control them better. The tools and techniques described in this book are well suited to the creative performer. They will allow them to deal with the periods of intense pressure without destroying their inner creativity. In addition, there is a good argument that taking part in performance events is a good intervention in itself.

When examining creativity it is not possible to ignore the potential negative aspects of a fully creative approach. Convergent thinking has its place. The next section of this chapter will examine two of the potential problem areas: risk and thinking errors.

Mental toughness and risk

The challenge component certainly has a risk flavour about it. It is clear that individuals high on challenge are drawn to controlled risk. Maddi (2004) examined risk taking from what might be called an existentialist perspective. He argued that life was a series of decisions. In making decisions, individuals face a choice between repeating the past by choosing the familiar path, or striking out in new directions (ie more risky but also potentially more rewarding). Nesti (2004) developed a similar theme, but related this to sport. He argued that choosing the past 'tried and tested methods and approaches' can be comforting, but tends to lead to stagnation. Regularly choosing the past can mean missing important opportunities for personal growth, and appears to be linked to individuals who do not learn to operate outside their own comfort zone.

Crust and Keegan (2010) carried out a study examining risk-taking attitude and scores on the MTQ48. They concluded that a willingness to take risks was an important attitude that characterizes mentally tough athletes. They also found that overall mental toughness and the sub-scales of challenge and confidence in abilities were significantly and positively related to attitudes to risk.

However, these relations were limited to attitudes towards physical risk taking. Indeed, only the mental toughness sub-scale of interpersonal confidence was found to be significantly related to attitudes towards psychological risk. They argue that tough individuals appear to be future-oriented decision-makers who seek out challenges, take risks and approaches rather than avoid potentially anxiety-producing situations.

Thinking errors – are the mentally tough less prone to error?

This is a very important question. For example, when selecting people for safety-critical jobs, should you go for the tough, develop toughness or does it matter? We believe that toughness may be a critical feature in understanding how people deal with decision making, especially under pressure.

We are all prone to errors in our thinking. Some of the main biases are summarized below.

- confirmation;
- gambler's fallacy;
- post hoc rationalization;
- status quo;
- negativity bias;
- projection bias;
- current moment;
- anchoring, contrast and Barnum effects;
- fundamental attribution bias;
- halo and horn;
- probability errors.

It seems likely that a data rational style will provide some protection against these biases, but obviously not a complete protection. We are, after all, only human.

To add to these individually-based errors there are proven group pressures that impact on decision making and risk. 'Group think' is a classic example. Here individuals are under pressure to conform to the will of the group. This often means that information is not correctly processed, alternatives examined, or contrary views expressed. At a time that has seen the importance of 'whistle-blowers' rise to prominence, the role of mental toughness in breaking group norms falls sharply into focus.

What of luck?

Luck and superstition give people a feeling of control over a very unpredictable world. It is very clear that some people believe themselves to be unlucky:

many fewer think that in fact they are blessed with good luck. It is very clear that perceptions of luck are based on faulty thinking. Whilst by definition there has to be the world's unluckiest person – it is a statistical certainty – most people have about the same amount of ups and downs in life. However, their perceptions and attributions are very different. Some people dwell on the good: others on the bad. Individuals low in control tend to wait for something to come along whereas the high controllers believe they will make it come along.

Professor Wiseman of the University of Hertfordshire is one of those who have seriously investigated luck. He identified four key principles:

1 Maximize chance opportunities: lucky people are skilled at creating, noticing and acting upon chance opportunities.

2 Listening to lucky hunches: lucky people make effective decisions by listening to their intuition and gut feelings.

3 Expect good fortune: lucky people are certain that the future is going to be full of good fortune. These expectations become self-fulfilling prophecies by helping lucky people persist in the face of failure, and shape their interactions with others in a positive way.

4 Turn bad luck to good: lucky people employ various psychological techniques to cope with, and often even thrive upon, the ill fortune that comes their way.

Superstition certainly gives a sense of control, but it is basically faulty thinking. The great behavioural scientist BF Skinner demonstrated that you could produce superstitious behaviour in pigeons. He fed the birds randomly. Obviously, at the time of feeding, the birds were carrying out some form of behaviours. Although these were completely irrelevant, they tended to repeat them consistently in the mistaken 'belief' that their actions would produce reward – lo and behold, a new superstition was born!

CASE STUDY   Examining the link between mental toughness, thinking style and risk at MMU

Reality testing refers to the preference to test critically the coherent credibility of beliefs (Irwin, 2004). Reality-testing deficits bias individuals away from analytical–rational processing towards intuitive–experiential interpretations of anomalous events. Believers in this context are dependent upon, or favour, intuitive–experiential processing and consequently, appraise perceptions and experiences less critically. Consequently, they are more inclined to report unusual perceptual sensations (seeing things that do not exist, hearing things when there is no apparent reason etc). Several studies report an association between proneness to reality-testing deficits and unconventional beliefs (particularly belief in the paranormal, endorsement of urban legends and conspiracism) (eg Drinkwater, Dagnall and Parker, 2012). It has been reported that emotion-based reasoning predicts level of paranormal belief (Irwin, Dagnall and Drinkwater, 2012). Thus, believers tend to endorse paranormal occurrences because of their emotional rather than rational appeal (Sappington, 1990).

It seems that individuals with high levels of paranormal beliefs have a different model of how the world works, based on a less 'classically' rational approach and a more emotion-led style. If these findings are linked with those that mental toughness is associated with, lower levels of emotional and passive coping mechanisms, we hypothesized that mental toughness would be negatively linked with paranormal beliefs, which in turn would be suggestive of a less realistic/rational decision-making style.

A pilot study was carried out by Neil Dagnall, Ken Drinkwater and Peter Clough in the Department of Psychology, MMU, in 2015. A convenience sample of 180 participants took part in the study. Participants were recruited via undergraduate and postgraduate health-care courses (nursing, physiotherapy, acupuncture, speech therapy etc) at MMU.

Three questionnaires were used: the MTQ48, the PRI (risk) and the MMU-N. The MMU-N is a 47-item scale based on the eight paranormal factors (hauntings, superstitions, religious belief, alien visitation, ESP, PK, astrology and witchcraft). A brief summary of the findings is reported in Table 11.1.

TABLE 11.1 The correlations between mental toughness and paranormal beliefs

Mental toughness	−0.22**
Challenge	−0.22**
Commitment	−0.18**
Control	−0.28**
Confidence	−0.12*

The results show that more mentally tough individuals appear to be less drawn to paranormal beliefs. This is as predicted and suggests that mentally tough individuals take a more reality-based approach.

We then went on to examine risk, paranormal beliefs and toughness. This produced a much less clear picture. Individuals with higher levels of paranormal beliefs were more risky and saw themselves as more risky. This is what we expected. Mental toughness did not relate to risk-taking behaviour or perceptions directly. However, indirectly there may be a link, as mental toughness does relate to paranormal beliefs. Risk and toughness seem to be intimately linked, but it is up to research teams like the MMU group to really get under the skin of this. Physical risk and toughness seem to go together well, but other areas are far from clear.

The work at MMU is in its infancy but it does promise much. It will begin to explore how mental toughness may be linked to decision making. This may allow us to identify individuals at risk of decision-making errors and, perhaps more importantly, allow us to provide cognitive and psychological interventions. This may have a wide number of potential applications, for example, managerial behaviour, health behaviour, sports performance and health and safety system compliance.

Mental toughness and fatigue

12

The impact of mental toughness on the development of fatigue

Mental toughness and fatigue are closely related concepts. As described in the earlier chapters of this book, mental toughness is a multidimensional concept incorporating components of challenge, commitment, control and confidence.

Like mental toughness, fatigue is also an important part of the stress process. Where mental toughness is known to be a potential moderator of the stressor/strain relationship, fatigue is a significant part of the resulting strain. In short, fatigue is the state of tiredness which follows a period of dealing with a stressor, eg heavy mental workload or physical demands. So, along with anxiety, fatigue is a core 'product' of the human stress response.

With regards to the complex interaction between mental toughness and fatigue, people who are mentally tough may be less likely to suffer the performance and health-related consequences of stress-induced fatigue; and possibly less likely to experience the state of fatigue itself.

These two propositions have important implications in the worlds of business, sport, education and occupational health. This chapter will initially present an overview of fatigue, explaining what fatigue actually is and the likely consequences of fatigue. Following this, the relationship between mental toughness and fatigue will be considered and the conclusion of the chapter aims to offer some practical considerations for readers to better understand their own stress response and minimize the impact of their personal stressors.

What is fatigue and why is it important?

Fatigue is a familiar and commonplace occurrence. Most people regularly experience some degree of tiredness following a difficult day at work, a particularly challenging work-out, a bad night's sleep, illness, or as a consequence of dealing with a difficult emotional problem. But, despite the familiarity of the fatigue experience, psychologists working in this field are still debating many of the issues surrounding the concept, even the most basic issue of 'what fatigue actually *is*'. Also, there is still lively debate as to whether the 'fatigue' which develops after exercise is the same as the 'fatigue' which develops after a difficult work day or emotional challenge.

As long ago as 1921, Muscio comprehensively outlined the fundamental problem associated with studying fatigue as the difficulties associated with measuring it. To explain the impact of the measurement issues, hypothetically consider an everyday example. Imagine that scientists could not measure temperature. Without a reliable measure of temperature, it would be very difficult indeed to understand the weather, understand how the weather patterns change over time and how to predict changes in the weather. The problem is the same with fatigue. Psychologists have struggled to find an accurate measure of fatigue and without this, it has been extremely difficult to understand changes in fatigue and what factors influence these changes.

Despite these difficulties, it is not at all surprising that fatigue research has been sustained as real people still experience fatigue and it continues to be associated with poor performance, errors, accidents and ill-health. In response to this enduring and real-world problem, there is a global academic interest in all aspects of fatigue which can be categorized into areas of practical and academic interest (for a comprehensive discussion of current research see Ackerman, 2011; Hockey, 2013). These areas are:

- Causal factors – understanding the development of the fatigue state and what makes people tired. What are the conditions in the workplace, for example, which make people tired? How are people affected by factors such as workload, exercise, autonomy, social support, noise and lighting?

● Moderators – exploring the personality factors which can moderate the state. Is the development of fatigue different in people who are high in traits such as mental toughness, trait anxiety, or conscientiousness?

● Measurement issues – the development of tools and techniques for measuring changes in fatigue. Can questionnaires adequately measure levels of fatigue? Are there any reliable physiological changes which can be used to estimate, or even explain, fatigue? Can we measure differences in distinct types of fatigue, such as mental, emotional and physical fatigue?

● Consequences – understanding and minimizing the consequences of fatigue for performance (in the short term) and for health and wellbeing (in the longer term). What can organizations do to maintain high levels of performance in safety-critical jobs such as those in frontline medical professions, or those in important monitoring roles such as air-traffic controllers? What factors lead to significant health issues such as burnout?

Each of these areas has huge relevance in the modern world.

But, what *actually* is fatigue? Well, although there is no universally accepted definition of what fatigue is, it is now generally accepted that fatigue is a *state* which is generated by engaging in some form of heavy or prolonged demands/work. Although early theoretical models of fatigue represented it in terms of some form of depleted energy (like a run-down battery), modern views of fatigue characterize it as an adaptive motivational control process – an aversive state which prevents us from continuing to focus on unrewarding activities and to engage in new and relevant goals. This fatigue is associated with *feelings of tiredness* and, importantly, also by a strong desire to stop. Whether or not we listen to these impulses may be influenced by many factors, including mental toughness.

The following section will explain the implications of fatigue, before going on to consider the role that mental toughness plays in the process.

What happens to us when we are fatigued?

The process of fatigue should really be considered at two levels or stages: the short-term effects and the longer-term effects.

Short-term fatigue effects

Consider the two options which are generally available for an individual who is facing ongoing demands and feeling fatigued: they can choose to 'listen' to their body, submit to feelings of tiredness and take a break; or they can choose to ignore the feelings of fatigue and continue with the task in hand.

The reasons for choosing to submit to the fatigue or, alternatively, to override these feelings and continue, are relatively simple. Consider the conditions which would result in you choosing to stop working on a task when you feel tired, or keep going in spite of these feelings. The key is motivation – how much do you want (or need) to keep on going? What will be the cost of not continuing? These are the sorts of questions we explicitly and implicitly ask ourselves continuously.

If the answer we provide ourselves is that 'it can wait' and circumstances allow us to take a break and rest, we are likely to directly reduce our level of effort and the feelings of fatigue may dissipate. However, we can (and do) choose to override these feelings and continue to invest effort. Under these circumstances, we are likely to face a number of consequences (for a full description of this process see Hockey, 2013).

In the first place, the feelings of tiredness are likely to continue and build, and the desire to stop may become increasingly persistent and uncomfortable. In addition to these feelings are the subtle and less well-known changes in the way we think: in essence, being in a state of fatigue typically leads us to increasingly adopt low-effort strategies and ways of working which rely less on higher-level thinking (particularly working memory).

To provide a test of this process, we recently carried out an experimental study to investigate the roles of motivation and effort in the fatigue process (Earle *et al*, in Press). The aim of the study was to demonstrate how fatigue develops under conditions of sustained effort, which was manipulated through enhanced motivation: essentially, if people are sufficiently motivated and committed to a task, they will invest more effort and are consequently more likely to experience the feelings and consequences of fatigue.

The participants in the study were required to manage a complex process control simulator, similar to managing the life-support system in a power plant, aircraft or submarine. Half of the participants were given standard operating instructions (relating to the system and the task goals) but, while the other half of the participants were given exactly the same workload task, they were given modified instructions emphasizing the importance of task success and the consequences of poor task performance. As predicted, the second group of participants were more successful in terms of task goals, but experienced a higher level of state fatigue and, crucially, a higher level of fatigue after-effects. In the context of this experiment, the after-effect of increased effort and associated fatigue was an increased reliance of low-effort problem-solving strategies when faced with a further task. Fatigued participants were more likely to make a quick guess when solving a problem than to systematically work through the possible choices and make an optimal decision.

Therefore, the consequences of sustained high effort and a fatigued state are a tendency to make quicker and less well-thought-out decisions and an increase in risky behaviour. In the real world, this suggest that a fatigued person is less likely to carefully think through options, and is more likely to just guess, or make a quick decision without fully considering all of the consequences. Furthermore, if the decision requires action, fatigued people are likely to be heavily weighted towards a decision which requires less effort on their part. Interestingly, this shift towards quick decision making is typically accompanied by an increase in our subjective confidence in our decision!

In general terms, it is this shift towards low-effort strategies of thinking and behaviour which characterizes the fatigued individual. It is not difficult to imagine the consequences of fatigue in all working environments, particularly those with a safety-critical setting. However, while the impact of fatigue in safety-critical settings is worrying, this 'low-effort' approach has implications for any environment where performance is an issue. As described above, these changes are more likely to lead to risky behaviours, poor decision making and increased risk of accidents.

Thus, fatigue has clear relevance in all occupational settings, sporting environments and within the educational sector. It also has relevance within the realm of normal life, eg driving safety.

Longer-term fatigue effects

While the fatigue state may be uncomfortable, inconvenient and occasionally dangerous, it does have an adaptive value. That is, it can serve to protect us from the development of longer-term health problems.

Although psychologists do not currently fully understand the link between dealing with prolonged strain (stress) and the development of longer-term health problems, there is sufficient evidence to strongly suggest that if we consistently override the feelings of fatigue there will undoubtedly be health consequences. The most commonly reported consequence is that of burnout (Maslach, 1976), which constitutes a significant and enduring health problem associated with emotional exhaustion, depersonalization and a reduced sense of personal accomplishment. Other potential conditions include high blood pressure, heart attacks, stroke, gastrointestinal problems and even cancer.

In summary, fatigue may be a commonplace and familiar phenomenon, but in the short term the state of fatigue can subtly and subconsciously influence the way that we all work and in the longer term, the decision to consistently override the desire to stop can have catastrophic health consequences.

Next we consider how mental toughness interacts with fatigue, and finally what *you* can do to minimize the negative consequences of fatigue.

How does mental toughness impact on the development of fatigue?

As stated earlier, mental toughness comprises a combination of components which have been found to moderate the stressor/stress relationship. However, the relationship between these two familiar concepts of mental toughness and fatigue may be surprisingly complicated.

On first consideration, it seems plausible (although counterintuitive) that mentally tough people are in fact more likely to suffer the consequences of fatigue, as they may be more inclined to override the desire to stop. However, this idea would clearly be contrary to the literature on mental toughness and against the broad underpinnings of the concept. It is a central assumption in the mental toughness literature that mental toughness somehow 'offsets' or reduces the impact of stressors on the individual (Jones *et al*, 2002). Nonetheless, there is little direct research evidence which explains how these concepts are interrelated. In consideration of this, an experimental study was undertaken to directly investigate moderating effects of mental toughness on the responses to physical work and the development of fatigue.

CASE STUDY   Experimental case study on mental toughness, workload and fatigue

The study aimed to find out how individuals would respond to physical work and whether this process was different for people who were high or low in mental toughness. How would the demands of the work affect them physiologically? How would they evaluate the demands of the work? How would the individuals differ in their ability to maintain focus on an additional mental task? And what level of fatigue would they experience?

The study – what did we do?

Physical work was simulated by using stationary cycling activity which we could manipulate to represent different levels of activity. This was varied at three levels of intensity or weight resistance, representing low, medium and high levels of workload. This three-level workload approach was used so that we could see how people responded at different levels of demand, as it has been suggested that the advantages of mental toughness may be most relevant under stressful conditions. So, it was considered important to look at the effects of mental toughness across varying levels of stressor.

It was also very important to ensure that the physical workloads were equivalent for everyone, ie that one person cycling at the low level would be experiencing the same level of physiological demand as all the other participants cycling at the low level. To set the levels of workload for all, the fitness of each person was tested prior to the experiment. The levels of workload were then set for each individual based on their own level of fitness – *low workload* was calculated as 30 per cent of their own maximum, *moderate workload* was calculated as 50 per cent of their own maximum, and *high workload* was calculated as 70 per cent of their own maximum.

Each participant experienced three experimental sessions, each representing one of the three levels of workload. Each session included 30 minutes of stationary cycling at one of the three levels, assessment of heart rate throughout the cycling and the additional mental task of an auditory reaction time task. This task required the participants to pinch together their finger and thumb when they heard a high-pitched alarm. (The fingers were fitted with electrodes to measure their response times and this measure was taken to represent the impact of the cycling task). Finally, the participants completed two types of questionnaires. The first of these was the Borg measure of subjective workload (Borg, 1978) which required participants to rate demands on a 20-point scale at three intervals during the cycling. The second questionnaire was the state fatigue scale (Earle, 2004) which uses 15 items to assess changes in state fatigue.

The participants in the study were 24 students (mean age 24.3 years). Of these, 12 were categorized as being high in mental toughness and 12 were categorized as low in mental toughness. This categorization was based on their responses to the MTQ48.

The results – what did we find?

1. With regard to the physiological impact of the cycling, heart rate increased with workload, showing that there was a clear and significant difference in the impact of the different levels of the cycling on heart rate (see Figure 12.1). However, as illustrated in the figure, the average impact of the cycling was not different for those who were high and low in mental toughness: there was almost no difference in the average heart rate for the two mental toughness groups.

FIGURE 12.1   Mean heart rate as a function of workload and mental toughness

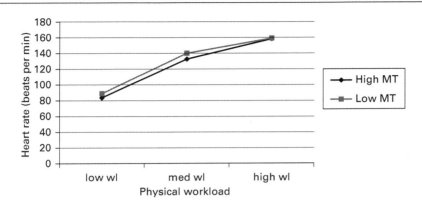

The relevance of this finding is that we can deduce that any subsequent differences in either the performance or fatigue may be explained by *psychological* variables. Interestingly, this is demonstrated, to some degree, in the data for the auditory response time task.

2. The data illustrated in Figure 12.2 highlight a trend that, as physical workload increases, the response time (to the auditory alarm) increases steadily for the low mental toughness group; whereas the response times in the high mental toughness

FIGURE 12.2   Mean alarm response times in milliseconds for the two time periods as a function of low/medium/ high physical workload and mental toughness

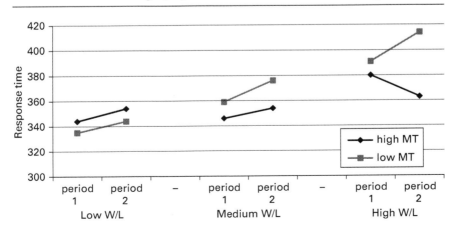

group are less affected by workload, and do not increase linearly with the demands of the task. This suggests that the physical task had less impact on the more mentally tough participants, who had greater concurrent mental resources to respond to the auditory alarm.

Furthermore, the largest difference in reaction times between the two groups occurred in the high physical workload period, supporting the argument that *mental toughness is particularly important when facing high levels of a stressor.* Although these differences were not found to be statistically significant, the data do provide the first layer of evidence that individuals with increased mental toughness can perform more effectively in adverse conditions. So, while the participants experienced the same level of objective demand of the cycling, with no differences in heart rate, the impact of cycling was greater for those who are less mentally tough and impacted negatively on performance on a simple current task. This is further supported by the subjective data of post-task overall workload assessment.

3. As one would expect, there was a significant impact of physical workload on ratings of workload, ie the higher the level of cycling, the more demanding the participants rated this task and both groups reported increased physical demands as the workload increased.

However, the positive impact of mental toughness was again highlighted when the individuals were working at the highest physical workload. As illustrated in Figure 12.3, there were no differences between the ratings of workload at low

FIGURE 12.3   Mean physical demand ratings as a function of physical workload, period (10-minute intervals) and mental toughness

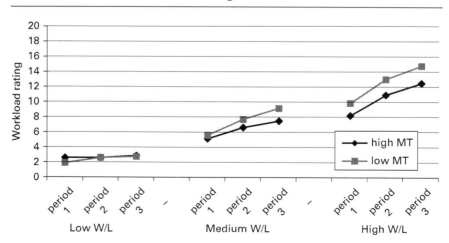

levels of demand for the two mental toughness groups. So when the task was relatively easy, being mentally tough did not provide an obvious advantage.

However, there was an increasing divergence in workload ratings, with workload ratings being slightly higher for the low mental toughness group at medium load and the gap between the two groups increased under high load. Although this finding was again not found to be statistically significant, this is a thought-provoking trend.

4. Of particular relevance to this chapter is the reported change in state fatigue. That is, the extent to which feelings of tiredness increased as a consequence of dealing with the physical stressor of cycling. The findings shown in Figure 12.4 illustrate that, for those who are low in mental toughness, subjective physical fatigue increased as workload increased. However, while physical fatigue in the high mental toughness group did increase from low- to medium-workload conditions, it did not increase from medium- to high-workload conditions. (NB: a negative fatigue score indicates a reduction in reported fatigue from the start of the cycling to the end.)

FIGURE 12.4   Mean change in physical fatigue (on a 5-point scale) as a function of workload and mental toughness

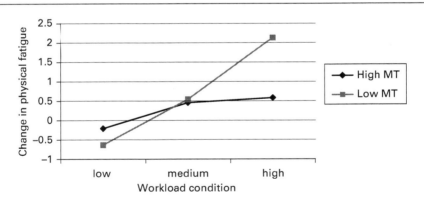

The analysis of this data revealed a significant interaction between mental toughness and workload, with workload having a different effect on those who are high and low in mental toughness (significant at the 5 per cent level). That is, the demands of 'heavy' cycling (at 70 per cent of maximum) only resulted in substantially increased fatigue in the low mental toughness group. This is a very important finding, as this is direct evidence to support the proposition that stressors have less of an impact on those who are mentally tough!

Summary

In summary, the experimental case study presented here gives us a direct comparison of the stress process in people who are high and low in mental toughness. Following on from the results presented above, the impact of the cycling on the two groups was measurably different. Although the physiological impact was the same (in terms of heart rate), the faster response times of the mentally tough group (under high levels of load) suggest that this stressor resulted in a greater 'pull' on the cognitive resources of the less mentally tough.

This was also consistent with a higher evaluation of workload in the low mental toughness group and a greater increase in the level of resulting fatigue. Therefore, people who are high in mental toughness are less affected by stressors and are, consequently, less vulnerable to the development of fatigue.

How does fatigue affect people with different levels of mental toughness?

The relationship between mental toughness and fatigue is complex. We know that fatigue is a state associated with subjective tiredness, feelings of task aversion and shifts towards strategies which require lower effort processing. We also have strong evidence to support the argument that more mentally tough people are less likely to experience fatigue and its consequences. However, we can currently only hypothesize about the underlying mechanisms of this relationship. To enhance our understanding of this important issue we can consider the relationship between fatigue and each of the 4 Cs separately.

- *Challenge and fatigue* – the concept of challenge within the mental toughness framework refers to approaches to facing difficulties. It is this appraisal process which has clear implications for the development of fatigue. If a situation or task is not appraised as a stressor, then the development of fatigue is less likely. Therefore, we could hypothesize that individuals who are high (specifically) in challenge are less likely to experience stress and the strain-related consequences of stress, including fatigue and anxiety. With regards to practical applications, organizations would benefit from understanding the nature of individual differences in challenge, making allowances for the fact that individuals will differ in the way they appraise and respond to difficult circumstances, such as organizational change. Support for individuals who are low in challenge could be beneficial for both the individual and the organization.

- *Control and fatigue* – similarly, individuals who are higher in control are also less likely to develop fatigue. Personal control is a recognized moderator of the stressor/strain relationship, with control minimizing the impact of stressors on the development of fatigue. However, irrespective of an individual's personal level of emotional and life control, enhancing opportunities for control and decision latitude within working environments would be universally beneficial.

- *Confidence and fatigue* – the relationship between confidence and fatigue may be more complex. While a 'high challenge' profile is clearly associated with imperviousness to stress, and 'high control' is known to minimize the impact of stress on the individual, confidence may work in two different ways. An individual's level of confidence would impact on their willingness to undertake various challenges. At low levels of confidence a person may be less willing to take on additional tasks and therefore be less prone to task-related fatigue. However, low levels of confidence are closely associated with anxiety, particularly with regards to interpersonal confidence. The stress associated with difficult interpersonal situations may result in greater fatigue proneness in those with low interpersonal confidence. Conversely, however, individuals who are very high in confidence may be more prone to task-related fatigue, if they are overly ambitious in evaluating the level of work they can realistically undertake.

- *Commitment and fatigue* – the relationship between commitment and fatigue is particularly interesting. This group are particularly prone to overriding the warning signs of tiredness. As discussed earlier, the aversive of subjective experience of fatigue is believed to have a protective function, particularly with regards to longer-term health. Therefore, people who are high in the commitment component of mental toughness may persist with their chosen goals in spite of considerable adversity and beyond that which may be reasonable. Behaviour such as this will undoubtedly attract compensatory costs in the medium and long term. So, individuals who are particularly high in commitment would benefit from regularly evaluating the current validity of their goals, taking into account short-, medium- and longer-term costs.

Understanding your own process of fatigue – three recommendations for action

What remains of this chapter is a consideration of how we can use the 100 years of research on fatigue to understand our own fatigue processes. In a general sense, it is important to understand the changes that you are likely to undergo when fatigued.

1. Monitoring your fatigue

As reported earlier in the chapter, the feelings of tiredness and irritability are often the first indicators of fatigue. They are our warning signs that a rest should be considered. In themselves, they are not particularly worrying, but these feelings are typically associated with changes in the way we think. Although the pattern of these changes may be slightly different for everybody, we are all likely to experience a subtle shift towards low-effort thinking.

An understanding of this is extremely important, as it is often a subconscious process with potentially catastrophic consequences. This shift can lead to reduced attention to detail, risky behaviour and faulty and biased decision making. In a work context, this can result in poor work performance and an increased likelihood of accidents. In education this might mean a reduced capacity to revise and produce good coursework and so on.

However, an awareness of this process may be sufficient to minimize the impact that fatigue has on our attitudes and behaviours. An explicit knowledge of this process during a fatigued state could offset these changes, at least for a short period of time!

If you are aware that fatigue is likely to make you take 'short cuts', this information could be important in deciding whether to take a break or alternatively, consciously increase the care you take over tasks which are important to get right.

2. Identifying its causes

The second consideration worthy of mention is to evaluate what it is which makes us tired. Again, this may be slightly different for everyone. Some people are more prone to physical fatigue, some to emotional fatigue and some people are particularly affected by heavy or prolonged mental demands.

It may be a worthwhile exercise to consider what it is that makes you as an individual tired, ie is it certain tasks, particular working conditions or specific times of day. If you can reorganize your work or life demands to minimize fatigue, this may be the best way to stop fatigue developing.

A fatigue awareness exercise: understanding your own fatigue patterns

The demands of the modern working world mean that it isn't always possible to take a break when we are tired. Therefore, it is important to recognize what makes us tired and how we respond to being fatigued. Consequently, it is important to develop effective coping strategies to minimize the negative effects of feeling tired and/or worn-out:

- be aware of what makes you tired, ie certain tasks, time of day etc;

- be aware of the short-term psychological consequences;

- if you can reorganize your work, do so;

- if not, be aware that your judgement may be affected and that you may be more inclined to take risks and jump to conclusions.

Use the following questions to identify what makes you tired, how you normally react and what coping strategies you could develop to deal with them better:

What typically makes you tired?

How do you react?

What might be a better potential coping strategy?

There are different types of fatigue: mental fatigue, emotional fatigue, physical fatigue, morning tiredness and evening tiredness. It is useful to discuss your coping strategies with your manager/coach/mentor or a friend or family member.

3. Understanding yourself: are you particularly susceptible?

Finally, in the context of the current chapter, it may be interesting to consider how the process of fatigue may be different for people at the two extremes of the mental toughness spectrum.

First, the people who are low in mental toughness are arguably more sensitive to life's demands. Stressful circumstances and events are likely to lead to a greater stress response in people who are low in mental toughness. Therefore, this group may be more prone to the negative consequences of fatigue and it may be particularly important for people in this group to consider changing the circumstances which lead to fatigue, or better still, to consider ways in which they could improve their level of mental toughness, leaving them less vulnerable to the effects of life's stressors.

Conversely, the people who are high in mental toughness are less likely to experience stress when facing difficult circumstances and are hence less likely to develop fatigue. However, these people may be less likely to listen to the warning signs that the fatigue state provides. While this may offer regular short-term gains in terms of task completion, there may eventually be a performance cost in the medium term and even a health cost in the longer term.

Mental toughness and the world of work (1)

Stress, motivation and aspiration, leadership, coaching and teamworking

13

Stress, motivation and aspiration

The world of work is a major source of stress, pressure and change for most people. Even if the work itself is not particularly stressful, the environment can often provide the stressors and pressures. People tend to work within organizations, large and small, and there are very few organizations that are so secure that they do not feel the effect of competitive pressures.

The stress model shown in Chapter 2 (Figure 2.1) illustrates the fact that stressors can arise from almost anywhere and from almost anything we do. And, as previously noted, the world of work is not just full of stress and pressure, it is often abundant with opportunity (which is, for some, the source of a positive type of pressure). For the ambitious and aspirational, this represents a challenge. Again it chimes with Maslow's assertion that the higher-order needs are important motivators for many – particularly a sense of belonging (working in a team is part of that) and self-actualization (striving to be the best that you can be and realizing your potential).

Since its launch in 2003, the MTQ48 has been used in occupational settings more often than in any other area. This has provided a rich source of case studies and in recent times the beginnings of carefully controlled research. These consistently show that mental toughness has a significant role to play in the performance and wellbeing of individuals, amongst other things. However, equally important has been the observation that assessing the mental toughness of groups has also been useful and often revealing. The performance and behaviour of groups seems also to be influenced by the prevailing overall mental toughness of the group.

From the organization's perspective a key requirement is often to recruit and develop a workforce that performs to the best of its abilities and which develops a positive attitude towards the commercial and operational challenges that need to be dealt with. There is a growing awareness of the importance of culture in determining organizational performance. A consistent component of most organizations' preferred cultural position is to have a 'can-do' attitude throughout the organization. Possessing such a positive attitude is always likely to bring about a better performance than the absence of such an attitude.

This is perhaps more important these days given that most individuals and organizations have access to the same plant, equipment and technology. Similarly, as education, training and development have improved, equal access to skilled and competent employees has produced a more level playing field. But you can still have two sets of employees with equal or equivalent skill, knowledge and experience working with similar equipment in similar environments and yet they will deliver two distinctly different performances. In general, the more motivated the workforce and more positive in outlook, the more likely it will consistently emerge as the higher-performing workforce.

We now understand very well that the motivation and mindset of a workforce are crucial interrelated ingredients for success. More and more time, money and effort are spent on examining and developing this aspect of the organization. Developing mental toughness is a significant part of the answer to creating a high-performance organization. This appears to be particularly effective when it combines with and supports other solutions.

It is not the whole answer to every such question. Nothing is. But it does emerge consistently as a core component which few organizations can choose to ignore.

Leadership

We now see much more attention given to leadership development. Leadership is a quality which provides motivation to followers to give up their discretionary effort and to do it willingly and enthusiastically. Discretionary effort is that part of what we do which goes beyond what we have agreed to do in, say, a contract of employment. In 'old money', what we used to call 'going the extra mile'.

This is a 'pure' definition of leadership. It focuses specifically on what leadership is about. Many combine it with other factors, such as creativity, authenticity, resilience etc, and that can often be useful, but the concept of leadership is something which needs to be understood on its own as a core function. The more that a leader can do to meet this core functional requirement of encouraging discretionary effort the more likely that the leader's highly motivated followers will achieve better performance and provide competitive advantage. The best organizations develop leadership at every level. The ability to deal with challenge, change and pressure is what mental toughness is all about. Mental toughness has a vital role in enabling both the leader and the follower to respond positively to the challenge of leadership.

In 2006 the authors completed, with the considerable support of Dr Nollaig Heffernan, a fundamental review of leadership theory and practice. Partly provoked by interest from the UK Institute of Leadership and Management, one of the world's leading qualification awarding bodies, AQR organized a study of 1,500 people in leadership positions in around 50 public- and private-sector organizations. The study looked at over 50 leadership models and found that all had their origins in the same components – six scales which represented different aspects of leadership style. Further research showed that there were three (higher-order) core competencies which are crucial for leadership effectiveness.

One important outcome was the development of the Integrated Leadership Measure – the ILM72 which is a reliable psychometric measure of these scales. The ILM72 was developed to assess these three qualities too. The term 'integrated' is used because it integrates almost every major leadership model.

Leadership style

All leaders adopt a preferred way of working. There is no right, wrong or ideal style which is always effective. We understand that style is situational.

TABLE 13.1   Adopted style measured across six leadership styles

Scale	Scale Description	Poles
Goal orientation	How important achieving goals is to the leader	The Means vs The End
Motivation	What the leader believes is the prime path to motivation	The Task vs The Person
Engagement	How leaders will engage with others	Flexible vs Dogmatic
Control	The extent to which leaders need to be in control	De-centralized vs Centralized
Recognition	The leaders preferred approach to recognition	Reward vs Punishment
Structure	How important structure is to the leader	Structured vs Organic

Usefully, ILM72 profiles can be aggregated to form a picture of the leadership style of a group. ILM72 measures adopted style across six scales representing the six aspects of leadership style (Table 13.1).

It is not difficult to see how the different factors (the 4 Cs) in the mental toughness model might come into play within each of the scales. Adopted style is influenced by mental toughness and mental sensitivity. For instance, control and engagement, which is characterized by delegation and empowerment (de-centralized and flexible), implies a need for a degree of mental toughness challenge and confidence.

The global scales – core leadership competencies

Our work found evidence that there were three factors which did seem to emerge consistently when looking at effective leadership. These are shown in Table 13.2.

It is not difficult to map these scales to many leadership models eg Covey, Adair's Action Centre Leadership, Fiedler's model. And again, it's not difficult to see how mental toughness maps to each of these scales, particularly when one looks at determination to deliver.

TABLE 13.2 Effective leadership factors

Determination to deliver	This describes a single minded determination to achieve. Most satisfaction – the individuals' and the followers' – is derived from this
Engagement with individuals	This describes enhancing the capability, confidence and commitment of individuals to enable them to perform and to fulfil themselves
Engagement with teams	The emphasis is on cross-functional teamworking – a leader knows and supports how people work together across the organization

Coaching

Probably the fastest growing area in organizational and individual development is that of coaching. In particular, organizations are taking up performance, leadership and executive coaching with an extraordinary zeal. The belief is that coaching is a superior way to develop individuals and it is an excellent vehicle for engendering employee engagement (a core competency in leadership development).

Again, the main goals for much coaching practice are improving performance, wellbeing, personal development and managing change. Mental toughness is relevant for each of these. We are beginning to be clearer that mental toughness is important for the coachee – and the coach! The most valuable outcomes for mental toughness activity emerge as:

- *Performance.* At every level of analysis we see a close relationship between the mental toughness of individuals and performance, however it is measured and assessed.
- *Wellbeing.* The more mentally tough, the more likely the individual will be able to deal with everyday stressors.
- *Positive behaviours.* People who are more mentally tough are more likely to be described or describe themselves as having a 'can-do' approach. They tend to assess risk and to accept risk with a more positive mindset.

The application of mental toughness to the work of coaches is examined in more detail in Chapter 20.

Group mental toughness – organizational development applications

This is an increasingly important application for the model and the measure. Organizations of all types are beginning to appreciate the importance of culture. Whether an organization is mentally tough or mentally sensitive is emerging as important. This is examined in much more detail in *Developing Resilient Organisations* (Strycharczyk and Elvin, 2015).

It is important for at least two reasons. First, the overall or prevailing level of mental toughness in an organization does seem to be a factor in the organization's success. It seems important to determine, to some extent, how the organization responds to setbacks and, just as importantly, how positively it responds to opportunity and change – especially in the fast-changing world we now inhabit. Secondly, culture does influence the individual. It is much more difficult to develop the mental toughness of individuals if the prevailing culture is one of mental sensitivity – giving up when things go wrong, despairing when the journey becomes difficult, losing confidence in the capability of the organization in the face of competition etc.

CASE STUDY   Group mental toughness

In 2008, we worked with a UK local authority based in the north of England which employed around 7,000 people. The organization had, in the previous three years, made significant progress in transforming itself from an organization which had been assessed as underperforming to one which was now seen as a high-performance operation. This transformation had also stirred an ambition amongst the top tier of the organization to achieve recognition as an excellent organization.

The first part of the journey had been achieved through the vision and commitment of the chief executive and a small group at the top of the organization. The culture had been variously described as 'top down', 'highly centralized' and even 'autocratic'. Senior management had correctly assessed that, although this had been appropriate to move the organization from its poorly-performing past, this would not be sufficient to move it to an excellently-performing future. A more participative and teamwork-orientated culture were needed to engage everyone in the organization in its success.

A substantial visioning and planning exercise was launched which involved all 97 members of the senior and the senior/middle management structures. The plans, though ambitious, were deemed realistic. However, when implemented, there was a poor response form the employees across the organization. The suspicion was that one element of this was the behaviour of the wider senior management group.

All 97 senior managers completed the MTQ48 measure and the results partially confirmed the original suspicion. Figure 13.1 shows the pattern of overall mental toughness scores.

FIGURE 13.1   Overall mental toughness

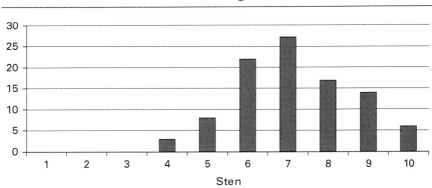

Studies by Marchant *et al* (2009) amongst others had shown that the more senior the manager the greater the level of mental toughness. We would have predicted that this group should show scores with a mean somewhere in the region of stens 7–8. The actual pattern is skewed to the left. Feedback and discussion with managers in the local authority confirmed that they thought the scores provided a reliable reflection of the situation at the time. One plausible suggestion was that the leadership style hadn't changed. Although all of these managers had participated in the visioning and planning stages of the organization development programme and had therefore been involved in its development, they didn't feel involved.

One interesting observation is that most managers didn't realize it was part of their role to champion and to implement the programme. One director observed: 'These are the results from self-report questionnaires. This is how we see ourselves. It's not going to be a surprise that the staff see us that way too!'

FIGURE 13.2   Mental toughness – challenge scores

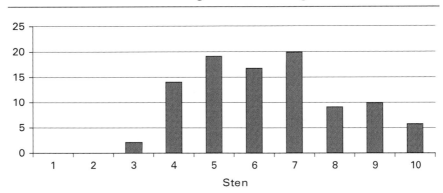

Analysing the scores for the individual scales was equally revealing. Figure 13.2 shows the pattern of scores for the challenge scale. This, if anything, is more skewed to the left than the pattern for overall mental toughness. This indicated that most senior managers (those scoring 7 and below, 72 out of 97), although they had been involved in developing the change programme, did not necessarily see the challenge as an opportunity to show what could be achieved.

Looking at the pattern of scores for commitment showed a similar pattern. This was lower than expected (Figure 13.3).

FIGURE 13.3   Mental toughness – commitment scores

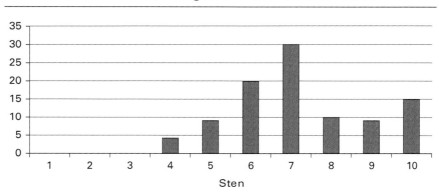

The analysis provoked a review of the organization's development strategy. Amongst actions taken were the provision of coaching opportunities for managers in this group and more attention paid to ensuring that managers better understood their role as managers and leaders in the organization. To some extent they had not moved their thinking from seeing themselves predominantly as functional managers.

Although appreciating the value of developing culture, atmosphere and attitude, this had always been 'handled by the HR department and senior management'.

Other analyses revealed that most managers didn't feel engaged with the organization and with other managers and that there was a poor focus on delivery of key organizational goals. Mental toughness wasn't the only factor in the failure of the programme, but it was a significant factor. The analysis also indicated strongly what might require attention to make the desired breakthrough.

By 2010 the organization had achieved its desired excellence (4-star) status.

Mental toughness and teamworking

We have often found ourselves, when operating as organizational development consultants, engaged in business improvement programmes which have the development of teamworking as a core component and belief. Curiously, a casual observation in many instances has been that senior management teams, which decide they would like to see a teamworking culture develop throughout the organization, can often provide the least compelling example of teamworking themselves.

More recently, an important study in the world of secondary education (St Clair-Thompson *et al*, in Press) found that mentally tough individuals formed peer relationships more readily and more effectively than did mentally sensitive individuals. This has provoked research into teamworking, in particular how mental toughness might plausibly play a role in developing interpersonal relationships. This is a valuable finding, especially in situations such as project management, where teams are often required to form quickly and then to deliver often complex outcomes within tight timescales and in challenging circumstances. It probably has an application in any form of teamworking.

Many team-building programmes devote attention to the potential difficulties in getting people of different personalities and with differing behaviours to work more effectively together. There are many models which are useful here. These focus on understanding differences and learning how to deal or cope with those differences.

The study suggests that there may be an additional approach worth considering – developing the mental toughness of participants who, by dint of that development, are much better able to deal with differences and take them in their stride. It might be that the mentally sensitive focus more on the team's goals than they do on the inner dynamics of the team. This might explain why teams at a senior level function with behaviours (like challenging each other often bluntly) which would be disruptive at other levels where there may be more mentally sensitive folk.

Our work with developing mental toughness within organizations and within teams has led us to some interesting and hopefully useful observations. First, we are generally convinced of the benefits of effective high-performance teamworking. We interact with others all day long. We are important and we influence others. We can be helpful, supportive or destructive. The way we behave sets standards for the rest of the organization – especially when we are in leadership and management positions.

So what do teams do for organizations? They:

- accomplish complex tasks – they tend to achieve high levels of performance;
- enable problems to be solved close to their source – usually more efficiently and more effectively;
- can be very good at co-ordinating the efforts of diverse but related groups and individuals;
- cover weaknesses with the strengths of others.

Developing teamworking can be a key component of the business strategy for many organizations. It figures widely in leadership and management theory and practice.

Mental toughness can have a big impact on both the performance of the organization and how teamworking and team-building is developed. Our experience suggests that there are two issues to be considered: organization development and culture, and teamworking behaviour and individual mental toughness.

Organization development and culture

When organizations are concerned with improving their performance it can be a very effective tactic to set about developing the mental toughness of their people. However, it is possible to develop the mental toughness of an individual or individuals and find that their effectiveness is limited because of the pattern of mental toughness within the organization.

The function of the organization development report available with the MTQ48 is to show the pattern of mental toughness within selected groups.

This report will often show that a group whose overall mental toughness is comparatively low can, over time, impact on the mental toughness of performers who are higher than the norm and 'wear them out'. Those with exceptionally high levels of mental toughness will not necessarily wilt but they may respond to a mentally sensitive culture with frustration and annoyance.

The challenge here is to support the development of mental toughness across the entire group or the team. One solution is to consider the use of coaches or mentors who, equipped with a toolkit of suitable interventions such as those described elsewhere in this book, work with members of the team to develop their mental toughness. Another is to provide learning and development around mental toughness to the whole team and not just selected individuals. In the world of education, the Scottish colleges have been experimenting with just these options. Do you provide support only to those whose scores suggest they need it or do you provide a broad range of support to everyone?

Teamworking behaviour and individual mental toughness

People who rise to the top of an organization are almost inevitably more mentally tough than the average person. However, being mentally tough usually implies a degree of personal achievement and a degree of mental insensitivity – a tendency to be 'thick skinned' and not to be too sensitive to things that might get in the way of performance. Not, at first sight, the best recipe for teamworking!

Senior management and board meetings can be interesting affairs. Conversation and exchanges can be very blunt and direct – to the point of appearing rude. Yet the participants will often take it in their stride and think no more of it. I well remember my first presentation as a junior/middle manager presenting a proposal to develop our operation with my colleagues. We had 15 minutes to put our case, the questioning was incisive and pressured and bruising. We were down-hearted on leaving the presentation only to learn later that the board had approved our proposal.

Examining the behaviour of high performing teams – whether they are from the sports, social or business worlds – shows that there are certain characteristics that are consistently present if that team is truly 'world-class'. These characteristics fall into five broad and interrelated areas as shown in Figure 13.4.

FIGURE 13.4   Characteristics of a world-class team

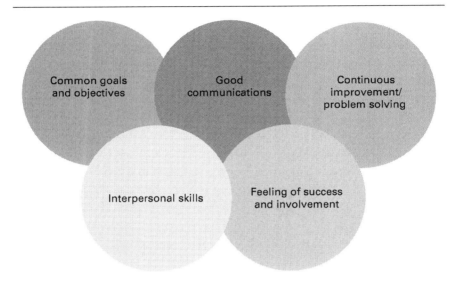

A truly first-class team must perform well in all five areas – anything less is not highly productive, effective and efficient teamworking. If we examine each area in more detail we can see more clearly why these are critical areas for success.

Developing team toughness

There are a number of actions that a team of mentally tough individuals can adopt which will enhance their teamworking. It is not necessarily desirable to change the mental toughness of the team members. It is after all one of the qualities which has brought them to the top of the organization, and may be a significant contributor to their individual and their group success.

The key here is to develop self-awareness and to enhance their understanding of their impact on others. And then to enable them to agree to adopt a common set of behaviours which better represent teamworking and send a stronger signal to others that they believe in teamworking and are prepared to adopt at least some recognizable teamworking behaviours. This can be expressed as a 'team charter'. Typical activities adopted to enhance team toughness and teamworking include the following.

Control

- Agree on who is doing what.
- Accept that setbacks are normal occurrences.
- Agree on a plan together and support each other in sticking to it.
- Give each other the space/time/support each needs to recover from setbacks.
- Some things will always be outside or your control – work as a team to work around that which you cannot change.

Challenge

- Review and prioritize work together.
- Communicate with each other.
- Identify each other's strengths and weaknesses – coach and delegate where necessary.
- View challenges and obstacles as opportunities at both a team and individual level.
- Break down assignments into smaller manageable chunks and delegate.
- Recognize when you need to take time out and recharge as a team and as individuals.

Commitment

- Take time to recognize each other's contributions and give praise where due.
- Accept that some tasks can't be completed. Review resources and energy – could they be better directed?
- Identify what motivates you as a team and as individuals and incorporate this into your planning.
- Agree on your goals and deadlines. They should be specific, measurable, achievable, relevant and time-bound (SMART).
- Don't be afraid to ask each other for help when you need it and encourage each other to suggest ideas.
- Have regular meetings/contact to monitor progress. Things change and so might your goals with them.
- Listen to each other and ask each other questions. Communicate.

Confidence

- Recognize each other's strengths, acknowledge them and use them.
- Don't dwell on mistakes and over-generalize them. Not everything is black and white – mistakes can be learned from.
- Beware of over-confidence.
- If confidence is knocked, recognize the need for time off to recover. Give each other the additional support needed.
- Give constructive criticism, corrections and encouragement instead of verbally beating someone down.
- Give teammates the support they need to improve their skills and increase their confidence.
- If a teammate or colleague needs chastising, do it in private and provide them with the opportunity to remedy their error.

A team must have: a shared sense of purpose; aspiration; effective ways of working with each other; a willingness to work together; personal independence; and a collective identity. If a team behaves carefully it can improve things for its colleagues and show others – by example – how to be more effective.

There are two steps to be taken. First, reflect on and discuss with colleagues key issues such as described below. Once done, this should lead to the completion of a team charter. Typical issues for reflection include:

- What can we do as a team to increase team toughness for others and ourselves?
- What can we do as a team to reduce stress for others and ourselves?
- What can we do as a team to achieve peak performance?
- How can we work more effectively with each other?
- How can we work more effectively with others outside of the team?
- Can we genuinely commit to doing something about it?
- How will we implement and publish it?
- Which actions are absolutely key?

A typical team charter might look like this:

Team charter

Set out below the key behaviours everyone in the team will adopt to improve the way the team performs:

- We will avoid the use of strong language at all times.

- We will publicly support all group decisions.

- We will respond promptly to all questions and queries.

- We will not apportion blame to any person or group when something goes wrong.

- We will keep all appointments – and be on time every time.

- We will visit a department of the business at least once a week for at least one hour.

Summary

Leadership, teamworking, developing motivation and aspiration are all activities which are vitally important for all organizations. Whilst all provide a source of opportunity they are all also sources of stress and pressure. The mental toughness of the organization as a whole will be as important as individual mental toughness in dealing effectively with those stressors and in bringing about a successful outcome.

Mental toughness as a concept is made for application in the world of work.

Mental toughness and the world of work (2)

14

Assessment and development, and talent management

There are several areas where the model adds considerable value. It provides a practical description of core competencies for many jobs. This means that it has value in recruitment, selection and especially in talent management, succession planning and promotion.

Recruitment and selection

When used in recruitment and selection, the model must be used with care. Mental toughness must be shown to be a key requirement for the role, although we would argue that it is an essential or important requirement for many roles. The nature of business, whether it is private- or public-sector, means that all employees at all levels should be open to change.

The MTQ48 measure is a valid and reliable measure and it is a normative measure, and therefore has potential to be useful in recruitment and selection. Like any high-quality psychometric instrument it should only be used in conjunction with other sources of information about the individual's mental toughness. It is widely used to assess resilience, openness to learning and confidence. Once again there is a need for caution. Mental toughness is a plastic personality trait. This means that someone who emerges as mentally tough in the recruitment process can, in some circumstances, find that their mental toughness diminishes as time goes by – hence its application in developing staff. Conversely, someone who is mentally sensitive can develop their mental toughness if needed.

All things being equal and generally, if someone matches the job specification in all or most other respects, understanding the mental toughness of a prospective employee is primarily a very useful piece of information and should be treated as such.

Of course if the mental toughness factors are key to success in a role, then a mentally sensitive individual may not be suited to that role and the recruiter can perhaps give more weight to information about their mental toughness provided it is corroborated with other sources of information. One of the MTQ48 reports has been specifically designed to provide the user with a battery of questions to help the user probe someone's mental toughness.

One area where the MTQ48 is widely applied is in assessment and development centres.

Assessment and development centres

The objective of assessment and development centres is to obtain a clear and accurate picture of an individual's qualities such that they may be matched against the requirements of a job or jobs. Managers will recognize this as a common approach to a wide range of human resources activities and initiatives. However, there are three main areas of application:

- selection;
- management development;
- talent management.

Assessment centres work on the principle that it is possible to identify and isolate many of the key requirements for a particular job. Subsequently, techniques such as tests, interviews, exercises and simulations are devised which have as their focus one or more of these criteria. By asking someone to undertake these tests it is possible to obtain some measure of the qualities of the person, ie do they demonstrate relevant behaviours or do they have the potential to acquire them quickly? Cross-referencing information from a variety of sources – tests, simulations, discussions and exercises – is one of the elements which enable centres to make good predictions about the individual. In a sense then it is possible to simulate elements of a new role or job (or even an existing job) and to judge a would-be jobholder according to the criteria which are thought to be appropriate to that job.

There is now a wealth of evidence to show that assessment and development centres are an extremely effective selection and development tool. Although set-up costs can be high, the tool remains a cost-effective way of acquiring valid information that is often difficult to come by through other means. Its capacity to predict future behaviour is higher than almost any other technique. And its use is now being extended as a device for identifying clearly and accurately the training needs of employees in their current roles.

Assessment centres

An assessment centre is most often used in a selection or recruitment situation where the organization seeks to discover as much relevant information as possible about a person in order to select one or more for a specified role. This often means that there is one (or more) 'winners' and that there are often 'losers'.

If the participants are external to the organization then they may get little more than the experience of participation. The logistics of the process means that they may not receive deep feedback. If the participants are internal then there is often more scope for constructive feedback to be given.

Development centres

A development centre provides both the user and the employees with the opportunity to find out more about their current skills and future potential – particularly those which are crucial for current or future job performance and therefore business success.

The objective here is to assess where the employee has existing strengths suited to a future role and where there may be gaps. In the latter case the outcome is usually to identify training and development needs and to secure commitment to a development plan – from both the employee and the organization. In this sense there are no 'losers'. Everyone emerges with valuable feedback and a structure through which they can improve – everyone 'wins'. Furthermore it helps to focus development activity on those areas that ensure those key skills and competencies are acquired as quickly and as effectively as possible.

Competencies

Most recruitment and assessment and development activity in the 21st century is based on the use of competencies. Here again the structure and the clarity of the mental toughness model provides some strengths which support the effective application of competency frameworks.

Whilst mental toughness is often identified as a competency in its own right, its elements often underpin other important competencies. Table 14.1 illustrates this potential.

TABLE 14.1 Mental toughness model – relationship with important competencies

Competency	Short Descriptor	Control	Commitment	Challenge	Confidence
Self-efficacy	can-do	×			
Emotional management/ poise	managing presence	×			
Goal orientation	purpose		×		
Tenacity	sticking to the task		×		
Openness to learning	open- mindedness			×	
Positive attitude	cup half full			×	×
Resilience	copes with setbacks	×	×		
Self-belief	... in abilities				×
Assertive	influential				×
Leadership	motivational	×	×	×	×

TABLE 14.1 *Continued*

Competency	Short Descriptor	Control	Commitment	Challenge	Confidence
Empowering	delegator				×
Interpersonally skilled	how the person involves others	×			×
Structured	organised		×		
Team worker/ team builder	building teams	×	×	×	×
Strategic thinker	big picture thinker	×		×	

Employee development and talent management

Arguably the greatest value of the model perhaps lies in employee development, in leadership and management development and in coaching activity to which it is very well suited. This is examined further in two later chapters: 'Can mental toughness be developed?' in Chapter 19 and in the section on 'Coaching' in Chapter 20.

In development activity generally, work has been carried out which confirms that the effectiveness of much training and development activity is due in some part to the mindset of the individual entering training and development programmes. Unsurprisingly, if the individual enters a development programme with trepidation and perhaps even fear, they are unlikely to get from the programme what they could. This is particularly true in organizations where staff and managers are 'sent' on training programmes. Those who adopt a positive attitude will inevitably optimize the learning experience. Their approach is to get the most out of the time they have to spend.

In some forms of education and training, eg apprenticeship programmes, there is a link between mental toughness and completion rates; or in more common parlance, drop-out rates. This is one of the areas of greatest waste in very many organizations but can be reduced through assessing a learner's mental toughness and responding accordingly.

In 2011 Adam Smith College in Scotland carried out a study on 400 students and found that they could reduce drop-out rates by 7 per cent overall from 15 per cent to around 8 per cent. This meant that an additional 28 students were being retained through to completion of the programme who might otherwise have not finished the course.

In terms of talent management, particularly where this is concerned with identifying and developing people who can work at higher levels in an organization, a study (Marchant *et al*, 2009) on 504 managers who were in junior, middle and senior manager positions found a clear correlation between mental toughness and level in the organization. Those in senior management roles had generally the highest levels of mental toughness. Those in middle management had lower levels of mental toughness and those in junior management roles had, on the whole, lower levels still. In all three cases the level was greater than the global norm.

The study didn't explore causality. Did the role make people more mentally tough or did the mentally tough travel higher up the ladder? Though, given that there is evidence of the link between mental toughness and aspirations we can perhaps suggest that many of those who aspired did so because they were mentally tough.

Finally, understanding mental toughness and incorporating relevant material into most soft skills programmes can significantly enhance the content of those programmes. This will include leadership and management programmes and interpersonal skills programmes of all types. It is especially valuable in leadership skills, presentation skills, sales skills and time management programmes. An individual's mental toughness is relevant to the way he or she approaches all of these activities.

Employability

A key issue for the 21st-century employer and employee

15

Employability – what is this concept?

This is a widely used term for which there is not yet a universally agreed definition, although there is a good understanding across the piece that it is important. Moreover, it has a core element which is perceived slightly differently from the perspectives of three important groups: employers (including their training, development and coaching resources), actual and potential employees, and those involved in career guidance.

As Kieran Gordon, CEO for Career Connect, states: 'At its simplest employability is the ability to get employment and maintain it. Increasingly, sustaining gainful employment is becoming as challenging as the act of getting employment in the first place'.

At AQR we have begun to use a slightly more descriptive definition based on the work of Professor Mantz Yorke:

> Employability is a set of qualities – operational skills, understandings and personal attributes – that, firstly, enable individuals to gain employment and, then, to be successful in their chosen occupations and in their long-term career development. This produces benefit for the individual, employers, society and the economy.
>
> Yorke, 2004

Both descriptions are useful. They explicitly link recruitment, career management and talent management. They are all elements of a potentially seamless process.

Employability also applies to those who are self-employed, are enterprising and are entrepreneurial. This is increasingly important. A greater proportion of people, the world over, are now opting, for one reason or another, for self-employment of some form. It is becoming an element of economic strategy for many governments.

From the *employer's* perspective, operational skills, understandings and personal attributes are often the personality-based attributes which identify the ideal employee. The most common response when asking an employer 'What makes a great employee?' is the single word 'Attitude'. They know what they mean but can rarely describe it further. Very rarely do they assess people for it either before employment or equally importantly, during employment. A major study to define and operationalize this is described on p 000. An interesting observation on the behaviour of many employers is that many will recruit people on the basis of their qualifications and knowledge but when they are fired it's on the basis of their attitude. Employers of all types want employable staff – employability matters.

From the *individual's* perspective, employability describes one of the most important sets of qualities they should develop and present to a prospective employer. It's equally important once in employment. Employability factors are almost always important in career development and talent management programmes.

When we speak about transferable skills, employability skills and attributes are amongst the most desirable and the most transferrable. Developing these skills not only enhances an individual's prospects within a job but is one of the most effective things an individual can do to deal effectively with adverse events such as redundancy and job loss.

From the *career guidance professional's* perspective, employability changes the emphasis of their work from guiding or directing individuals to jobs and careers to developing employability in their clients to enable those individuals to manage those careers. The world of work is changing and a job or career that exists today may not exist in 10 years' time. Conversely, it is now estimated that at least 40 per cent of jobs that will exist in 10 years' time don't exist today. How can you guide someone to a job that doesn't exist? Answer: You show them how to manage that situation when it arises by attending to their employability – employability is the universal need that doesn't change.

The situation for all three perspectives is further complicated because of change, especially technological change, and importantly because of the pace of change and the emergence of Gen X/Z/Millennial individuals who have a different set of needs than did previous generations. This adds complexity to change – together they represent a considerable challenge:

- by 2020 there will be 5 million fewer low-skill jobs in Britain than there were in 2010;

- today's school and college leavers will have between 10 and 14 jobs on average by the age of 38;

- the top 10 jobs in demand in 2010 did not exist in 2004.

And competition will increase. By 2020, China will produce more university graduates than leave the UK education system, at all levels, each year. Few economies are any longer protected in any way from international competition. Many jobs can be carried out effectively from anywhere.

People entering the world of work now arrive with different expectations:

- They are IT natives – and use technology in everything they do.

- They are better educated and better informed and are less likely to settle for jobs without change and interest.

- Knowledge is no longer an issue – Google and other search engines solve that problem.

- They communicate freely and do so round the clock – and expect prompt responses.

- They are less pay-orientated and more interested in the nature of what they do – Maslow's Hierarchy of Needs is now increasingly relevant.

Employability – what does this mean and where does mental toughness play a part?

In 2012/13 AQR, in conjunction with the Carrus Partnership, carried out a major exercise to consult with almost 500 employers in the UK to identify exactly what was meant by attitude. The Carrus Partnership is a federation of three of the leading careers services in the UK – Career Connect (north-west England), Inspira (north of England) and CXK (south-east England).

An initial survey posed the question: What were the important factors in the behaviour and performance of a high performing employee? The initial findings confirmed that many employers looked at qualifications and ability when recruiting people but, once established, they gave little weight to an individual's qualifications unless there was a technical imperative for this.

As stated earlier almost every response confirmed that attitude was a major determinant of success as far as employers were concerned. Within this initial phase we also sought to identify what employers meant by attitude. Around 30 themes/factors emerged which formed the basis of the second phase of the study. In the latter survey we asked employers to rate how important each of these factors was when describing attitude. Now a clearer picture emerged which identified 16 factors which appeared consistently as essential or important qualities. Curiously one factor which hardly figured at all was obedience – that is, responding to instructions without question. It may be that empowerment and engagement is now widely accepted in the UK.

The 16 factors are summarized in the following section and in Tables 15.1 to 15.4 and, unsurprisingly, four of the factors are the 4 Cs which make up the mental toughness model. There is now a good deal of research and case studies to show that mental toughness is a significant factor in performance, wellbeing and positive attitude. All high on the list of wants for most employers. This is discussed elsewhere in this book. The survey nevertheless indicated its importance in the context of employability.

> We are after people with a can-do attitude, enthusiasm, and interpersonal skills ... For us, it's less about what you've studied and more about why you want to work for us and what you can bring.
>
> Theresa McHenry, HRD, Microsoft

Employability factors – what does a good attitude entail?

The 16 factors arranged themselves around four major themes – mental toughness, the ability to deal with problems, motivation and drivers, and interpersonal skills – each with four elements or scales.

Mental toughness

The mental toughness factors emerged as essential qualities for the vast majority of respondents to the survey. Employers of all types – private sector, public sector and third sector – recognized that they operated in a changing, highly competitive world and engaging with their staff was hugely important in creating a responsive organization. In the words of the quotation about nature often attributed to Darwin: 'It is not the strongest of the species that survives, nor the most intelligent that survives. It is the one that is the most adaptable to change.' This seems to apply to business and commerce too.

Arguably the mental toughness factors also interplay and underpin the other three other three themes.

TABLE 15.1 Employability factors – mental toughness

Mental toughness		
Employers value those who can deal with stress, pressure, challenge and opportunity and respond positively to most situations		
Resilience – dealing with adverse situations	**Control**	Having a sense of 'can-do and maintaining poise when needed
	Commitment	Preparedness to make promises and to keep promises – goal orientation
Adopting a positive approach to what you do	**Challenge**	Being prepared to stretch oneself and develop – and learn from mistakes
	Confidence	The self-belief in one's own abilities and in dealing with people

Ability to deal with problems

TABLE 15.2 Employability factors – ability to deal with problems

The ability to deal with problems		
Employers value people who can recognise problems and look for opportunities to do things better by either attending to them or contributing to the solution. >90% of problems and issues can be dealt with by a responsive individual.		
Developing and possessing the skills to deal with problems	**Problem solving**	The extent to which you will actively identify, confront, analyse and solve problems
	Creativity	The extent to which you seek to add new ideas and innovation to your work
Wanting to do things in the right way and to do them better	**Organization**	The extent to which structure and order is important to you
	Continuous improvement	The extent to which you reflect on what you and others do and seek to improve on this

This also identifies a major part of the case for employee engagement. Increasingly organizations understand that most minor queries and issues arise 'at the coal face'. Furthermore, most employees who interface with the clients/customers will know how to deal with most of them. In the past the query would be passed up to a team leader, supervisor or manager who would work out a solution and either deal with it or pass the solution back down the line. This was inefficient and often ineffective in producing prompt response for the client. And it meant that so-called supervisors and managers were doing no such thing. Their days became cluttered with activity that could be better handled elsewhere.

As organization structures have flattened, the middle management of organizations has come under more and more pressure. Of course passing a problem upwards has been an easy option for some employees. Even a problem they are capable of handling comfortably. The desire from most employers is for employees who, willingly and enthusiastically solve problems, identify where systems and processes can be improved and offer their ideas for improvement.

The links with control, challenge and confidence from the mental toughness model are fairly clear.

Motivation and drivers

TABLE 15.3 Employability factors – motivation and drivers

Motivation and drivers		
Employers and educators value people who possess a degree of self-motivation and who approach what they do with a sense of wanting to be there		
The desire to do whatever they do in the right way	**Conscientiousness**	The extent an individual is guided by rules, standards and values
	Concern for standards	The extent to which an individual desires to work to a high standard
Prepared to take responsibility for own development and to achieve potential	**Ambition**	The extent to which an individual will desire attainment or seek to be 'the best'
	Personal development	The extent to which you take responsibility for own learning and development

This, for many employers, is an increasingly important area. Quality in the sense of 'total quality' is almost a given in the 21st century. If an organization promises something it must keep that promise. An organization generally delivers its offer through its people. Those people need to be motivated around the same standards. Moreover, where employers will support employees with their development, it is increasingly understood that the employee has an equal responsibility to be accountable for their development – especially in maintaining their employability.

Again here there is a link with mental toughness's commitment and challenge scales.

Interpersonal skills

TABLE 15.4 Employability factors – interpersonal skills

Interpersonal skills		
Almost everything that can be achieved has to be done with others. Employers value those who can appreciate this and who build effective relationships with others – colleagues, clients, tutors, managers etc		
Skills in dealing with people and being aware how others respond to you	**Teamworking**	The extent to which individuals work willingly with others to achieve the group's goals
	Altruism	The extent to which an individual wishes to act in the best interests of others
Being able to influence others and to co-operate when needed	**Emotional intelligence**	Your awareness of your and other's emotions and understanding how to respond
	Assertiveness	The extent to which an individual is determined to influence others

Long understood to be important, this theme grows in importance as more and more employees find themselves interacting with others, clients, suppliers, colleagues etc. The emergence of altruism is interesting and warrants a closer examination. We can see a connection with commitment and confidence in offering good interpersonal skills.

FIGURE 15.1 The employability cycle and its relationship to mental toughness

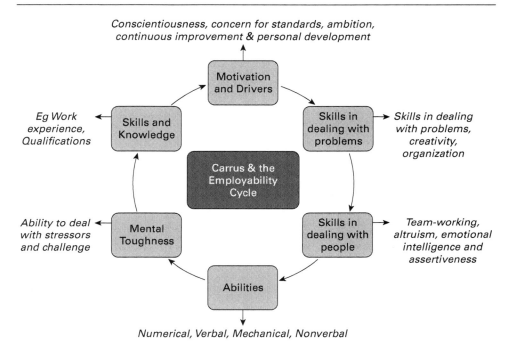

Many employers think that skills (what you can do) and personal qualities (what you're like as a person) are as important, if not more important, than paper qualifications.

BBC News, 2014

The 12 scales which revolve around the latter three themes are now embodied in a psychometric measure called Carrus which sits on the same platform as the Mental Toughness Questionnaire. The Carrus instrument also offers the optional capability to assess four areas of abilities in which most employers are interested – verbal, numerical, spatial and mechanical. Figure 15.1 provides an overview of employability and identifies where mental toughness sits.

Self-employment, enterprise and entrepreneurship

In 1995, AQR, working with CareerDecisions (a forerunner to Career Connect) and Merseyside BusinessLink in the UK, carried out a qualitative study on enterprise development. CareerDecisions and BusinessLink arranged for AQR Ltd to work with 39 individuals who had started their own businesses over the past three or four years. The individuals had started businesses which ranged from the ordinary (hairdressing) through to leading-edge (an educational software developer).

These individuals had been identified as successful. Although two were involved in highly creative activity most were establishing businesses which were variations on a theme already created elsewhere – hairdressing, account-ancy and book-keeping, landscaping services etc. For this exercise 'successful' was defined as:

- had been in business for 3 or more years;
- had increased turnover in each of those years;
- the individuals were involved full-time in the enterprise and were making a living from it;
- their business had recruited or were in the process of recruiting at least one person.

The last criterion was the real point of the exercise. It was felt that sponsor-ing lots of small potential employers might be a useful approach to economic regeneration rather than just encouraging a single large investor to set up in the region and employ lots of people.

Focus groups were held with the participants who described their experi-ences in getting their enterprises underway. All described the first two years as being very demanding. One actually spoke about the need for 'mental toughness' although we had not, at that stage introduced the term. All spoke of the pressures and challenges arising from:

- the unexpected happening (always apparently at the wrong time), eg customers changing their minds about their needs – often at short notice (challenge);
- working to targets – often from an unsympathetic bank or customer (commitment);
- dealing with setbacks (confidence);
- working long hours because they had so many things to do and they only had themselves as a resource (control).

These responses suggest that mental toughness is an important quality for those who wish to enter the world of self-employment, enterprise and entrepreneurship.

In summary, it would appear that mental toughness is a key factor in employability whether the individual takes up employment with an organization or engages with that organization though a different form of relationship. The latter is of increasing interest. More and more employers use a variety of approaches to manage their human capital needs in the short and the long term. Some of that resource will be employed on a full-time basis, some will be employed on a part-time or contracted basis and some will be in the form of associateship or partnership.

Mental toughness and the world of education and the development of young people

16

Children and young people face a number of daunting challenges. Golawski (2014) identified a number of these:

- bullying;
- self-esteem;
- pressure of distorted media images;
- celebrity culture;
- studying;
- exam pressure;
- career choices;
- friendship and relationships;
- peer pressure;
- changing family dynamics.

Mental toughness has the potential to make a significant impact on all of these important aspects of the world of education. This is true all the way from early years through to further education. Indeed as Paul Tough suggests in his very readable *How Children Succeed: Grit, curiosity, and the hidden power of character*, the earlier the intervention the more effective the outcome. Moreover, it is very much in step with global interest in the importance of mindset, character, grit and resilience which is being understood and adopted all over the world, and particularly building on some of the pioneering work by people like Dweck (mindset) and Seligman (learned optimism) where the mental toughness model is seen as an overarching concept which succeeds in bringing together many of these approaches. This gives it an operational strength valuable for practitioners.

Furthermore, at a technical level mental toughness clearly overlaps with a number of concepts that have proved useful within the educational domain. These include resilience (eg Putwain *et al*, 2013): buoyancy (eg Martin and Marsh, 2006, 2008); the concept of grit (eg Duckworth *et al*, 2007); self-efficacy (eg Boggiano, Main and Katz, 1988) and many others. The 4 Cs model offers one way of encapsulating all of these into an easily operationalized context.

Our work around the world has shown that mental toughness is valuable with a wide range of topics important in the development of young people. This includes transition, retention, wellbeing, attendance and behaviour, aspirations, development of peer relationships as well as issues such as bullying. Many of these factors are interrelated, showing that developing young people can be a complex affair and requires a holistic approach for true and sustained difference.

This chapter consists of a mix of illustrative research and case studies which supports the idea that there is a 'toughness advantage' in education. There are many more. Institutions are now introducing mental toughness development programmes in order to maximize the potential of all their students. Likewise, many parents are attempting to achieve the same outcomes.

Performance and attainment

Clearly, mental toughness is associated with better performance in a number of domains. Modern education is, for better or worse, a performance environment where attainment of qualifications is seen as the prime output. We would expect mentally tough children to do better – and they do. Sensitive children have a harder road to travel – but also much to offer the education system. Unfortunately, the focus on assessments in education may mean that they cannot always express their skills and talents to the fullest extent.

Case studies in secondary, further and higher education consistently show a close relationship between an individual's mental toughness and their performance in exams and tests. Two important studies in secondary education (one in the UK and one in the Netherlands) indicated that up to 25 per cent of the variation in a young individual's test performance can be explained by their mental toughness (as assessed through MTQ48).

In 2007, Knowsley Metropolitan Borough Council in the UK introduced a significant initiative to use the concept of mental toughness in the development of young people to explore the barriers to learning. One of the key goals for the oncoming programme at that time was that all schools in Knowsley achieved results above the National Challenge benchmark which required that at least 30 per cent of pupils achieved 5 A*–C grade GCSEs including English and mathematics. Knowsley schools moved above the National Challenge benchmark during the period in which mental toughness had been initiated. Improvements of 3.4 per cent and 3.6 per cent were made over the period 2007–9, and this trend continued with another rise in the 2010 results.

One observed pattern was that pupils who had higher mental toughness scores tended to achieve better scores than predicted, while those with low mental toughness scores tended to achieve lower grades than predicted. This is similarly observed in vocational (further) education. The research into vocational education in Switzerland carried out at the University of Basel showed that mentally tough students performed better than mentally sensitive students and that the mentally tough improved their mental toughness during their exam year, whereas mentally sensitive students became more mentally sensitive. In higher education, a study on sports psychology students at the University of Hull showed a correlation between mental toughness and exam performance and, interestingly, that mentally sensitive students would choose 'easier' options during their studies.

What about the mentally sensitive young person? They can be provided with a 'toughness' toolkit, allowing them to compete on a more even playing field. It can also be important to provide them with the care and support they clearly need to function in an environment that is not best suited to their skill sets. This has implications for teachers and leaders in education. They can usefully learn about mental toughness and reflect on their own mental toughness – it will have an impact on the development of young people. The same is true of parents and guardians.

We are not saying all young people should be tough; rather we are saying that the differences need to be recognized and appropriate actions taken.

Wellbeing

The higher the level of mental toughness, the more the individual is able to deal with the pressures, stressors and challenges of everyday life. They are able to deal more easily with even the most difficult days. Pilot work shows that this translates into outcomes such as better attendance, less stress and lower reported bullying.

A 2010 pilot study at the Depression and Sleep Research Unit at the University of Basle in Switzerland showed that in adolescents, favourable sleep patterns and favourable mental toughness seem to be related. The study also looked at exercise and sleep patterns and found no significant correlation. Whereas the underlying mechanisms remain unclear, the study concluded that it seems conceivable that improving both sleep and mental toughness should confer increased wellbeing. This initial work was followed up by a number of studies by this group. They consistently report that higher levels of toughness are related to better sleep and wellbeing in a broad spectrum of adolescent samples.

In the UK, Elizabeth Stamp has shown the link between toughness and wellbeing in a university sample. These studies are reported in more detail in the Chapter 26 of this book on research. Taken together they show that it is not simply about performance. Mental toughness is about enjoying life and fully optimizing potential.

Attendance, behaviour and peer relationships

Research led Dr Helen St Clair-Thompson, Dr Myfanwy Bugler and Dr Sarah McGeown has looked in depth at the possible impact of mental toughness in the secondary school system in the UK. In a series of studies, they examined the relationship between mental toughness and different aspects of educational performance in adolescents aged 11–16, focusing on academic attainment, school attendance, classroom behaviour and peer relationships. They showed:

- Clear links between several aspects of mental toughness (but particularly life control) and academic attainment and attendance. A major project in the UK (delivered by Career Connect) working with around 4,000 young people with poor attendance records and which was focused on improving attendance (amongst other objectives) showed that introducing mental toughness development activity led to an improvement in attendance from a low of 68 per cent to the target of 95 per cent. In turn this translated into higher attainment. The programme involved assessing the mental toughness at the start of the programme, providing feedback to create self-awareness and then introducing selected interventions over a period of six weeks.

- Significant associations between several aspects of mental toughness (but again particularly control of life) and counterproductive classroom behaviour.

- Significant associations between aspects of mental toughness (confidence in abilities and interpersonal confidence) and peer relationships. This has proved to be particularly interesting, providing the first real evidence that the mentally tough might be more open to developing relationships with others. This perhaps indicates that the mentally tough are less sensitive to others' differences and might be more accommodating of others.

As is often the case, this has provoked a desire to carry out more research – it carries the possibility that mental toughness has a key role to play in effective team working.

Together these studies suggest that mental toughness is a useful construct to consider in educational settings, and that mental toughness interventions have the potential to have beneficial effects upon several aspects of adolescents' educational experiences. It is interesting to note that the commitment and life control sub-scales have perhaps the clearest impact on educational success.

The higher the level of mental toughness the more the individual demonstrates positive behaviours. They will adopt a 'can-do' attitude and there is clear evidence that the higher the level of mental toughness the more likely the student will engage in the class and the school (asking questions, engaging in discussion, volunteering, engaging in extra-curricular activities etc). Studies in the occupational world show exactly the same thing.

Curiously, two studies have also indicated that some teachers in secondary education routinely discriminate between male and female students in terms of engaged behaviour. This is often perceived as a 'good' behaviour when demonstrated by males but as 'troublesome', 'difficult' or 'lippy' when the same is demonstrated by females. This appears to be the case whether the teacher/tutor is male or female.

Retention

This is a significant issue in further and higher education where students enrol on programmes but, for a variety of reasons, will drop out at an early stage. The following describes a case study in a Scottish college of further education. FE colleges can be characterized as places where diverse groups of learners of different ages from a range of (often non-traditional) backgrounds come together to pursue a wide variety of programmes of study. This work was carried out and written up by Craig Thompson who was Principal of Adam Smith College at the time.

CASE STUDY Adam Smith College – using MTQ48 to direct interventions

In Adam Smith College, a research project was set up with the aim of using the Mental Toughness Questionnaire (MTQ48) to direct a range of interventions with learners. The plan put in place for the 2010/11 academic year involved testing 10 per cent of the college's full-time FE learners (FE provision in the college has tended to show weaker levels of retention than HE, and full-time FE is, in turn, weaker than part-time). The class groups involved in the pilot were selected to reflect a range of different curriculum areas and to cover SCQF levels 4 to 6.

In focusing on groups, the college departed from the more standard approach adopted in interventions directed by MTQ48 where the focus is solely on the individual. This was done to allow the initial pilot to play a dual role. On the one hand, it was aimed at achieving improvement with the pilot groups. On the other, it provided the opportunity to familiarize staff and students with the approach and to allow open consideration of how the move to an individual focus might be achieved. The staff were initially concerned that the approach might single out or place an inappropriate focus on vulnerable learners. The research design therefore included a communication and engagement strategy to ensure that discussion and developments were clearly understood.

The initiative also grappled with the difficult issue of nomenclature. 'Mental toughness' was considered an explicit but stark term and the project was named in line with its core intention, adopting the title 'Stay and Succeed'.

Learners were helped to think across the 'Stay and Succeed' components (control, confidence, challenge and commitment) and to reflect and work on how they could:

- be better prepared for what life 'throws at them';

- cope with difficulties and challenges;

- be more resilient;

- be better organized and able to plan their life;

- adopt positive thinking;

- consider how they perceive things;

- bounce back from setbacks.

Records of subsequent CPD sessions held with staff show that the outcomes of the interventions and student/staff discussions helped to move the debate within the college on from concern about individual interventions to consideration of how the interventions could be individualized.

While the methodology employed did not focus on individuals, the results in terms of improved early retention in the 2010/11 academic year proved to be encouraging. The 18 class groups involved in the pilot covered courses in construction, a range of creative subjects, sport, engineering, welding, hospitality, hairdressing and access to nursing studies.

The results were initially analysed in three dimensions, comparing them with figures for the previous year, college averages and sector averages. Of the 18 courses, 11 showed improvement with previous years, 11 improved relative to sector averages and 13 showed improvement when compared with college averages.

Although these results can be viewed as encouraging, suggesting that the interventions had a positive effect, they have to be treated with caution and cannot be presented as conclusive. Further analysis was therefore carried out with retention figures for each course compared against three-year averages for the course. Figures for each of the academic years 07/08, 08/09 and 09/10 were extracted from college records and average retention rates were established. Three-year averages could not be calculated for five of the courses, as these had not run over the full period, having been established in their current form relatively recently. For the remaining 13 that had been in place for the full three-year period, 11 showed improvement while 2 did not.

When these results are scrutinized within the context of the performance of other full-time FE courses in the college, they offered further cause for optimism relating to their potential impact. In 2010/11, early retention rates for those full-time FE student groups not tested for mental toughness fell from 85 per cent to 84 per cent. In contrast, early retention results for the groups tested for mental toughness increased from a pre-intervention average of 81 per cent to a post-intervention average of 88 per cent.

An associated trend was also found from a small sample where there were dual occurrences of the same course. In three cases, courses selected for the project were run in two distinct class groups, one of which was given the mental toughness test while the other was not. The average early retention rate for the three groups not tested for mental toughness was 74 per cent while the average for those who were was 92 per cent.

At the University of Lincoln, Dr Lee Crust and colleagues found that students who survived their first year compared to those that failed their first year of study were found to have significantly higher levels of mental toughness. In addition, the actual academic performance of students with high mental toughness was found to be significantly higher (ie mean year grade) than those with low levels of mental toughness. In combination, these results indicate that students with high levels of mental toughness are more likely to pass and proceed (rather than fail and drop out) and achieve higher grades than students with low mental toughness.

In a complementary study of 168 undergraduate students in the UK, Elizabeth Stamp reported that mental toughness was a significant predictor of psychological wellbeing. Taken together these two example studies reveal that the mentally tough undergraduate is more likely to stay, succeed, perform better and be happier.

Transition

Whilst transition is an issue impacting on further and higher education retention rates, it is an equally significant issue at two other points in a young person's journey through education.

Arguably one of the most important is the transition from junior education to secondary education. This usually occurs around the ages of 11–13 in most countries, and it is the change of environment which unsettles most. One minute they are in very familiar class groups which won't have changed for many years and often with the same teachers for all subjects. They often sit in the same classrooms in small buildings. A few weeks later they will go to a much larger school which often draws pupils from several 'feeder' schools. As a consequence the young people now find themselves in unfamiliar surroundings having to change classroom for each new subject (and a much wider range than before) and a different teacher for each topic. Worst still, the composition of the class may change for each lesson. It might be one of the most dramatic changes most people make in their lives.

Case studies in the UK, the Netherlands and the United Arab Emirates all show that when assessed, the mentally tough student makes that transition more effectively than the mentally sensitive. The Dutch study in particular provided an indication that this might be a long-lasting effect too – impacting in time on examination results in later years.

Clearly staff in junior education can do much (and often do) to prepare a young person for this transition. Working on the mental toughness of the student might be a useful intervention.

Moving from secondary to further and higher education is another significant transition point which provides difficulties for some. This is a likely explanation for the significant drop-out rates in UK colleges and universities (which are mirrored elsewhere in Europe and the rest of the world) where up to 16 per cent of students drop out of study within 10 weeks of starting a new course.

The other major transition is the move out of education into the workplace. We look at this next.

Employability

We use the term 'employability' in its widest sense. For many it will be getting a job and embarking on a career. For an increasing number, self-employment is an option. For others a move into a half-way house of apprenticeships and traineeships is yet another. Arguably this is the true purpose of education. Focusing on qualifications is too narrow a goal. Ultimately it represents a transition from the world of formal education to the world of work or the wider world in some way.

Employers will commonly complain that the education system doesn't provide work-ready people. Educators complain about the lack of engagement of employers. Both can be right but both can miss a point. For good reasons young people have been accustomed to the values and behaviours expected in the world of education. For the rest of their lives they need to build on those. Again this can represent a dramatic change for many. Once again case studies show that there is a relevance to mental toughness here.

In 2010, the Scottish Funding Council carried out a project on the employability and employment behaviours of around 100 young people who had graduated from two programmes at Adam Smith College and Stevenson College – Hospitality (Housekeepers) and Creative Media (Editors). Amongst the many findings were two observations: the more mentally tough the graduate, the more quickly they got a job; the more mentally tough the graduate, the more quickly they settled into a new job.

Working with around 3,500 disadvantaged unemployed young people, Reachfor, a federation of career services in the UK, used the Mental Toughness Questionnaire together with development activity over a period of 10 weeks to help young people improve their employment prospects. They found, again, that employability was correlated with mental toughness and that developing mental toughness was associated with job-hunting success.

More mentally tough individuals are more likely to recognize the recruitment process as a competitive one. They will approach important elements of the process in a more positive manner. For instance, they will enter an interview with the mindset that they will show the interviewer(s) what they are capable of offering. Less mentally tough persons will see an interview as a trial. The mentally tough will also recognize they need to compete and outperform others to get their job. They will also be more realistic about the job-hunting process.

Many universities and colleges are putting mental toughness development at the heart of their employability and transferable skills agenda. This is discussed in more detail in Chapter 15 in this book.

Aspirations

Again perhaps closely related to employability, aspirations reflect the extent to which the individual believes or expects that he or she can achieve employment and even a certain level of employment. The socioeconomic and family environment will often be significant in shaping an individual's expectations. It's not a big call to suggest that someone who has gone to a very good private school will have high aspirations. Or that graduating from Oxford or Cambridge universities raises one's expectations.

In that context the study carried out in Knowsley Borough Council, described on p 000, provides an interesting insight here. Knowsley contains areas of significant deprivation with high unemployment stretching over generations. The study showed that the more mentally tough the student, the higher the aspirations. The most mentally tough aspired to professional careers, the next most mentally tough aspired to careers in drama and entertainment (the college was one which offered drama as a specialization). Both these sectors are demanding (see Figure 16.1.)

The next category was attracted to blue-collar work and finally white-collar work (clerical etc) seemed to attract students with the lowest mental toughness scores. This shows a clear link between mental toughness and career aspiration. Mental toughness could usefully be incorporated into career guidance activity.

FIGURE 16.1 Career aspirations and links to mental toughness

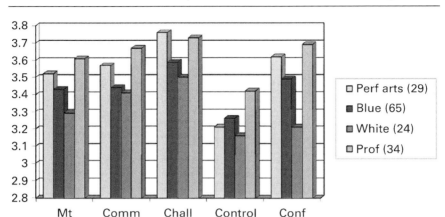

Social mobility and working with the disadvantaged

Social mobility, or the lack of it, is one of the biggest problems facing the UK at the moment. As we travel around the world it's a challenge for almost every society. Apart from the impact on those who are prevented from realizing their potential by dint of the factors that lead to disadvantage, it is a waste of an economy's most important resource.

Young people from well-off backgrounds are twice as likely to achieve good GCSE results as those from poorer backgrounds. Identifying possible reasons for the discrepancy, and finding ways of reducing the 'achievement gap', is an increasingly important focus of all involved in education.

A major application of the mental toughness model and measure is in working with the disadvantaged. Most of that work deals with the socially or economically disadvantaged particularly with those from deprived areas. This might reveal a cultural consideration. If most people in an area believe they have little or no chance of escaping their circumstances, does this impact on the individual's mental toughness? Most psychologists and sociologists believe this to be the case.

The model provides a framework through which facilitators can provide their interventions and explain them to their clients. The measure provides a means of assessing firstly, mindset, and secondly, changes in mindset after intervention. This also helps facilitators to monitor progress and the response to their interventions.

For both authors this is an important application for their work. Both Doug and Peter were brought up in areas of economic and social deprivation. Doug from Govan in Glasgow and Peter from Hunslet in Leeds. Both learned at first hand of the challenges and issues that faced those seemingly trapped in those environments.

Bullying

The mental toughness model and measure provide an interesting insight into bullying, a big issue in the world of education. Undoubtedly there is bullying activity in schools and colleges which can be extremely destructive and harmful.

In the Knowsley study, analysis of mental toughness scores and the tutor's assessment of students showed that there was a clear and strong relationship between the student's belief they were being bullied in some way and their level of mental toughness (Figure 16.2).

FIGURE 16.2   Bullying behaviour and links to mental toughness

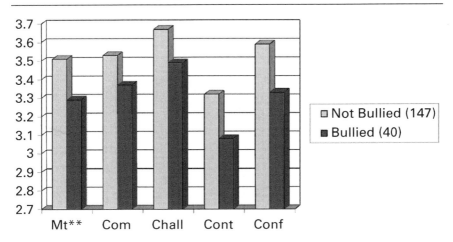

This confirms the finding of a major study at Hull University (published by Dr Iain Coyne) which showed very similar results in the workplace. This indicates that mentally tough people might perceive other behaviours in a different way than the mentally sensitive perceive it. A casual slight may be brushed off by a mentally tough individual whereas a mentally sensitive person might take it to heart. The likely explanation is that mentally tough people shrug off other people's behaviour or actions and don't feel bullied or threatened by it. Mentally sensitive people on the other hand appear to respond negatively to any level of provocative or challenging behaviour from other people (even when not deliberately aimed at them) and will feel intimidated by it. For some a solution to feeling bullied may lie in developing mental toughness strategies.

Anti-social behaviour

Studies with young offenders show that the lower the level of mental toughness the more likely the individual will adopt anti-social behaviours. A possible explanation is that these individuals are less able to deal with life's stressors, pressures and challenges and either respond poorly to those pressures or are more easily influenced by gang leaders who appear to be more effective at dealing with life pressures etc.

It is likely that assessing and developing mental toughness in young people can translate into valuable outcomes such as better social behaviours and reduced re-offending.

Mental toughness and parenting

Much of the focus in the research community has been on examining the impact of mental toughness in educational establishments. This, however, tends to distract from the important role of parenting.

Parents have the biggest influence on their children – for good or bad. Many parents have an intuitive grasp of the concept of mental toughness. They both value it and try to develop it in their offspring. Interventions cover a wide spectrum, ranging from discussions through to participation in organized sports. The 4 Cs model also offers parents a structure to help them develop their children's toughness.

We believe that mental toughness has a major genetic component. Therefore, we can speculate that some children will be brought up in 'tough' households whereas others will be from 'sensitive' environments. The impact of this in later life is unclear and is an area that Professor Clough and his colleagues hope soon to explore. In the interim, it is likely that parents and their offspring will benefit from making use of the tools and techniques that are included in this book.

Leisure activities – sport and outdoor activities

Sports involvement and outdoor-based leisure activity has long been seen as a way to toughen up and develop character. Taking part in sports is clearly linked to toughness. Perry (2014) writes:

> By its very nature, sport provides challenge. Sport requires great commitment in training to reach one's potential. It presents high-pressure situations, which require great control, and it pushes people to their limit, which requires great confidence. It is for these reasons that sport is a prime way of developing mental toughness in young people.
>
> Perry, 2014, p 189

However, the relationship between sport and toughness is complex. For example, researchers at the University of Basle have shown that tougher adolescents are more likely to participate in sport and suggest that toughness training may be a way to get more youngsters to exercise. In other words, the causal direction is not always clear.

The question remains as to whether or not there is something unique about sports involvement, as against taking part in other non-physical activities. Clough *et al* (1989) showed that the motives for running shared much in common with motives for other leisure activities. All types of leisure appear to satisfy similar psychological needs. Doing something appears better than doing nothing! Mental toughness, we would argue, can be developed by participation in a wide range of leisure activities. But perhaps toughness may need to be developed in order to help people participate.

Primary education

Until recently, most of the work on mental toughness and its impact on education had focused on secondary, vocational and higher education. That's partly because that's where the most immediate need lay and partly because the MTQ48 measure used in research and evaluation is presently only suited to young people above the age of 10 or thereabouts. However, there is every indication that the 4 Cs model holds good for those below this age and indeed, there is fast-growing interest and educators, researchers and practitioners once again recognize the value of early intervention.

The development of a measure suited to this age group is underway and the next edition of this book will certainly contain information about what we find. It appears common sense that toughness interventions in early life will be the most effective but we need to establish the facts with caution and care.

Conclusion

It is clear that there is a mental toughness advantage in education. It is also perhaps equally clear that current systems are not particularly conducive to the development of the more sensitive child. All over the world educators are developing ways of both developing mental toughness and supporting the more sensitive students in their care. We hope, and expect, that this will allow the full potential of many more students to be reached.

Developing psychological or emotional resilience and mental toughness is now well understood to be a very important life skill. As one director of children's services in the UK put it: 'Not only can we, in many cases, enhance a young person's performance; these particular skills are useful for just about everything else that person is going to have to do in life'.

Returning to the themes of performance, one observation from the early research is that the MTQ48 generally emerges as a good predictor of exam success. Sometimes a better predictor than the tutors' assessment. In some ways this is not surprising. In the occupational world there is similar overwhelming evidence that judicious use of psychometrics helps managers to make better decisions about people – even when they have worked for some time with those people.

It is important to add the standard cautionary note that tests such as MTQ48 should never be used on their own. They are not designed to do that. A psychometric measure is most effective when teachers, tutors, coaches and counsellors use it with other sources of information to make the best assessment of the person in front of them.

In summary, the evidence overwhelmingly suggests that examining mental toughness as a factor in the development of young people has the potential to be a valuable and rewarding activity. The development of the measure enables the concept to be better understood and allows the user to make better assessments.

Moreover, the concept is reasonably accessible to most practitioners in this field and many of the appropriate interventions are known to many. A common observation from many is that this has helped them to better direct their efforts to help the student or young person.

Mental toughness in sport
A case study in developing mental toughness

17

Mental toughness and sports psychology

The first published work on the MTQ48 was a chapter in *Solutions in Sport Psychology* in 2002 by Peter Clough, Keith Earle and Dave Sewell. On re-reading this chapter it is clear how far the work has come and also how relevant the model still is to its starting point: sport.

Entering any professional sporting organization, irrespective of the sport, can be extremely difficult and surrounded with problems throughout all levels. In his book *Psychology in Football*, Mark Nesti proposed that the 'sport psychologist must get ready to be insulted, misunderstood, ignored, denigrated, seen as a mole, a threat, as unreal, not sufficiently performance focused, and peripheral and lightweight.'

This rather negative perception of sports psychology needs to be addressed from the outset of any encounter with an interested organization. Therefore, having a strong theoretically-based concept with a clearly-defined relevance to performance outcomes is a strong starting point. Certainly the use of mental toughness as a conceptual framework and the use of the MTQ48 as an informational base can be seen to be both theoretically and practically valid and valuable.

We use the mental toughness structure and assessment in most of our applied sports psychology work. It allows us to quickly identify the issues and provides us with a vocabulary that we, and the athlete, can share. This common ground allows us to move the process forwards quickly. This is vital when dealing with elite athletes as often they are faced with rapidly upcoming key events. We have introduced toughness assessments and development to a number of athlete groups including:

- rowers;
- figure skaters;
- rugby league and rugby union players;
- soccer players;
- ski jumpers;
- snooker players;
- elite swimmers;
- speedway riders;
- dressage riders;
- gymnasts;
- track athletes;
- field athletes;
- golfers.

The basic process undertaken by a sports psychologist can be summarized as:

- Diagnostics – what are the issues? These can encompass individual, team, club and organizational factors.
- Discussion – Confirming and extending the diagnostic stage.
  Even when the athlete disagrees about the assessment, the act of disagreement facilitates useful dialogue.
- Tailored interventions – targeting the resource to meet individual needs.
- Reviewing and reassessing – the measure and related interventional techniques provide an excellent framework with which to evaluate success.

In 2002 we wrote:

> The model described here is the result of the synthesis of practical sports psychology and, as such, provides a useful starting point for discussions with players and coaches. It means that the practitioner does not need to start with what interventions are available, but can determine whether mental toughness is the problem ... Too often a comprehensive psychological skills training package is used as a universal panacea for any psychological problem.
>
> Clough, Earle and Sewell (2002) p 41

The use of the model and the MTQ48 allow us to understand what the problem really is. The old adage 'don't fix it if it ain't broke' is key here. But we would suggest: 'First find out what is broke ... then fix just these bits'.

Psychological skills training is the bedrock of sports psychology. It provides a range of interventions, tools and techniques that can be used with athletes. Over the years we have added to these in our mental toughening programmes, but they remain at the heart of many of the interventions we use. The skill is using the right ones, at the right time and with the right people.

Much of our initial and continuing work has involved rugby league. To many people this is the epitome of a tough environment. In our model development we merged psychological theory with practical examples, often drawn from this demanding sport. For example, we supported the ecological validity of the model by identifying important issues encountered by Super League sides. These included:

- control: reaction to mistakes;
- control: reaction to fluctuating performance;
- control: coping with biased crowds;
- commitment: attitude to training;
- challenge: response to injuries;
- challenge: bad press;
- confidence: being on the bench;
- confidence: disagreements with the coach.

Case studies

The remainder of the chapter is devoted to two case studies that show both the work of a sports psychologist and how mental toughness can be incorporated. One is in rugby league, the other in soccer.

CASE STUDY   Applied case study 1 – the mental toughness framework

A season with Hull Kingston Rovers (a rugby league club)

An example of where the 'mental toughness framework' was used is work with Hull Kingston Rovers (HKR) who play in the top tier of professional rugby league in the UK (Super League). The following account describes the process of embedding a mental toughness training programme into HKR and details some of the applied consultancy work that was undertaken at the club.

Of greatest interest to the coach was the concept of mental toughness and how this could be integrated into the team's training regime. As a former Australian rugby league player, he had previously experienced the use of psychologists within the game and was well aware of the potential benefits of incorporating a more psychological approach to team and individual development. Therefore, it was agreed that a multifaceted approach would be taken at the club that would incorporate assessment of the players, team development and, where appropriate, would use individual player sessions.

At the start of pre-season the players were given a brief overview of sports psychology and the way it was going to be introduced into the club. There was an opportunity at this point for the players to ask questions and make their views known about the introduction of psychologists into the club environment.

Before the mental toughness framework was introduced it was decided that the players should express their views on the concept, what they thought mental toughness was, and the importance of the concept in terms of its relationship to both team and individual performance.

Player's definitions of mental toughness

'Person's ability to counter any negativity in the mind and keep focused, positive and persist with the activity.'

'Is the ability to perform at the highest level, pushing yourself past its regular threshold despite the internal demons and exterior factors.'

'Pushing your body through the pain barrier. Your mind will tell you to stop, if you are mentally tough you will ignore it and push yourself to levels not yet achieved personally.'

'Perform under adversity and effort under fatigue.'

'How much until you mentally break.'

'Putting your mind to things and getting through the harder things by thinking about it.'

'Blocking things out and playing through the pain barrier. Mental toughness is being able to play through the pain barrier and still perform to your best and overcoming things.'

'The ability to push your body through pain or fatigue. To be resilient to negative people and things that happen around you.'

'Keeping your focus in a difficult situation.'

'Pushing yourself beyond the pain barrier. Not giving up when it gets tough.'

'Overcoming obstacles that are not in your usual routine.'

'Not moaning about things all the time.'

'Maintaining a good attitude, not cracking under pressure.'

'Testing the mind and body and being strong in showing your strength not weakness.'

'Being able to deal with ups and downs in your career and at the same time maintain a high performance every training session in the week to head into a game at the weekend, and then starting to go again Monday morning.'

'Not giving up when times get tough eg tired, things not going well, mistakes.'

'Pushing through the barrier.'

'Is being able to work mind over body. So whatever challenge faces you, you never give up.'

'No matter what obstacles are put in front of you it won't have an effect on the outcome.'

'The ability to remain relaxed and focused under pressure.'

'Is not giving up when things get difficult and the easy option is to quit.'

'Being able to overcome hard times during training, playing and in your everyday lifestyle.'

'Is like a shield around my mind – in a rugby match people are constantly trying to break the shield, getting me to quit. The thicker the shield the tougher I am.'

'Finding the reason and will to do something your mind and body tell you not to, all for a greater cause.'

'When things get tough eg fatigue, soreness etc, you block it out and carry on.'

'The ability to continue to carry out the task in the face of adversity and under physical and mental strain.'

'Being able to make hard decisions with no fuss.'

'Mental toughness is being able to contribute significantly to the team when under fatigue.'

'Not giving up when things get hard, never giving up on the task.'

'Is the ability to keep on fighting and keep trying in the worse possible conditions to yourself.'

'Being able to turn on absolute focus when under pressure'.

Irrespective of the actual definitions themselves it does highlight the fact that the concept of mental toughness is an extremely ingrained psychological construct for the players that relates positively to enhanced performance when under extreme physical and/or psychological pressure. Discussions with the players further cemented the notion that mental toughness was an intuitively comfortable model that they would be happy to explore through various assessment and intervention techniques.

Shortly following this initial meeting all first-team squad players completed the MTQ48. From the resultant analysis it was found that nine players scored high (sten 8–10) in mental toughness, 17 players scored in the medium range (sten 4–7), and one player scored in the low range (sten 1–3). This spread of scores is typical of professional sport, as you would expect the enduring process of rising through the senior ranks of professional sport to be usually only successfully completed by athletes who were already mentally tough or by athletes who had quickly adapted themselves to the professional environment and performed sufficiently well to pursue a professional career in their chosen sport.

A group session was held with the players to discuss the results and explain exactly what the scores meant (both total mental toughness score and the four sub-scale scores were detailed to the players). This process included defining mental toughness and its components and describing in detail the key aspects of each of these areas, examples of which are:

- challenge: seeing challenges as opportunities rather than threats;

- control: recognizing that setbacks are normal occurrences in a sporting environment;

- commitment: developing a clear goal-setting strategy;

- confidence: consciously seeking to build up your feelings of self-worth.

Each player was given their own personalized profile with suggested recommendations for the enhancement of each of the core elements of mental toughness. These profile reports would be used as the framework for the individualized sessions for the players. These individualized sessions were not compulsory and were, in all cases, initiated by the players.

Although the information from the MTQ48 reports was used as a starting point during the individualized sessions, the sessions were not merely restricted to the development of mental toughness. Everyone was encouraged to hold these sessions in an environment where all issues impacting on performance could be freely discussed in an open and confidential manner (strictly adhering to BPS code of conduct guidelines).

Although individual sessions cannot be reported in this chapter, it was generally thought (by the players and coaching staff) that they were useful in formulating future action planning in areas such as goal setting and anxiety control.

To further illustrate the importance of mental toughness the players undertook a unique biofeedback challenge that incorporated the use of the Mindball Trainer. This piece of kit measures, via detecting alpha and beta brainwaves, the ability of individuals to both concentrate and remain relaxed – both key features in sport at whatever of ability and level. Each player completed the task, which involved wearing a headband with electrodes attached. The electrodes are connected to a biosensor system that measures the electrical activity in the brain (EEG). This was converted into a signal which enabled a small ball to move on a magnetic table. The movement was a function of the extent to which the individual concentrated and remained relaxed.

The goal of the task therefore was to be as relaxed and focused as possible to enable to move the ball away from the player to the intended target in the shortest time possible. Players could monitor their levels of relaxation and focus by a connected screen (detailing levels of both relaxation and focus) or by viewing the movement of the ball itself.

Preliminary analysis of the data showed a positive relationship between overall MTQ48 scores and Mindball Trainer times. This relationship was in fact even more strongly shown in the sub-scale control (incorporating emotional control) which showed a strong statistically significantly relationship between the variables of MTQ48 and time.

As well as providing interesting results, this practical demonstration showed it also provided an exciting and interesting method of introducing sports psychology into a team environment. Breaking down the barriers between psychologist and athlete (specifically in male-dominated team environments) is a key factor in the successful implementation of any sports psychology intervention programme.

This initial practical session laid the foundations for the mental toughness training programme, which took place over the whole of the season. The following describes in detail three team activities designed to enhance and increase the awareness of the various components of mental toughness.

1. The line of positivity – confidence building

The aim of this exercise is twofold. First, to create an awareness of differing levels of confidence in the squad, and secondly, to provide a sound basis for developing a confidence enhancement strategy.

This exercise involved the team members forming a line, in order of their perception of their own positivity/confidence – this process was most enlightening as debate reached fairly heated levels as a number of scores were considered to be over-inflated. After much discussion consensus was achieved over final positioning for all participants in the exercise.

At this point the players were asked to write down three positive self-affirmation (PSA) statements designed to enhance differing elements of their psychological make-up. These statements were then used as self-affirmation reminders throughout the year. Furthermore, the players were then asked to create self-affirmation statements for any members of the squad that they chose. These statements were collated by the psychologists and then individually delivered to each player where appropriate. This process uses the well-researched sources of confidence building ie social support and positive self-talk.

2. Performance profiling – commitment enhancement

This is a technique that uses a structured goal-setting approach to identify important training needs and maximize the motivation levels of the athlete to adhere to the resultant training programmes.

The process starts with the squad members dividing themselves into small groups (ideally with a mixture of youth and experience) of similar positional players (eg forwards, backs). Each player independently produces a list of the qualities (both technical and psychological) that typify a player in his particular position. The list for a scrum-half may include such attributes as speed, good decision making, communication, passing technique, determination and confidence, amongst others. Once this is completed the list of attributes is discussed with the other members of the group to ensure that all the key qualities for that specific position are covered appropriately.

As soon as this is done for the whole group, each player independently rates on a scale of 1–10 (1 being not important, 10 being vitally important) the importance of each of these attributes in order to create the 'perfect player'. For example, a scrum-half may feel that communication is the most important facet of his play and would therefore rate this as a 10. However, he may feel that confidence is not so important and only rate this as an 8. Once all the attributes had been given a rating based on their importance, the player then rates himself in relation to the list of attributes. This self-rating is discussed within the original small groups and a final self-rating is then decided.

As with all good goal-setting technique the importance of agreed targets cannot be over-emphasized – the ownership of these goals is key to the effectiveness of the future training programme. The final performance profile then clearly provides a representation of the player's strengths and potential areas of improvement. This can be then discussed with the coach/trainer and integrated into the overall training programme.

3. The egg-drop – challenge and confidence

This is an exercise designed to highlight a number of facets within teamworking. The task itself involves designing a method that would enable a raw egg in its shell to be dropped from a height of 10 metres, without breaking the egg.

The squad was split into teams of around six players, and each team given a number of articles that could be used in their design. The materials included ten sheets of newspaper, a strip of sticky tape, four short/two long pieces of string, an A4 leaflet, a parcel tag, bulldog clip, two paper clips and a rubber band. The teams were given 30 minutes to build their design and then the eggs would be dropped – in this case from the upper tier of the Roger Millward Stand. Throughout the exercise the teams were closely monitored to enable a discussion of learning points from the task, although at the time the teams' only task was to protect their egg from gravity and concrete!

Once the 30-minute design phase was completed and the various attempts at dropping the eggs were undertaken (some more successful than others) then the whole squad returned to discuss the process. In this instance, the following learning outcomes emerged:

- Generally, insufficient planning was devoted to the exercise – some teams had finalized their design within 10 minutes. The whole 30 minutes could have been broken up into sections to ensure the best use of time (5-minute individual thinking time, 5-minute group discussion, 15-minute build time, 5-minute review).

- The importance of including everyone in the decision-making process. It was noted that in some groups certain individuals looked uninterested and not did not become engaged with the task. There were various reasons for this including inappropriate seating arrangements that hindered good working relationships and lack of leadership that resulted in only limited ideas and views being expressed (quiet thoughtful people also generate ideas – and often the best ideas!).

- Focus on the task in hand. There were numerous occasions where players were spending a great amount of time on irrelevant issues and materials (eg how to use paper clips and what to write on the parcel tag!). These issues further highlight the importance of good leadership and having appropriate interpersonal confidence to be able to direct efforts in a more efficient and productive manner.

- Finally, the design of the 'egg safety device' is all but irrelevant (although encasing the egg in a cone-shaped crumple zone with a parachute attached seemed to be the most effective design). It is all about the process and good leadership, incorporating ideas gathering and a review process, is key in this particular task.

The season-long mental toughness training programme delivered a comprehensive package of psychological skills to the players that could be targeted to enhance any aspect of their overall mental toughness. The toolkit essentially consisted of those tools and techniques described in the development section of this book.

This toolkit for sporting performance created an awareness for the players of how, when faced with difficult circumstances (eg lack of confidence, pre-game anxiety), they can effectively deal with these issues. The head coach of Hull Kingston Rovers commented:

I believe we are the first rugby league club in the UK to benefit from such a comprehensive package of psychological support. The concept of mental toughness and its relevance to our game cannot be underestimated – any attempt to enhance this aspect of our game can only be advantageous to the club.

The season initially saw mixed results with the team sitting outside the top eight and out of the play-offs half-way through the season. In the second part of the season, the ship was steadied somewhat and Hull KR achieved a second consecutive play-off place, ending the regular rounds in 7th place. This led to a play-off game away at the KC Stadium to deadly rivals Hull FC, which Rovers won comfortably 21–4 to record their first ever Super League play-off win. The 2010 season ended at Wigan Warriors a week later when Hull KR were defeated 42–18 by the eventual winners of the Super League Grand Final.

CASE STUDY   Applied case study 2 – the role of mental toughness

Legia Warsaw – winning the Polish Premiership title

Legia Warsaw is a professional football club based in Warsaw, Poland. Legia is one of the most successful clubs in Poland winning a total of 10 Polish Premiership Champions titles, a record 16 Polish Cup trophies and a record 4 Polish Super Cup matches. However, they had not won the Premiership since 2005 when they decided to introduce a new element into their training and preparations for matches. In 2011 and 2012 they won their 9th and 10th Premiership titles and acknowledged that the application of mental toughness had been significant in those successes as well as enabling them to deal with the challenge of participation in the European Champions League.

Team preparation, whilst embracing physical training and tactical or technical awareness, now also embraced mental training. In 2009, working with the consultancy 4Business & People, the club adopted a programme called Mental Win, which shapes mental toughness. (4Business & People is a Warsaw-based consultancy specializing in coaching activity in a range of sectors. They have incorporated the mental toughness model and MTQ48 measure into much of their work.) Patrick Sitek from 4Business & People commented:

> Today, everyone knows that to win you have to have a winning mentality. Not many know exactly what that means and how it can be measured and grown. Our partnership with the AQR and Professor Peter Clough in the UK has given us the opportunity to fully operationalize the mental toughness approach. We started at Legia Warsaw with the Mental Win programme based on the use of MTQ48 to explore mental toughness and an AQR training programme called UCanWin. Elements of this programme have already been used in clubs such as Fulham and Blackburn Rovers.
>
> At the start of the programme players completed the MTQ48 which measured their mindset through factors such as the approach to challenges, a sense of control, commitment and confidence. Through feedback, this enabled the identification of specific situations in which players may feel uncomfortable and which affected their attitude on the pitch, training, but also in life. This led to individual development sessions normally held once a week or so.

For the club directors and the coaching staff, continuing the mental training of players is one of the most important projects in the club. CEO Leśnodorski said:

> Right after joining the club, director Jacek Mazurek told me about the talks with the guys offering Mental Win. I knew that this involved some risk, but we are a club open to new initiatives and I was very positive about this.

Player X, a member of the first-team squad, commented:

> We are still young players, our career is gaining momentum, we won the first title and we are aware that the demands on us are increasing. Participation in the programme helps us to focus on important things, realize and correct errors arising in the head. The programme, combined with hard work in training, definitely helped us to get the League and Cup double after 18 years.

Dariusz Nowicki is one of Poland's leading sports psychologists and uses MTQ48 in a range of sports. He is responsible for the preparation of many outstanding Polish sportsmen including world champions. He commented:

Using MTQ48 to analyse strength and resilience, in conjunction with a feedback session with a player, saves time primarily on the specific diagnosis of possible weaknesses in performance.

The practitioner's perspective

Generally, the approach to developing an athlete is broadly the same as development in any other field. Indeed many of the most effective interventions were developed and polished in the world of sports coaching.

As set out at the beginning of this chapter, before making an intervention it is important to carry out some form of diagnosis – the mental toughness model is an excellent framework for part of that process – then to have some discussion to agree what might need attention and what are the desired outcomes.

In sports, the outcomes are typically performing in competition, training, enjoying what you do and balancing what you do with the rest of your life. In other domains such as the world of work, these might become performance, wellbeing, development and work/life balance and in education these become attainment, study and learning, wellbeing and balancing your life.

The goal here is to make the mental toughness model and, in particular the 4 C components, relevant to the desired outcome. In this way the individual can see the connection and become more likely to be motivated to apply what comes next.

Figure 17.1 illustrates how that kind of mapping can be achieved. It's drawn from AQR's UCanWin programme which is applied to athletes of all types and of all ages.

The figure shows how the four mental toughness scales relate to areas we want to improve, examples of which are listed in each column. You will be able to think of others. Translating the output from a discussion into a set of outcomes which are mapped to the 4 Cs enables interventions to be selected which can themselves be mapped back to the 4 Cs.

Almost all interventions are common to all walks of life. Many are described in later chapters.

FIGURE 17.1 Mental toughness – relationships to areas for improvement

TRAINING AND SKILLS DEVELOPMENT

Dealing well with a poor performance – it's an opportunity to learn – I can do better next time.
You can't win until you learn how to lose – Kareem Abdul-Jabbar, highest-scoring basketball player in history

Developing new and different skills and technique as opportunities to move me on.
The principle is about competing against yourself. It's about self-improvement, about being better than you were the day before – Steve Young, American Football Star

Being prepared to practise to make sure I learn new and different skills.
The harder I practise the luckier I get – Gary Player, golfer (on winning the Open with a remarkable putt which was judged to be lucky)

Managing my time so I can do all my training and skills development properly.
Desire is the most important factor in the success of any athlete – Willie Shoemaker, champion jockey

COMPETITION

Entering a competitive situation believing I will do well.
You miss 100% of the shots you never take – Wayne Gretzky, ice hockey great

Looking forward to proving myself – I want to push myself to achieve a best-ever performance.
When I go out to race, I'm not trying to beat opponents, I'm trying to beat what I have done – Ian Thorpe, swimming champion

Setting a realistic but stretching target and then doing whatever I need to do to get there.
I've always made a total effort... I never quit trying; I never felt I didn't have a chance to win – Arnold Palmer, golf legend

Believing I can do it! And not reacting poorly to any setbacks.
If you have everything under control, you're not moving fast enough. Mario Andretti, F1 World Champion

CONFID-ENCE

CHAL-LENGE

COMMIT-MENT

CONTROL

FIGURE 17.1 Continued

ENJOYING WHAT I DO

Having the confidence to know I can do well and that I can enjoy what I am doing.
Success is ... most of all, the love of what you are doing or are learning to do – Pele, Brazilian Football Legend

Enjoying the challenge of competing with and meeting new people in new places.
Being your best is not so much about overcoming the barriers in front of you as it is about overcoming the barriers we place in front of ourselves – Kieren Perkins, Olympic Gold Swimmer

Enjoying setting goals and then doing what it takes to get there. It's great to celebrate success.
A champion is someone who is bent over, drenched in sweat at the point of exhaustion when no-one else is watching – Anson Dorrance, US Women's Soccer Coach

Enjoying developing the sense that I can do it and I can show others too.
I am tired of hearing about money ... I just want to play the game, drink Pepsi, wear Reebok – Shaquille O'Neal, Basketball Star

OTHER IMPORTANT FACTORS – MY LIFE

I know I have the ability, I am going to take this opportunity.
You have to expect things of yourself before you can do them – Michael Jordan, Basketball Star

Setting big goals for me – I want to do well and win medals, competition, etc.
It's lack of faith that makes people afraid of meeting challenges, and I believed in myself – Muhammed Ali, Boxing Legend

Making time for friends, family and relaxation.
You owe it to yourself to be the best you can be – in baseball and in life – Pete Rose, Baseball Star and Coach

Not worrying what others will think – I am in charge of me! I can keep things in perspective.
Success isn't permanent and failure isn't fatal – Mike Ditka, American NFL Star and Coach

CON-FIDENCE

CHALL-ENGE

COMMIT-MENT

CONTROL

Conclusion

Sport provided the foundation for the development of the 4 Cs model. The sporting environment is performance-driven and often stressful. It therefore offers a natural home for those interested in mental toughness. We have now moved this concept out of the 'sport silo' and into the wider world.

Whilst this paradigm shift has happened, mental toughness continues to be highly relevant when working in the sports domain. It has been used in many team and individual sports and is the focus of many research studies (described in detail in Chapter 26).

Sport does have a dimension which is often confused with the notion of mental toughness. That is, aggression can often provide a competitive advantage. In sport there can often be a win–lose scenario. In most other aspects of life, there are many more benefits in a win–win scenario.

Sport offers many lessons for the non-sporting world for which it is increasingly a good metaphor. From our experiences with mental toughness, we can also definitely say the non-sporting world has many lessons for sport too. Not least in the notion that in life we can all be winners.

Mental toughness and its link to the social and health sectors

18

Perhaps one of the most satisfying achievements in our work with mental toughness has been to broaden its applications from a narrow focus on sport to an understanding that it is a fundamental aspect of human personality and that it has application everywhere.

After all, stress, pressure, challenge and targets are not unique to the world of sport. They impact on all of us at some time. Towards the end of the first decade of the 21st century everyone saw a major global upheaval as the social and economic certainties of the past 15 years of apparent stability suddenly became very uncertain. Whether you were working, studying, at play, dealing with a personal or social issue, the ground rules changed and life became more challenging for everyone the world over. Since 2010, we have witnessed an exponential interest in mental toughness as a concept which has a role to play in the health and wellbeing of individuals and society. Often described as character, resilience or grit, it is becoming an important component of many development programmes – particularly in working with the disadvantaged and very much so in supporting social mobility.

This has spawned a huge number of research projects and of pilot applications in these areas. Most such programmes realistically are long-term in nature. The issues they address cannot be resolved sustainably overnight. It is too early to report outcomes and conclusions from most of them but there is evidence emerging to support the notion that developing mental toughness has a role to play in this area.

In the UK, where much of our work started, programmes such as New Horizons (Career Connect working with 3,990 young people who have been taken into care) and Right Track (Reachfor working with 4,550 young people who were underachieving) have been unqualified successes. They are both essentially mental toughness development programmes. Both programmes have produced outcomes around attainment of qualifications, improving attendance in vocational programmes and achieving employment. In both programmes, this was achieved with groups of individuals who either did not believe they were capable of doing this or who had not previously shown the determination to achieve in these important areas.

These results are being replicated in smaller programmes in the UK and in programmes around the world – in the Netherlands, Poland, the Gulf region and in Australia. At the time of writing we are preparing to do similar programmes in Canada.

This chapter describes where we are in applying mental toughness into these areas. We are confident, on the basis of the work done in other sectors and the emerging evidence from work in these sectors, that mental toughness is a significant and valuable concept in most if not all of those applications too. The kinds of issues being examined in terms of a link with mental toughness in health include:

- recovery rates from trauma and operations;
- general health and fitness;
- occupational health – helping people back into work;
- links to treatment of conditions such as eating disorders and ADHD;
- links between mental toughness and the incidence of mental health problems;
- supporting people recovering from certain forms of mental illness;
- stop-smoking activity.

Issues in society include:

- examining worklessness – where significant work has already been carried out with encouraging results;
- building aspirations in areas of socioeconomic deprivation;
- social mobility – helping people, especially young people, to believe in themselves to grasp the opportunities that the changing world is providing;
- examining anti-social behaviour including offending patterns;
- minimizing re-offending rates for young offenders and adults in custodial sentences;
- developing programmes for carers etc.

The work is truly global too. For instance, in the Gulf region we are working in Oman, the UAE and Saudi Arabia on what is locally called the 'Arabization' agenda which is to do with reducing reliance on ex-pat resources and supporting the development of the local population in the uptake of work and occupations which aren't traditionally in their province.

So what forms the basis of our confidence in these areas?

Mental toughness and health

There has been extensive work on mental toughness and health, which can be broken down into mental health and physical health.

Mental toughness and physical health

It is clear from our studies that mental toughness and physical fitness positively co-vary. Mentally tough people tend to do more exercise. As Dienstbier showed us earlier, we already know that physiological toughening can lead to psychological toughening. The causal link is unclear at the moment. Mental toughness may drive the exercise or the exercise may drive the mental toughness!

Exercise is for many people physically uncomfortable. In fact this discomfort is the second most cited reason why people don't exercise – the first reason is the fairly empty statement of 'not having the time'. Surely this is a phrase that an individual with a high level of commitment would not use?

Early in the development of the MTQ48 we carried out a study that aimed to assess the influence which mental toughness has upon an individual's ability to tolerate physical discomfort. The MTQ48 model predicts that an individual's ability to endure physical discomfort will significantly and positively correlate with mental toughness and its sub-components. The study was undertaken with 41 males with a mean age of 21 years. All were assessed for their suitability for undertaking the physical endurance task, which constituted a standardized method of assessing physical endurance.

Participants were instructed to lift a dumb-bell using their dominant arm in an over-hand grip from its resting position on a desk to a holding position, and maintain this position for as long as possible. The dumb-bell was standardized to weigh approximately 1.5 per cent of the participant's own body weight. This low resistance was chosen to produce a gradual increase in physical sensations during the task. The holding position required participants to hold the weight suspended with a straight arm directly in front of their body and over a desk, with a 90° angle between arm and torso. Performance was timed until participants were unable to maintain the holding position.

The findings showed that there was a significant correlation between total mental toughness and duration (r = 0.34). Individuals who scored higher on total mental toughness, control and confidence were significantly more likely to tolerate the physical endurance task for longer than those individuals who scored lower on these factors.

Perceptions of discomfort

Antarctica and the Arctic are two of the most challenging environments within which humans perform. An individual's ability to cope with these demanding environments is of significant importance as not only is perform-ance affected, but both an individual's and team members' lives will be at risk. One study we carried out followed a team of 12 scientists training for a long-haul expedition within the Arctic Circle to collect environmental and medical data. This training took place within the Arctic Circle over 10 days, and consisted of long-distance trekking, hauling equipment and camping. Team members also ran through scientific protocols and procedures.

As part of the study, team members completed the MTQ48 prior to starting this training programme. At the end of each day, participants rated their perceptions of the emotional, mental and physical demands during that day. This was achieved through a simple 7-point rating scale (Table 18.1).

Total mental toughness was significant correlated with ratings of physical, but not emotional or mental, demands experienced during that day. Specifi-cally, individuals with high levels of mental toughness rated the physical

TABLE 18.1 Correlations between mental toughness demands

	Demands		
	Emotional	Mental	Physical
Mental toughness	.008	−.059	−.391*
Emotional demands		.772*	.383*
Mental demands			326*

* Significant correlations

demands they experienced during the day as significantly less than those individuals lower in mental toughness.

Recovery from injury

An athlete's ability to cope with physical injuries and successfully adhere to rehabilitative regimes is of great interest to those looking to improve rehabilitation success and ensure continued participation. One study followed 70 athletes throughout a 10 week rehabilitative regime for sports injuries (Levy *et al*, 2006).

In the initial stages of rehabilitation, participants completed the Sport Injury Rehabilitation Belief Survey (SIRBS), the MTQ48 and the Sport Inventory for Pain 15-item (SIP-15). Physiotherapists measured adherence via attendance and completion of clinic rehabilitation activity using the Sport Injury Rehabilitation Adherence Survey (SIRAS). Participants were informed to record their adherence to home-based rehabilitation activities.

A number of external measures were used:

- Adherence – attendance to scheduled rehabilitation appointments was calculated by dividing the number of rehabilitation sessions attended by the number of rehabilitation sessions scheduled.

- Sport Injury Rehabilitation Beliefs – the SIRBS is a 19-item questionnaire assessing severity, susceptibility (threat appraisals), treatment efficacy and self-efficacy (coping appraisals).

- Pain – to assess pain the SIP-15 was used. This measures three factors concerning how athletes respond psychologically when in pain.

The results are shown in Table 18.2.

In summary, these findings suggest that the more mentally tough an individual is, the less susceptible they believe they will be to further injury. This finding was replicated with regard to pain in that more mentally tough individuals were better able to cope with pain during rehabilitation by using more direct coping methods.

In contrast, low mental toughness individuals were found to be more likely to dwell upon the pain during rehabilitation and potentially despair when the pain was unbearable. In respect of rehabilitation adherence, greater attendance at rehabilitation sessions was displayed by those who had higher levels of mental toughness, who also demonstrated higher levels of adherence to procedures whilst within the clinical environment. Importantly, mental toughness was associated with greater adherence to home-based exercises and procedures as well.

TABLE 18.2 Correlations table for MTQ48 and rehabilitation measures

Measure	Mental Toughness	M	SD
Susceptibility	−0.31*	23.01	3.83
Treatment efficacy	0.20	71.21	2.46
Rehabilitation value	0.22	5.10	1.10
Severity	−0.30	20.10	2.62
Pain – direct coping	0.43**	17.53	3.55
Pain – catastrophizing	−0.32**	15.46	1.79
Pain – somatic awareness	0.07	10.30	2.16
Clinic adherence	−0.30*	273.10	74.96
Home adherence	−0.28*	89.46	33.95
Attendance	0.25*	91.77	9.04

The finding that individuals who are low in mental toughness were less able to cope with their injuries and were also less likely to participate in rehabilitation has important implications for both sporting and occupational settings. Of particular importance are the lower perceptions of future injury risks.

For athletes and sport rehabilitators, the knowledge that high levels of mental toughness are associated with successful participation in rehabilitation regimes is important for promoting future programme success. By identifying low mental toughness individuals, appropriate efforts can be made to support them to ensure successful rehabilitation outcomes. This finding also adds weight to the proposition that highly mentally tough individuals are better able to deal with stresses and setbacks. This is clearly a central issue for the mental toughness construct.

In occupational settings, it would be important to note that low mental toughness individuals could potentially be vulnerable to poor health outcomes following illnesses, which represents a double detriment for such individuals: 1) low mental toughness individuals are more likely to report worse health outcomes; 2) these individuals seem less likely to be able to deal with illnesses and successfully adhere to advice.

A summary of the mental toughness and exercise findings

It is clear from the findings reported here, and many others carried out by ourselves and others, that mentally tough individuals are more likely to exercise. They are better equipped to deal with the physical demands.

The study relating to injuries is potentially very important. Although it used a sample of elite exercisers, there is little reason to suppose that its findings are not applicable to non-elite athletes and health issues in general. Current research using the MTQ48 is attempting to move the health agenda forward. Dr Lee Crust at the University of Lincoln linked mental toughness with the flow experience. Flow, a term developed by Csikszentimichalyi, is the feeling of getting lost in an event. Everything goes right and time just flies by. You lose yourself in the moment. This type of experience is very pleasurable and motivating. Dr Crust's work shows that tougher individuals are more able to experience flow, offering another explanation as to the draw of exercise for them.

A recurring theme in this book is the need to treat individuals as individuals. Attempts to get the population to exercise or be healthier or to give up smoking have tended to fail or at best produce disappointing results. It is estimated that around 14 per cent of the population exercise on a regular basis. It is reasonably clear that the exercise experience is different for sensitive and tough participants. If we wish to attract more people into a healthier lifestyle we have to tailor the incentives to their experience of the activity.

Mental health

Mental health problems are widespread. Around 1 in 10 individuals will suffer from a significant mental health issue in their lifetime. It is important to be clear here. The MTQ48 is designed to be used in a normal population. It cannot be used with people with severe clinical problems. Similarly, the interventions outlined later in the book are designed for the 'average Joe or Josephine'.

It would be patronizing to suggest that the techniques could be effective with someone who has clinical issues. It is important that if you have significant and recurring depressions or anxiety that you seek out the appropriate medical help. This book, the model and the measure may help you identify that you have a problem – but that is as far as we can take it.

In Chapter 4, we discussed the original construct validation work of the MTQ48. Part of this work showed that the measure was positively related to self-esteem, optimism, self-efficacy and life satisfaction, and negatively related to trait anxiety. Each of these variables has been consistently related to mental wellbeing. It is perhaps therefore not surprising that mental toughness scores also link directly to mental health.

Many of the studies we have carried out over the last 10 years have used the General Health Questionnaire (GHQ) as a measure of mental health. The GHQ is a standardized screening instrument to assess the probability of minor psychiatric disorders, and is a common measure used to give insight into an individual's present state of mind. For example, we carried out a small-scale study looking at mental health issues within the prison service (prison officers) and higher education institutions (lecturers). A summary of the results is shown in Table 18.3.

TABLE 18.3 Correlations between the MTQ48 and the GHQ

	GHQ
Overall MT	−0.70
Commitment	−0.52
Control	−0.54
Challenge	−0.71
Confidence	−0.57

Correlations indicate that higher levels of mental toughness as measured using the MTQ48 were associated with better mental health. Similarly in a sample of 83 teachers there was a clear and consistent pattern relating to the beneficial effects of mental toughness. Tougher teachers were less likely to report being anxious (state anxiety). The high toughness teachers utilized different coping strategies, being more likely to use active coping techniques, planning and restraint.

Teaching is widely acknowledged as a stressful occupation. Clark (1980) tried to identify why this was the case, identifying pupil behaviour, time demands, working conditions and staff relationships as key stressors. Borg and Riding (1993) suggested that certain types of teachers were particularly vulnerable. They reported cognitive style and experience as important factors.

An opportunity to compare teachers in a school specializing in children with emotional and behavioural difficulties and a mainstream school became available. The results showed that the special-school teachers were significantly tougher, as we had hypothesized. When considering mental health issues in the workplace it is important to recognize the matching of people with the job.

In 2015, a study in Northern Ireland with approximately 100 teachers working with young people with special educational needs found that those who were more mentally tough dealt better with the challenges arising from their work than did those who were more mentally sensitive, although they rated the challenge in the same way as sensitive teachers. Ideally, the job should be fitted to the person. In reality this is not always achievable and this rarely happens – it becomes a matter of fitting the person to the job. Some people are better suited to working in stressful environments. It should be noted here that a stressful environment is a subjective term. What you find stressful I might not and vice versa.

Mental toughness and sleep

There are clear links between mental toughness and physical and mental health. An interesting study from colleagues in Switzerland (Brand *et al*, in Press) examined the sleep patterns of adolescents. There is clear evidence to show that favourable sleep patterns are related to favourable psychological functioning such as curiosity, lack of depressive symptoms, and to increased physical activity. In the study 98 adolescents (mean age 18.36 years; 66 females) completed a series of questionnaires related to mental toughness, optimism, depressive symptoms, perception of pain, physical activity and sleep. Increased sleep complaints were related to low control, low confidence in one's abilities, and low challenge, amongst other things.

In adolescents, favourable sleep and favourable mental toughness seem to be related. The authors concluded:

> Whereas the underlying mechanisms remain unclear, it seems conceivable that improving both sleep and mental toughness should confer to increased wellbeing.

Social responsibility and mental toughness

At first glance, the concepts of social responsibility and mental toughness do not seem to go hand in hand. In Chapter 1, the caring side of mental toughness was touched upon. It is true that mentally tough individuals are often driven and dynamic. Thus the mental toughness stereotype is often seen as akin to the Gordon Gekko character in *Wall Street*. There is also clear evidence that they are by nature active copers. They are less likely to express, or perhaps even feel, emotion, preferring doing something concrete as against sharing their emotions. Neither approach is wrong or right. It's just different. However, sometimes it appears that the mentally tough are seen as disinterested onlookers.

This is not an accurate stereotype and misrepresents what mental toughness is. You can be a caring, mentally tough person, or an uncaring, mentally sensitive one. It's not a black and white, all or nothing phenomenon.

We are building up our research in this area and the work is at a relatively early stage, compared to other aspects reported in this book. In the remaining part of this chapter we would like to introduce a small number of studies and also briefly describe where this type of work is leading. It covers a wide array of areas including:

- voluntary work;
- Alzheimer's carers;
- bullying;
- anti-social behaviour.

Voluntary work

A study carried out by Kate Halstead and Peter Clough investigated the motivation of student volunteers. It is obvious that people have greatly differing reasons for giving up their time to help others. In this study 72 volunteers completed two questionnaires: the MTQ48 and the Volunteers Functions Inventory. The latter questionnaire looks at six main functions of volunteering: values, understanding, social, career, enhancement and protective functions.

The findings were fascinating. Most of the students who volunteered to give up their free time to help others were more mentally sensitive. Of the sample, 25 had low mental toughness scores, 39 average scores and 7 achieved high mental toughness scores.

It was also clear that there were differences in why they volunteered. The more sensitive individuals were more likely to do so for social reasons and also to protect their ego. This latter motivational category is all about feelings of guilt and self-worth. At this point it appears that the more mentally tough are unlikely to give up their time to help others. However, the ones who did volunteer were more likely to work longer hours, suggesting that when they do something 'they really do something'.

Where does this leave us? It is clear that more sensitive individuals are more likely to help out others in society. It is interesting to speculate why this is the case. It's unlikely that the mentally tougher are simply bad people or less caring about others. The data from this study perhaps give a clue towards a better understanding of what is happening here. The tougher individuals are less likely to feel guilty and feel bad about themselves. Much of the promotional and advertising activity used by charities and third-sector organizations uses the 'guilt card' fairly robustly. However, this may be leaving a large percentage of the target audience unmoved.

The second interesting suggestion to come out of this research is that the tougher individuals, when they do volunteer, do and achieve more. It might be argued that the goal of the charitable work is to aid the person who is need of support, not to make the volunteer feel good about themselves. These conclusions have to remain speculative, but they do raise interesting questions. It is the intention to carry out more research into this complex area.

What of the carers?

We are living in a time when our population is ageing rapidly. This has seen a rise in many health conditions, especially dementia. Currently 1 in 6 people over 80 and 1 in 14 people over 65 have some form of dementia. With the growth of this terrible disease comes the growth in the need for carers.

Many carers are not volunteers. They are simply people who find themselves in this dreadful situation. Mental toughness was designed to understand performance in high-pressure environments. There can be few higher-pressure environments than trying to help people in the later stages of dementia. The pressure is unrelenting and there is no foreseeable 'good' end point.

Sarah Sykes carried out an investigation into the impact of mental toughness on the wellbeing of carers. Twenty-two carers were asked to complete four questionnaires: the GHQ, the Carer Strain Index, the MTQ48 and the Ways of Coping questionnaire.

The results were illuminating. The carers' scores indicated that they were experiencing high levels of stress, anxiety and depression. There was a clear negative correlation between the mental results and the MTQ48. It appears that mental toughness gives some level of protection to the mentally tough individual.

Again there were differences in the coping mechanisms involved. Mentally tough individuals were less likely to adopt avoidance strategies. They faced their problems head-on. This clearly links with the findings of Lee Crust and Adam Nicholls, and also to the cutting-edge brain structure approach that clearly identifies the reality-testing centres of the brain as being more active in the mentally tough.

In the introductory chapter we were at great pains to point out that mental toughness is not simply about winning at all costs, winning games or making money. It is more fundamental than that. The findings relating to dementia carers raises the possibility that mental toughness training may help them cope better. Both the authors of this book are reasonably mentally tough. We are drawn to the active coping paradigm and have both experienced first-hand the impact of dementia in people close to us. We would like to offer a practical way forward. Not just sympathy, but practical solutions!

Bullying

The subject of bullying has received an increasing level of attention in recent years – particularly in terms of workplace bullying and in school-based bullying. A number of studies have now used the mental toughness model and the MTQ48 to examine bullying in the workplace and in secondary education. The results have been consistent and do provide a valuable perspective on this complex and troubled issue.

The most important result is that there is a strong correlation between mental toughness and the extent to which an individual perceives they are being bullied. It is important to understand that this does not necessarily mean that the individual is being bullied. Some involved with dealing with bullying may argue that this is an irrelevant distinction. It isn't. It helps us to understand how bullying arises for many and how it might be handled.

It must be stressed that this does not mean that bullying doesn't exist. It clearly does. In some (perhaps many) instances the act of bullying is a deliberate attempt by one individual to undermine or demean another for some unjustifiable advantage. However, the results show that for many, the perception of bullying may be just that – it's a perception that they are being bullied. In many cases it is entirely possible that the individual is sensitive to the words or actions of another and may attach a meaning to these which may not be there.

The people we meet in our life, our work and our play will adopt a wide range of behaviours. Some people will respond to some of these behaviours by feeling they are being bullied. Others will accept them as a normal part of life. Some will argue, with some validity, that simply because some aren't offended by another's behaviours means it isn't bullying behaviour. Again we are saying not saying it isn't a manifestation of bullying.

The suggestion here is that a bullying situation should be examined carefully from the perspective of the alleged bully's behaviour and the response of the apparent victim to that behaviour to come to a more measured view about what is going on and, importantly, what can reasonably be done about it.

The standard solution to dealing with bullying is usually to find a bully and deal with that person or persons. To take a more complete and more balanced view, we need to consider how the individual is responding to apparent bullying behaviour. It's this internal state that has often been underplayed – it often does not seem to be considered with enough weight when examining a bullying scenario. This is complicated further by an awareness that the same behaviour in one situation may be seen as potentially bullying where in another situation it is seen as normal and acceptable. We are not attempting to blame the victim. We are just trying to better understand the interaction and suggest that, on some occasions, no 'crime' has been committed.

In the sports arena a coach or manager will often shout at a person to stimulate a better performance. Back in the workplace, the same behaviour between the same people may be deemed unacceptable. Similarly, there is a hypothesis which has increasing support that many bullies are in fact themselves the past recipients of bullying behaviour and may also possess a higher degree of mental sensitivity. The bully may be just as much a victim as the bullied.

One important implication is that mental toughness development activity does appear to help individuals deal more effectively with situations where they perceive themselves as being bullied. This helps to provide a more holistic solution to a difficult and complex issue.

Workplace bullying

A study was carried out by Dr Iain Coyne (Coyne *et al*, 2006) looking at workplace bullying and the role of mental toughness. Presented at the British Psychological Society's Annual Conference in 2006, it assessed 93 individuals in the workplace using MTQ48 and the NAQ (Negative Acts Questionnaire).

The NAQ is a questionnaire relating to the experience of 22 bullying behaviours.

The study showed that mental toughness has a role to play in bullying and in particular a mediating effect on the relationship and physiological distress. Individuals low in mental toughness reported more incidence of bullying-type behaviours, showed more evidence of psychological distress and tended to use less effective coping strategies. Mental toughness training seems to improve an individual's ability to cope with a stressor.

Perceptions of bullying in a secondary school

The Knowsley study covered the entire year 10 group (age 16 years), some 240 pupils, from a secondary college based in an area of north-west England which experiences a degree of social deprivation. All pupils participated – no self-selection was permitted. Pupils were asked to self-assess in terms of being bullied. Tutors were also asked to rate which students appeared to be bullied and to what extent.

Analysis of mental toughness scores and the tutor's assessment showed that there was a clear and strong relationship between the student's belief they were being bullied in some way and their level of mental toughness. Focus groups showed that the same incident would be viewed differently by pupils depending on their level of mental toughness. A tutor who may shout in class to get attention would be seen as a 'shouty' teacher by the more mentally tough who would see it as an aspect of the teacher's behaviours with no specific implication for themselves. The more mentally sensitive would often see the shouting as directed personally at them even when they acknowledged that the teacher shouted at everyone. The likely explanation is that mentally tough people shrug off other people's behaviour or actions and don't feel bullied or threatened by it. Mentally sensitive people on the other hand appear to respond negatively to any level of provocative or challenging behaviour from other people and will feel intimidated by it.

Anti-social behaviour

A final area we wish to explore is mental toughness and difficult behaviour. This work is still in its infancy but it raises exciting possibilities. We have carried out one small study. The control group was made up of 22 participants, with a mean age of 29.91. The 'troubled' group consisted of 19 participants with a mean age of 30.42 (range = 15–57, SD = 9.32). The delinquency sample was recruited from a drug intervention programme (DIP) and youth offending team (YOT).

A significant difference was observed between the total mental toughness scores of the troubled group and the control group. The troubled group had significantly lower mental toughness scores. Significant differences were also observed between the two groups on the mental toughness sub-scales of challenge, commitment and control (life) (Table 18.4).

TABLE 18.4 Mental toughness and difficult behaviour – a comparison of group scores

	Troubled		Control	
	Mean	SD	Mean	SD
Challenge	3.5	0.47	3.9	0.31
Commitment	3.4	0.56	3.8	0.28
Control (emotion)	3.2	0.37	3.3	0.54
Control (life)	3.3	0.49	3.7	0.48
Confidence (abilities)	3.3	0.55	3.5	0.57
Confidence (interpersonal)	3.7	0.47	3.8	0.5

Occupational health

At time of writing this is an area which is receiving a significant amount of attention and where we are finding a very considerable interest in our work. There appear to be two drivers for this.

First, responsible employers recognize that some of their employees do find aspects of their work stressful and challenging and do not always cope well. In the UK the single most common reason for a 'sick note' from a doctor is for stress. It is cited as one of the most common reasons for absenteeism. Job re-design and allocation to duties more suited to the individual will form part of the solution, but also, it appears, is looking at the mindset of the individual. Occupational health programmes and work rehabilitation programmes are increasingly using the mental toughness model and measure for assessing mindset and as part of the preparation for return to work. This is perhaps what a caring, considerate employer should be doing.

Secondly, there is an economic case here. In 2008 the UK coalition government introduced the re-assessment of individuals who were registered with some form of disability and who were able to claim disability benefits. In 2014 it was reported that since 2008 nearly a million people who applied for or were in receipt of sickness benefit have been found fit for work, according to figures from the Department for Work and Pensions. The figure does not include those who successfully appeal against the ruling (one figure quotes 15 per cent of appeals are successful).

This is a delicate and often controversial area and there have been errors in the process. We are not making any political point here. It does seem to be the case, however, that there are people who are identified as 'unfit for work' who may not be unfit for all work and are capable of re-entering the workforce and becoming useful and productive members of society.

The assessments have focused, in the main, on physiological and medical factors. In discussions with one of the providers of the re-assessment service, they confirmed that they found that many were capable of returning to work but that the issue was not always about physical capability; it was often an issue of mindset – an inability to sleep was a surprisingly frequent occurrence.

There seems to us to be a good case for mental toughness development in order to prepare individuals for a successful return to work. Pilot and exploratory work is now underway.

Summary

The application of our model and the measure in the wider realms of society and in public and personal health in general is potentially the most exciting area of application.

For many, carving out a living and making a success out of life for themselves and for their families represent a major challenge and opportunity. It is patently a source of stress for many. In some parts of the world the challenge dwarfs those faced in the UK. Raising a family in central Africa is a vastly different proposition to raising a family in the western world. But for both this still remains a challenge.

The changing role of society and the inability to expect government to provide us with services will mean that many will have to fend for themselves in a manner not experienced since the Second World War.

It is interesting that one area in which we have seen a rapid growth of interest is in parenting. As we introduce mental toughness assessment and development into schools and colleges, we are increasingly being asked by parents to explain what we are doing and then to help them to apply this to their offspring. There is a realization that this is a vital life skill that all young people should develop. The state of the economy and the way that working life will shape up will ensure that stress management at least will remain a major issue in health management. Mental toughness already has a major role to play here.

But the interest in examining recovery rates from operations and trauma also provides opportunity. It is not too difficult to understand that the more mentally tough you are the more quickly you are up on your feet (providing that in doing so you don't undo what has been done). It is more likely that people who dwell on their circumstances may be supported back to full health more quickly through the application of mental toughness.

Health services represent scarce and valuable resources in any society. Anything that optimizes their use and delivers great performance has to be welcomed.

Can mental toughness be developed?

19

The practitioner's and psychologist's perspectives

Introduction

Having defined what mental toughness is and how valuable the concept can be in determining individual and group performance, wellbeing and behaviour, and in understanding better how to measure mental toughness, the million dollar question is: 'Can we do anything about it?'

Instinctively the answer is: 'We can.' Sports psychologists and sports coaches would argue that they have been doing this for many years with significant evidence of success. Coaches, trainers and mentors in other fields might argue likewise. More practically, the answer still appears to be: 'Yes, we can.' There is growing understanding about how this can be achieved and this is supported by an increasing number of case studies and research.

One key question to which we are beginning to find an answer is: 'are we changing someone's mental toughness or can we simply be equipping someone with tools and techniques that enable them to behave as a mentally tough person might behave?'

The answer appears to be that, where the individual or the organization wants to change or develop it is possible to change core mental toughness. We are not suggesting that anyone should or must develop their mental toughness. For those who see a benefit in their life or their work, there may be a good reason for doing this. And, as indicated earlier in the book, there do seem to be some valuable advantages in life and work for those who are more mentally tough than most. It depends on what they want to achieve and how they want to live their lives.

Again, it is important to note here that we are not suggesting that anyone should become very mentally tough. The value of the model and the MTQ48 measure is that they can help to identify which aspects of one's mental toughness are preventing or hindering him or her from attainment, achieving wellbeing or leading a more positive life. It is often the case therefore that developing an aspect of mental toughness is worthwhile. But that might mean a shift in mental toughness – not a dramatic leap to the extremes. It depends on the individual and their circumstances.

Given that we understand mental toughness to be a fairly plastic personality trait, we may find that an individual's mental toughness can go down as well as up. It can go down because of factors such as sustained exposure to stressors, significant setbacks, changes in personal circumstances and even health and physical fitness. Development activity here may be focused on restoring a level of mental toughness. Mental toughness is like a lot of attributes: it needs to be maintained. The very mentally tough can sometimes dig deep and sort this out for themselves. Most will need and will value some support to do this. It's one reason why it has become so popular in coaching and mentoring activity.

What about the mentally sensitive? The more mentally sensitive an individual the more difficult it is to make a change in their mental toughness in the short term. However, here we have a potential solution which, in fact, can apply to everyone. It appears that you can show individuals what a mentally tough person would do and support them in applying these approaches, tools and techniques – and they will achieve a significant benefit from doing this. It seems to work.

Introducing some of these techniques to some individuals as coping strategies can be effective. The mentally tough use the same techniques for dealing with stress pressure, challenge and opportunity. Of course, if someone begins to use some of these techniques and finds that they work for them, they may start to use them regularly. This becomes a habit which eventually impacts on their personality and they do change their mental toughness.

We have learned over time that a fuller answer is a little bit more complex than this. We need to consider questions such as:

● Which are the tools, techniques and interventions that really work?

● Do some work better than others? We know they don't all work for everyone.

- Is the person delivering the intervention a factor?
- Is the recipient a factor?
- What are the conditions needed to make them work?
- Can we explain why these work?

From a practitioner's perspective many of these may matter less than they would to a psychologist or academic researcher. Practitioners may be more concerned that *what* they do works but it's still important that they understand *why* something works. Especially when they find that something works in one situation but doesn't appear to have the same impact in another. The psychologist is generally more interested to know why they work. In this chapter we look at mental toughness development from both perspectives – they are mutually supportive.

The psychologist's perspective

There is some evidence that mental toughness may have a significant mental component. For example, Horsburgh *et al* (2009), using a sample of twins, showed that mental toughness not only had a strong genetic component, but was also influenced by environmental factors. Clough *et al* (2010) reported a positive correlation between higher mental toughness scores (measured by a questionnaire) and more grey matter tissue volume in the right frontal lobe, suggesting a genetic link, but certainly not precluding the influence of environmental factors.

In general, psychology has moved beyond the age old question: are we a product of nature or nurture? The fact is that clearly both have an influence. So some people are born tough, and others may develop it. This raises the very interesting question of how mental toughness is developed.

Various researchers have identified that critical life incidents can facilitate mental toughness (Coulter, Mallett and Gucciardi, 2010). Parental behaviour is clearly a key component in the deliberate or accidental toughening of children. The centrality of the role of the parent is highlighted by Thelwell *et al* (2010) who advocate educational programmes aimed at parents to help cultivate the most appropriate environment to support psychological development.

A truly fascinating study was carried out by Nicovan Yperen (2009) in the Netherlands. His prospective study was designed to identify psychological factors that predict career success in professional adult soccer. Two groups were distinguished: 1) male soccer players who progressed into professional adult soccer; 2) male soccer players who did not reach this level.

Differences between the two groups were examined on the basis of data gathered in the initial phase of their careers, 15 years earlier. In his discussion van Yperen writes:

> More remarkable is the finding that, relative to the unsuccessful group, successful participants had more siblings, were more often of non-white (or non-Dutch) ethnic origin, and more often had divorced parents. In speculating about these remarkable results, siblings may form a kin group bound by strong ties of trust and support, and may increase social skills which may be helpful to progress in team sports in particular. And being a member of an ethnic minority and having divorced parents may help to develop coping skills and attitudes that are helpful in dealing with all kind of problems or drawbacks.
>
> van Yperen, 2009, p 326

This fascinating insight into how people develop clearly shows that the hard knocks of life can bring forward toughness. However caution must be used. The individuals who experienced difficulties and used this energy to thrust themselves forward may have started with higher levels of toughness. It may be the case that sensitive individuals are more likely to be swallowed whole by traumatic events.

In a paper by Crust and Clough (2011) three further factors that might help enhance mental toughness were discussed:

- providing a challenging yet supportive environment;
- having an effective social support mechanism;
- encouraging reflection – emphasizing the importance of experiential learning.

It is clear that genetics and environment both play a role in the development of mental toughness. This leaves many questions unanswered, but the research base is moving forward rapidly and insights are occurring on a regular basis.

One question that we can begin to address is: 'Can formal training actually increase mental toughness?' There is certainly some evidence that mental skills training programmes can lead to increases in self-reported mental toughness (eg Gucciardi, Gordon and Dimmock, 2009b; Sheard and Golby, 2006).

The mechanism by which these interventions work can be explained as follows. Often mental toughness is described as a mindset. Whilst we feel this does not do justice to a far more complex picture it does suggest the possibility that cognitive interventions (eg imagery, positive thinking) may be able to influence it. As noted in Chapter 26 on research, Crust and Azadi (2010) reported that mentally tough individuals use more psychological techniques and skills.

Similarly, Nicholls *et al* (2008) found mental toughness was significantly and positively correlated with problem- or approach-coping strategies (ie mental imagery, effort expenditure, thought control, logical analysis) and significantly and negatively correlated with avoidance-coping (distancing, mental distraction and resignation).

This led to the AQR team developing a mental toughness training package. The approach is based on psychological skills train (PST) and cognitive behavioural interventions (CBI). The programme has proved both popular and effective.

The rest of the book is primarily focused on the techniques themselves. These include contributions from experts in the fields of relaxation, attention and fatigue. They are intended to provide you with the key skills needed to deal with the everyday pressures of the real world.

The practitioner's perspective

We now know we can understand better what mental toughness is and how important it is in determining our capability to perform to the peak of our abilities, our wellbeing and the extent to which we adopt positive behaviours and a positive mindset.

We also know that we are able, through the model and the measure MTQ48, to assess an individual's mental toughness in some useful detail.

The most important question for the practitioner is: 'Can I do something which helps my client develop mental toughness?' We know the short answer is: 'We can!' Other important questions for the practitioner include:

- If I do help someone to develop their mental toughness, how sustainable is this?
- In working with people, am I actually changing their mental toughness or showing them how to behave in a more (or less) mentally tough way?
- Are some techniques and approaches more effective than others? And is this down to the technique or down to the way it is delivered?

We will address these questions in the summary to this section.

Turning back to examine how we can work with people to develop mental toughness, we find that there are very many tools, techniques and approaches which seem to make a difference to a greater or lesser extent. Most of these appear in other areas of people and HR development. Indeed a lot of trainers, coaches and managers are familiar with many of these.

This can be reassuring to the trainer or coach. First, it means that the mental toughness model adds to what they know and understand. We are not introducing something so new that we are suggesting they throw away what they already know. Secondly, a very common response from trainers, coaches and managers is that they now understand better why some of their techniques and approaches work and, importantly, how to direct them better.

Interventions and exercises can often be found under labels such as psychology, sports coaching, cognitive behavioural therapy (CBT), neuro-linguistic programming (NLP), positive psychology etc. Some techniques and approaches appear in all of these places. Interestingly, many techniques also appear within and are practised by some of the major religions, most notably Hinduism and Buddhism. In a recent visit to India one response from a student to a description of a visualization technique was to say: 'We do that ...We call it prayer!'

Nevertheless what we have found is that virtually all the tools and techniques can be grouped under five major headings:

1 positive thinking;
2 visualization;
3 anxiety control;
4 goal setting;
5 attentional control.

The first four are generally well known to most trainers, tutors and coaches, and to many competent managers. Curiously, the fifth, attentional control, is still less well understood and less well known. Developing better attentional control can produce some of the most significant benefits for those to whom it is introduced.

One thing that we also know about most of these techniques and approaches is that they all seem to work to a varying degree but they don't always work for everyone and they don't work all the time.

So there is a clear need for effective practitioners to be aware of this and to monitor and assess the effectiveness of what they do. Very few do this! Many adopt a 'toolbox' of tools and techniques and use them relentlessly on a 'faith-based' approach, often relying on casual anecdotal evidence as the primary source of support for the technique. For example: 'Mary showed Mike how to ... and he tried it for a week and it changed his life in these ways ...'. This isn't good enough. It may seem to have worked for Mike but the change in Mike might also have little to do with what Mary did unless you can show a direct link.

Fortunately it is possible to do something more effective in terms of assessment and research. All of the psychological changes implied in mental toughness and developing mental toughness have a physiological counterpart. So we are able to (easily) measure changes in the body which reflect changes in mental toughness. This includes heart rate monitors (now commonly available in apps), galvanic skin response devices (which measure subtle changes in perspiration) and a variety of brainwave devices (which measure changes in alpha and beta waves). This is called biofeedback.

Finally, perhaps unsurprisingly, the MTQ48 and good feedback have also emerged as effective interventions in their own right. As in other areas of people development, self-awareness gives individuals better information with which to reflect on their position which can either help them to do something about it or understand better why something works and other things might not.

Developing mental toughness – guiding principles

The mental toughness model and the accompanying measure, MTQ48, provide the opportunity for a reasonably holistic approach to the development of individuals and organizations when combined with the use of appropriate tools, techniques and approaches. The goal is almost always focused on improving one or more of performance, wellbeing and positive behaviour. These translate into valuable benefits and outcomes, including amongst many others:

- attainment of goals and objectives;
- stress management;
- making the most of opportunity;
- handling transition and change;
- improving attendance and timekeeping;
- completing tasks and programmes – training, study, projects etc);
- better application of important skills (presentations, negotiation, sales, teamworking, coaching and mentoring etc);
- more effective leadership;
- employability;
- better social skills.

The MTQ48 model and measure also provide capability for measuring what you do and evaluating its impact:

- diagnosis;
- evaluation;
- research – identifying which interventions are most effective.

It's the holy grail of development activity – knowing exactly what works and what doesn't – and why. We often talk of evaluation and ROI (return on investment). MTQ48 and normative instruments like it are important elements in making progress towards a professional approach to training and development or coaching and mentoring.

So we can now describe a complete concept (Figure 19.1).

FIGURE 19.1   Development mental toughness – the complete concept

This concept applies equally in all areas of life from education (all levels) to an occupational setting (the world of work) through to health, sports and social applications.

We have also learned over time that mental toughness is more effectively learned rather than taught. It's one reason why it is so suited to coaching. It fits very well with experiential learning and, like a lot of developmental activity, it is a very good illustration of the Kolb Learning Styles model usually shown as a continuous cycle (Figure 19.2).

To develop mental toughness we start with self-awareness and establishing a need to do something together with the commitment to act. The learning process is initiated by doing something – experimenting with a new technique, tool or approach. It is very useful here to use interventions which can measure impact in some way what is happening. There are an increasing number of exercises, particularly online exercises and apps, which enable this.

The next stage is crucial – reflection: considering how and perhaps why the new approach is producing some benefit. If it is, then something that

FIGURE 19.2   Kolb Learning Styles model

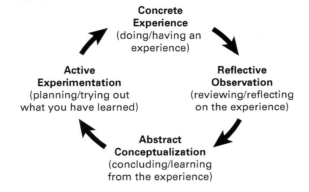

we learn from the world of sport is highly beneficial – the importance of purposeful practice. If something works then the individual should do it regularly and often until it becomes a habit. In the sports world coaches will work with their charges almost daily to ensure this happens. Without this, it is comparatively easy to fall back into old habits. And as Kolb suggests, it's a continuous process.

From the practitioner's viewpoint the process will look something like the diagram in Figure 19.3.

Although each of the 4 Cs is an independent component of mental toughness, they are of course connected through their relationship with mental toughness. An individual's needs will be unique to them. Several people with the same level of mental toughness will have different patterns of mental toughness in terms of the 4 Cs. The starting point for development will depend on the individual's specific needs.

There is, however, one scale, confidence, which sometimes requires particular attention. If confidence (in abilities and interpersonal) is low, it is sometimes harder to make progress with development on the other 3 Cs. Therefore, where confidence is low, that is often a good start point for development activity.

There can also be a flow in the way the scales and sub-scales impact with one another. This is shown in Figure 19.4. It can also act as a map for individuals to understand what a more complete development process might mean.

Unfortunately, as many trainers, managers and coaches know only too well, individuals will often fail to maintain the level of commitment and application to make change stick. And that, of course, can be a mental toughness issue.

FIGURE 19.3
Mental toughness – the continuous learning process

FIGURE 19.4   A mental toughness flow map

The measure is now used at the start of a training or development programme to assess key parts of the individual's mindset to identify whether they are truly ready to optimize learning. If the individual is not in the right frame of mind they are more likely to drop out of the programme, to approach learning in a minimalist fashion and fail to achieve buy-in to the outcomes even when they are apparently beneficial.

The relationship between the mental toughness 4 Cs is illustrated in Table 19.1 shown. This suggests that the mental toughness model and measure not only have an intrinsic value in terms of the content of many personal development programmes but they have an operational value for any development activity.

TABLE 19.1 Using the 4 Cs to identify readiness to learn

MT Scale	Descriptor	Approach to learning
Control	**Life control** I really believe I *can do* it – self efficacy.	Open to learning. I have a belief in my capability to learn
	Emotional control I can *keep my emotions in check* when doing it.	I will keep my frustrations to myself and get on with it.
Commitment	**Setting goals and targets** I *promise* to do it – I'll set goal and targets.	Will target learning both in terms of what they want to learn and in terms of outcomes.
	Conscientiousness I'll *do what it takes* to deliver it – achieving my personal best.	Will adopt a disciplined approach – do what the tutors, managers and coaches suggest. I may have to put some practice in to get the desired results.
Challenge	**Drive** I will *stretch myself* and take risks. The impossible is only that until it is done.	The desire to seek new experiences and opportunities – open to learning. Prepared to try new things that stretch me. Cup is half full.
	Taking success and failure in your stride *Setbacks make me Stronger.*	Accept that there is learning everywhere – even in setbacks and failure. Things don't necessarily work the first time.

TABLE 19.1 *Continued*

MT Scale	Descriptor	Approach to learning
Confidence	**Confidence in abilities** I *believe* I have the ability to do it – no one needs to tell me I'm good.	Self-belief – in my ability to learn.
	Interpersonal confidence I can *stand my ground* and argue my corner if I need to.	Happy to engage with others for the purpose of learning and, on occasion, to challenge others' ideas in pursuit of learning.

Another useful approach is to map mental toughness and its components to competencies. Competency frameworks are commonplace in many organizations and individuals can have a good understanding and appreciation of competency. Particularly where competencies and behaviours are used to describe what a high performing employee looks like. Table 19.2 shows an example of that approach.

TABLE 19.2 Mental toughness vs competency map

Mental toughness scale	What this means: what does MTQ48 assess?	Competency/behaviour – relationship with MT scale
Control	*Life control* – I really believe I can do it	1. ***Self-efficacy*** – the sense of 'can-do'
	Emotional control – I can manage my emotions and the emotions of others	2. ***Emotional management*** – presenting an appropriate face to others 3. ***Poise*** – managing difficult situations

TABLE 19.2 *Continued*

Mental toughness scale	What this means: what does MTQ48 assess?	Competency/behaviour – relationship with MT scale
Commitment	*Goal setting* – I promise to do it – I like working to goals *Achieving* – I'll do what it takes to keep my promises and achieve my goals	**4. *Goal orientation*** – a sense of measurable purpose **5. *Tenacity*** – sticking to it **6. *Planning and organizing*** – setting about tasks systematically
Challenge	*Risk taking* – I will push myself – I am driven to succeed *Learning from experience* – even setbacks are opportunities for learning	**7. *Open-mindedness*** – open to learning **8. *Change-oriented*** – prepared to go with 'the new'/change **9. *Positive attitude*** – setbacks as well as success make me stronger
Confidence	*In abilities* – I believe I have the ability to do it – or can acquire the ability *Interpersonal confidence* – I can influence others – I can stand my ground if needed	**10. *Self-belief*** – nothing is beyond me just because I don't know **11. *Assertiveness*** – I influence others more than they influence me **12. *Working with others*** – a contributor

Mapping enables users and individuals to understand how the mental toughness model links to ideas and language that may already predominate in their environment.

Using the mental toughness model and the MTQ48 in coaching and mentoring

20

The mental toughness model provides an insight into how people respond to the world around them. It helps individuals to be self-aware about the potential reasons for their responses, and more specifically, how and why they respond to events and situations which contain stressors, challenge, opportunity and pressure.

As described earlier in this book, this insight is provided to a significant and valuable degree of detail – through the 4 Cs – and to a more detailed level given that each of the four components has sub-scales. This enables the coach to undertake a significant degree of analysis and feedback in an area important for the development and performance of many individuals.

A good deal of coaching and mentoring activity is focused on three areas:

- improving or developing performance – including dealing or coping with specific events;
- creating or enhancing wellbeing;
- developing, usually positive, behaviours.

Given that mental toughness is a significant factor for each of these areas, the model provides, for the coach and the coachee, a useful framework for the exploration of an individual's responses when facing those challenges and opportunities. The MTQ48 questionnaire provides the ability to carry out some form of reliable and valid assessment which contributes to understanding what is going on.

Given that the coaching process and activities associated with it are themselves events, the model and measure have at least two opportunities to contribute to coaching and mentoring. First, by providing insight into the coachee's response to the change or issue at the heart of the coaching activity; secondly, and equally usefully, by providing insight into the coachee's mindset or attitude towards the coaching process or the coach. As with most such approaches, if the individual isn't up for coaching or mentoring, he or she will get little from the process. That attitude can be determined to some extent by the individual's mental toughness.

The mental toughness model, the 4 Cs and the kind of reports that can be generated are described earlier in this book. Assuming that the coachee has completed the measure, the coach/mentor has an important source of information with which to proceed with coaching activity.

The first step should be to use the output from the measure to check that the individual: 1) understands the model, its relevance to the task at hand, and the purpose of the questionnaire; and 2) agrees (or otherwise) with the outputs and what might be being suggested or implied. The second step is to create a degree of self-awareness that enables the individual and coach to feel that they can proceed usefully.

As with all feedback, first ensure that the use of the MTQ48 is relevant to the particular case. A high level of mental toughness is a quality that is not always needed in a particular role – many people will have the 'right' level of mental toughness to carry out their roles and lead a reasonably comfortable life. In working with a coachee it is important, at the outset, to:

- provide feedback about the scores and what they indicate;
- check that the coachee is comfortable with that description of him or her at the present time – a coachee will frequently challenge the picture that is being offered, which is perfectly fine, as it provides data for the coach;
- confirm that the description has or has not changed in recent times;
- if a change has occurred, fully explore this.

Prior to a feedback session the coach should:

- plan the schedule to ensure that the coachee is given adequate time;
- read the relevant reports thoroughly and construct an outline plan for the session;
- identify ways of illustrating what he or she wishes to say;
- provide the coachee with a copy of the (candidate or development) report or with sufficient time to read it before the discussion.

Is there evidence for mental toughness and its effectiveness in coaching?

The evidence around the relationship between coaching and mental toughness is encouraging. Studies do indicate a relationship between coaching and the elements that constitute mental toughness: self-efficacy, cognitive hardiness, enhanced goal-striving, higher expectations about outcomes and environmental mastery (Grant, 2009). A 2007 study found that coaching can increase cognitive hardiness (mental toughness) and hopefulness in high school students (Green, Grant and Rynsaard, 2007).

Coaching has also been shown to enhance goal-striving (Spence and Grant, 2007), increase self-efficacy and heighten expectations about outcomes (Evers, Brouwers and Tomic, 2006). We can be reasonably confident that coaching has an important role to play in supporting people to develop appropriate levels of mental toughness and that this is useful to the coachee.

How can a coach apply the mental toughness model in their work?

We set out below an illustration of how the model can be used to support a coaching process. There are many useful coaching models around. For the purpose of illustration we are using the GROW model but it works equally well with others such as OSCAR.

This material is drawn from AQR International's *Coaching Workbook*. This is a resource developed to support coaches and coaches on their journey. The material is designed to support a flexible coaching approach for both parties to the coaching discussion. It is often used as a workbook for reflective notes when working with the support of a coach. It is particularly suited to the style of coaching that might use 'step-by-step' models and focus on goals and outcomes.

Coaching is a continuous process which is used to bring out the best performance in others. Coaches guide and support people who possess the knowledge, skills and abilities they need to perform effectively but may need help to:

- recognize where they need to improve and develop their performance;
- overcome barriers to effective performance improvement;
- achieve long-term and sustainable change;
- develop strategies that help sustain their potential.

Identifying the outcome of a coaching intervention is often a vital component for measuring success. One of Stephen Covey's 'Seven Habits' states: 'Start with the end in mind'. How often do you set out on a journey without knowing where you are heading off to? Rarely, we would guess. So this is sound advice and it is equally important that you enjoy the journey that takes you to your chosen destination.

Coaching is the very opposite of telling someone what to do. It is frequently described as non-directive, although some would argue that simply by asking questions, even open questions, the questioner is bringing some direction to the conversation. The best coaches use questions to:

- raise self-awareness;
- develop understanding;
- provoke thinking;
- help to form actions.

Coaching is based on the use of good open and structured questions. The material in AQR's workbook seeks to do that and to provide the structure for the coachee to record and use the answers to those questions. This is illustrated below. Primarily developed to support the work of the coach, this workbook can, with careful use, be used as a stand-alone device by the coachee.

The GROW coaching model

First, just a few words of introduction to the GROW model. The GROW model (Whitmore, 2002) is perhaps one of the more familiar models used to structure a coaching conversation that is focused around clear outcomes or goals. It proposes that a coaching conversation can proceed purposefully through four distinct stages:

1 *Goal* – at the start of the process we define the goal or outcome – this helps us to stay focused.

2 *Reality* – this is about what is happening now that you would like to change and establishing what this would be like in the future.

3 *Options* – identifying and exploring the options available, barriers and how they might be overcome and challenges you might face.

4 *Way forward* – commitment to specific actions and an action plan for building motivation.

Whilst described as a linear process it is actually iterative and coaches may find themselves moving backwards and forwards between the stages to clarify and refine the best course of action. This can be diagrammatically shown as:

FIGURE 20.1 The GROW process

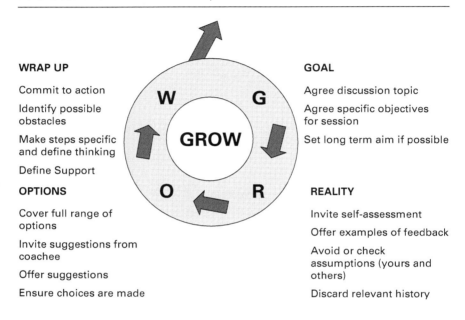

WRAP UP

Commit to action

Identify possible obstacles

Make steps specific and define thinking

Define Support

OPTIONS

Cover full range of options

Invite suggestions from coachee

Offer suggestions

Ensure choices are made

GOAL

Agree discussion topic

Agree specific objectives for session

Set long term aim if possible

REALITY

Invite self-assessment

Offer examples of feedback

Avoid or check assumptions (yours and others)

Discard relevant history

Preparing the coachee for the coaching experience

A fairly fundamental step – the coachee must be ready for the journey. The MTQ48 measure can provide insight here as to the potential state of readiness. Read it carefully before considering the following:

> To what extent am I in the right frame of mind to get the most from this coaching process?
>
> What can I do to improve this?

If you think you can, you can. If you think you can't, you are probably right.

Henry Ford

G – Goals

Take a moment to think about what you want to achieve personally, professionally or from the results of your mental toughness questionnaire. Consider any challenges you are facing or potential changes that you might need to respond to, and when you are ready, answer the following questions:

What specifically do you want to achieve from working through this guide (short-term/long-term)?

How will you measure it?

How will you know when you have achieved it?

When do you want to achieve it by?

How will you best use your time on this workbook?

Goals – and mental toughness

Several of the components of mental toughness are relevant for this stage in the process. Table 20.1 provides a series of questions to consider under each component.

To what shall I attend to ensure that I am in the right frame of mind to set SMARTER goals?

TABLE 20.1   The GROW process – Goals

GROW component	Mental toughness component	Rationale	Questions
Goal	Control	To launch the GROW process, you need to have a sense that you know where you are going and that you believe that you can achieve. Others do it. So can you.	• To what extent do you believe that you are in control of your life and your environment? Or do you believe that it's the environment and others who shape you? • It's hard to set goals and targets: will you give up in a fit of pique or do you have staying power? • Will you be able to deal with all the actions you may have to implement?
	Commitment	This is at the heart of this stage.	• To what extent are you prepared to set challenging goals and targets for yourself? • Will you keep these at the front of your mind throughout the process? • How determined are you to succeed? • Will you be honest with yourself and monitor yourself against your goals and targets?
	Challenge	This is at the heart of the process of which this is the first stage.	• Does the process and the challenge that goes with it interest and excite you? Or does it already feel overwhelming? • How do you feel about the prospect of change? • Is there anything that concerns you about the process and the goals you are setting? • How good is your planning? Have you set milestones for the bigger goals?
	Confidence	This is about your readiness to deal with setbacks and challenge and ridicule from others.	• Are you prepared to deal with those who don't agree with what you are doing? • How will you deal with things that go wrong?

R – Reality

Consider what has got in the way of you achieving these goals previously and what is happening in your current reality that has an impact on your personal and professional goals and objectives. Then answer the following questions:

What is happening right now? (What, when, where, how much?)

Who is involved/Who do you need to involve?

What are the consequences of your current situation?

What will help you move forward? What will constrain you? How did you get here?

On a scale of 1–10, how do you feel right now about your challenge?

Reality – and mental toughness

The components of mental toughness that are relevant for this stage are listed in Table 20.2.

To what shall I attend to ensure that I am in the right frame of mind to create a reality where I am more likely to succeed?

Life is like a game of golf. Good golfers play the ball where it lies, not where they would like it to be.

Doug Strycharczyk

TABLE 20.2   The GROW process – Reality

GROW component	Mental toughness component	Rationale	Questions
Reality	Control		• To what extent do you feel in control of your life and your emotions? Is it enough to achieve your objectives? • What has felt outside of your control until now? How can you extend your circle of influence and bring some of this under your control? • Some of your reality will remain out of your control: how will you deal with that?
	Commitment		• To what extent have you set goals and targets for yourself? How have you done? • How easily do you give up? • What can you do to approach this more positively?
	Challenge		• How have you responded to challenges like this before? • What usually gets in the way of success? What typically helps you? • What generally gets you interested and excited? • What is it about this opportunity that is likely to get you 'buzzing'? Why?
	Confidence		• To what extent are you confident in your ability to succeed? What needs to be done to bolster that? • How do you deal with those who aren't convinced by what you are doing? • When things have gone wrong how has that felt? • How do you pick yourself up when things go wrong?

O – Options

Reflect on the current reality and then answer the questions in the box below to help you consider the range of options you may have. Keep open to new possibilities rather than limiting yourself to the obvious ones. Changing your environment might help – go for a walk, play some music and let the responses emerge.

What could you do?

What have others done in similar situations?

What haven't you tried yet that might work?

How might someone else tackle this?

What if you had more resource available – time/money/people etc?

What are the costs and benefits of taking action or of not taking action?

W – Way forward

Having taken some time to reflect on the reality and options of the situation you now need to consider the next steps in the process and the action plan that will keep you motivated. Answer the following questions in the box below:

What option or combination of options will work best for you?

What action will you take and when will you take it?

What obstacles might you meet and how will you overcome them?

What support do you need and where will you get it?

On a scale of 1–10 how likely are you to take this action? What needs to happen to make it a 10?

How will you feel when you have taken this action?

Options and the way forward – and mental toughness

The components of mental toughness that are relevant for these two stages include the following, set out in Table 20.3:

TABLE 20.3   The GROW process – Options and the way forward

GROW component	Mental toughness component	Rationale	Questions
Options / Way forward	Control		• To what extent are you happy to consider options? Or do you prefer to take things one at a time? • What can you bring into your control to ensure that you will succeed with your chosen path? • How do others do what you have found hard until now? • What remains out of your control? How will you deal with that?

TABLE 20.3   *Continued*

GROW component	Mental toughness component	Rationale	Questions
	Commitment		• To what extent have you set goals and targets for yourself? How have you done? • Are you content that you explored and evaluated all options and that you have selected the best one for your purpose? Are you hesitant in any way? • To what extent does your plan feel like a picture of success for you? • What factors will drive you forward to succeed? • What can go wrong and how will you deal with these? • Are you prepared to do what it takes to succeed? Is it important enough for you?
	Challenge		• To what extent does this represent an opportunity to improve your life, your work, everything? • Can you visualize a better person emerging from this process? • Did any other options promise the same? • To what extent do you want to do this?
	Confidence		• There will be setbacks: to what extent are you prepared for those? • Have you selected the best option? • How will you deal with setbacks? Is there support you can turn to? • Are you able to describe what you are going to do confidently to others ... and argue if they challenge you? • Will you be able to persuade and convince others to help you and to support you?

> To what shall I attend to ensure that I am in the right frame of mind to succeed?

CASE STUDY A case study in coaching using MTQ48

For 10 years Mr X had been a regional director for a large multinational operating in the educational and training field. His region had been acknowledged as the most successful of all the regional operations. He had been particularly successful at developing the consultancy aspect of the business – a significant contributor to turnover and profitability.

Following a global review of the operation the board took a strategic decision to drop the provision of consultancy services and focus on product sales. This created a problem for Mr X who argued that widening the offer was essential to doing business in his region, that it would also demotivate staff who enjoyed the spread of work. At that point he acknowledged that he was angry, confused and not in the best frame of mind to make good decisions. Also concerned that his behaviour would impact on the staff, he felt coaching would be valuable in helping him to work through the situation and support him in identifying how he wanted to respond to the situation.

A structured coaching approach was used, based on the GROW model. This started by setting goals for the coaching sessions then looking at an analysis of the current situation, identifying preferred outcomes and finally enabling action plans to emerge. MTQ48 was used to help understand his current mindset.

It was agreed at the outset that the most important outcome would be that the client felt that he wanted to know what to do in response to the prevailing situation and, if possible, to emerge with a plan of action.

Session 1

The self-reflection process used a form of abbreviated SWOT analysis to identify what he liked and what he disliked about his current position. He concluded that the change of policy had created two sets of problems for him. First, he had abilities in an area that the organization no longer wanted and didn't appear to value. He felt that he wasn't able to influence decisions made in any way. Secondly, he liked the freedom and the width of operation that he had previously enjoyed. Narrowing its focus diminished his feelings of contribution and success.

The SWOT analysis helped to crystallize his thinking and enabled him to look at the current situation rationally. The next step was to investigate the impact on mindset with MTQ48.

Session 2

This focused on feedback and reflective discussion around the results of the MTQ48. It gave the client a framework and a language through which he could reflect on his mindset.

First, he observed that his confidence had been diminished because he no longer felt valued. His sense of control had been affected by his seeming inability to influence the decisions made by the organization. This had then also impacted upon his emotional control. He recognized that addressing this was a priority in order to respond rationally to what was now happening to him. He later said that the realization of the extent of this impact on his mindset was the trigger for him to seriously consider his future in the organization.

Session 3

This focused on identifying options for the future and evaluating them to create an action plan. Having drawn up a mind-map of the possible options, he very quickly realized that the most viable options for the future all involved leaving the organization.

X made his decision: he now wanted to leave the organization. The final discussion was around how he would present this to his current manager. His goal now became forming his own consultancy.

Since then, X has left the organization and has become involved in setting up a consultancy in partnership with another company. He reports now that he is much more confident about his future and his ability to control his own destiny.

Mental toughness and its application to coaches

There is significant benefit for coaches in embracing the mental toughness model and examining its application to themselves and their work. The work of a coach is challenging and has its own sources of stress – not least the need to make a difference with another person who may not always be receptive to what a coach can offer.

The model and measure can be extremely valuable to coaches in provoking thinking about their own qualities in this area – and guiding them towards developing their skills, behaviours and attributes. Coaches who are mentally tough have the capability to withstand a significant amount of pressure. They have confidence in their abilities and are often willing to take on demanding tasks, believing they will succeed. They can usually shrug off criticism and not take others' comments to heart. They are likely to speak their mind when working in groups and are usually comfortable in many different social and work contexts. This positive approach to the coaching encounter is more likely to put the coachee at ease and allow the coaches themselves to have far more control.

More specifically coaches scoring high on mental toughness will tend to:

- set realistic goals, allowing them to avoid overwhelming coachees, or perhaps under-challenging the coachee;
- happily accept the more challenging encounters which offer them the opportunity to truly demonstrate their own abilities;
- feel in control, maintaining the belief that they can truly make a difference, despite setbacks.

Basically it can be argued that the coachee will respond better to a coach who is more confident, in control, committed and who is appropriately challenging. We suggest that mental toughness and mental toughness development are as important for the coach as for the coachee. It is literally a matter of 'practise what you preach'.

For coaches who may be mentally sensitive there a number of tools and techniques that can be used to facilitate the achievement of a successful coaching session. Development of these is described more fully in Chapters 21 to 25. They include:

- visualization:
- positive thinking:
- attentional control:
- anxiety control;
- goal setting.

Finally we remind users that mental toughness is not a universal panacea. The mentally tough coach will be better able to deal with the cut and thrust of challenging encounters but may not be as sensitive as some to the emotional content of their discussions. It may be harder for a truly mentally tough individual to fully empathize with the plight of someone who is, for example, very sensitive.

However, again, an understanding of your own mental toughness can be helpful. For example, a tough coach may need to clearly recognize that clients may not instantly have the resources to move their lives forward. It is indeed useful for such coaches to remind themselves of the fact that 'if it appears to be a problem to the coachee, it is a problem'. Driving too hard, or failing to acknowledge the coachee's feelings will severely impact on the coaching process.

Summary

In this chapter we've looked at the usefulness of the concept of mental toughness in the coaching and mentoring arena. It is often said that stress, pressure and challenge is endemic in today's society. While this emphasis on stress may over-inflate its importance, it is nonetheless obvious that many coaching sessions are instigated by clients under the umbrella of stress management.

There has been a considerable debate in the research literature as to what mental toughness actually is. It is obviously related to concepts such as resilience and hardiness, but provides a more specific hook onto which you can hang coaching interventions. The more mentally tough individual is better able to deal with the pressures of life and prosper within a competitive environment (eg Earle and Clough, 2001).

We believe the model of mental toughness and the mental toughness measure MTQ48 are robust and useable tools. They have four main components: control, challenge, commitment and confidence. Our view that mental toughness can be developed is driven both by personal experience of working as coaches and from clear empirical evidence.

In conclusion, mental toughness coaching offers the coachee the ability to deal with a whole range of pressures better and to 'become the best that they can be'. It also provides the coach with the opportunity to deal more effectively with the challenges and stresses that are often associated with this particular role.

Positive thinking

21

Henry Ford famously is claimed to have said: 'Whether you think you can do a thing or think you can't do a thing, you're probably right'.

Essentially he was describing the nature of positive thinking and its importance for our effectiveness. We are what we think. Positive thinking describes an approach that encourages ideas, words and images into the mind that are conducive to performance, wellbeing, growth and success.

We have an extraordinary power over ourselves as everything we know, feel and believe is based on our internal thoughts. We are often more aware of this in a negative sense than in the positive sense. Ask a group of people to list five things they have done well today and five things they have got wrong; most people will complete the latter fairly quickly but will struggle to complete the first part of the exercise. This occurs despite the fact that most of us get most things right most of the time. That is why any negative or demeaning statements you make about yourself, either to others or yourself, should be avoided. These self-limiting beliefs are reinforced every time they slip into your conversation or mind.

There are now hundreds of tools and techniques which support the development of positive thinking. They appear within CBT, NLP, sports coaching and positive psychology. This section describes some of those which are consistently found to be effective. They can usefully be grouped under three broad headings:

- learning to think positively;
- banishing negative thoughts;
- reframing – turning negative thoughts into positive thoughts.

Table 21.1 provides examples of intervention under the three broad headings. There are many more. Please note that some, such as mindfulness, may have an impact in more than one area – developing positive thinking and/or banishing negative thoughts.

TABLE 21.1   Positive thinking tools

Intervention	Description/Comment
Positive thinking	
Affirmations	Positive statements about yourself which are important to you.
Think three positives	At end of each day, record three good things which have happened. At end of week or month, summarize these to get a sense of all the good that is there.
Anchoring	An outside stimulus that activates a particular inner state or reaction within you. Place-kickers in rugby use anchoring when they adopt particular routines before a kick.
Touchstone triggering	A form of anchoring where you carry a small object around which you learn to associate with being content or happy. Originally a small pebble which people would carry around in their pocket.
What will I do tomorrow?	At end of each day, identify one, two or three things that you will accomplish the next day. Must be achievable. Pick up in the morning.
Looking at heroes/heroines	Identify people you admire and their key behaviours. Seek to emulate some of those.
Self-talk	In your head use positive language when setting out to do difficult or challenging things.
Self-hypnosis	Hypnosis carried out by means of a learned routine. Requires motivation, relaxation and concentration – the effort can be very worthwhile.
Slogans, quotes and sayings	Identify ones that inspire and put you in a positive frame of mind.
Banishing negative thoughts	
Physical thought stopping – elastic band	Short but painful reminder to stop thinking negatively. Thwack yourself with an elastic band if something negative has happened.
Mental thought stopping	How to say 'No!'
Mood-changing apps	Apps such as Mood Mint are designed to help you alter mood.
Self-talk	In your head eliminate negative words or phrases which enter thoughts when facing difficult or challenging tasks – commonly stop using 'if' or 'but'.

TABLE 21.1 *Continued*

Intervention	Description/Comment
Reframing	
Turning negatives into positives	Reframe negative thoughts or comments into positive ones (or those which have a positive component). 'I know this has happened to me but I can still ...' or 'I am still better off than ...'.
What have I learned from that mistake?	Seek the positive in any negative event: there is always something.
The Attitude Ladder	Shows ten phrases based on 'can do which progressively range from 'can't do' to 'can do', enabling individuals to map progress in change in attitude.

Learning to think positively

Making affirmations

These are short statements or phrases that mean something to you. When you are subjected to stress, pressure or challenge, their use can enable you to adopt a more positive approach. Affirmations are essentially a way of saying to yourself 'I can do it!' Examples of affirmations include:

- I am a calm, methodical and efficient worker.
- I can make a difference.
- I can achieve difficult tasks.
- I work well under pressure.
- I enjoy solving problems.
- I love that feeling of having achieved so much in a day.
- I enjoy being calm when others around me are not.

To make affirmations effective they should:

1 Be made in the present tense. Affirmations need to be stated in the 'now'. There is a temptation to make affirmations in the future sense – describing what you will do. 'I am ...' works much better than 'I will ...' because the subconscious recognizes 'I am' as something being done now, not in the future.

2 Have an emotional reward. Affirmations that are not personal to you won't work very well for you. So they should be expressed in the first person. Again this helps the subconscious mind recognize that this is something it is supposed to go to work on. Affirmations should begin with 'I' or 'my' instead of 'you'.

3 Be positively phrased. Affirmations rarely work when expressed as a negative. The mind isn't good at recognizing the concept of 'not'. Its use can inadvertently reinforce the behaviour you are seeking to change.

Affirmations work because it is broadly equivalent to someone else telling you that 'you can do it'. If you work with a coach or mentor who consistently reinforces your ability to do something, you will probably come to believe that it is so. You are creating a person 'in your head' who is doing exactly the same thing.

Self-talk

Widely used in sports coaching with considerable success, there is growing evidence that language and the way we process language can have a significant effect on how we approach tasks, work, challenges etc.

Words often conjure up images and meaning beyond the simple dictionary definition of the word. It is this 'additional' meaning that can influence us. A good example is the word 'exam'. The dictionary meaning might describe it simply as a test of ability. However, use the word 'exam' in conversation with students and you will get a range of responses. These will determine performance, wellbeing and success. Some students will hear the word 'exam' and will associate it with an eagerly anticipated opportunity to show the examiner what they can do. They associate the word with opportunity. The link provides a positive experience. Others will hear the word 'exam' and respond quite differently. They will associate it with something to be avoided. In their mind the exam is more than a test, it is a situation which will reveal how little they know about the topic being assessed. The two groups of students may have equal abilities and they may have attended exactly the same classes and programmes but their resultant performance will be quite different.

Where that association has come from is interesting and useful. It is possible that at a young age one group had been told to look forward to exams and to expect that they would do well. The others may have been told not to expect too much and maybe even expect to do badly. We see this behaviour replicated in every walk of life, whether it is an employee making a presentation, an athlete reaching their first championship final, someone being told they need an operation etc. The way they approach the 'presentation', the 'final' or the 'operation' may affect significantly how the event is handled.

Whatever the source of anxiety or pressure, try talking yourself through it. Examples include:

- 'These feelings will fade away – they won't last forever'.

- 'I know how to control these feelings. I must concentrate on relaxing myself'.

- 'I will begin to feel better soon'.

- 'No one is looking at me. I am not going to make a fool of myself'.

- 'This is perfectly natural and normal. I know what is happening to me'.

Exercise: Self-talk

Think of three positive statements which would work for you:

1

2

3

The MRI brain scan study confirmed that the challenge scale in the mental toughness model is closely associated with the fusiform gyrus. This is the part of the brain which is responsible for the visual word form (written not spoken) and semantic processing and language comprehension, all of which are likely to play a part in 'self-talk'.

Banishing negative thoughts

Thought stopping – physical and mental cues

Again widely used in sports coaching, this is a powerful and often quick-to-apply technique which is closely related to affirmations and self-talk. A cue is a device that you activate when experiencing negative thoughts. It is useful in dealing with worry, panic and anxiety. The essence of thought stopping is that you consciously issue a 'Stop!' command when you experience negative thoughts. The negative thought is then replaced with something more positive and realistic.

The way thought stopping works is straightforward. Essentially, it is a form of controlled distraction which abruptly and firmly turns one's thoughts from the negative to something that is more controllable. Without some form of positive intervention, negative thoughts can 'accumulate' and become the normal response. This will influence the way you behave and feel. If coupled with positive and reassuring statements, it is possible to break the pattern of negative thought.

Thought stopping can arise through the use of mental or physical cues or a combination of both. The process is typically as follows:

1 Identify a situation where you frequently find yourself thinking negatively.

2 Identify the negative statement you make when in this situation.

3 Prepare yourself with some form of relaxation.

4 Find a phrase or cue you can use to stop your negative thoughts.

A physical cue can be as simple as pinching yourself. Sports-people will use elastic bands on the wrist and 'thwack' themselves when a negative thought arises. Mental cues will include:

- positive statements which are activated when the negative thought arises;
- mentally or even orally shouting 'Stop!';
- replacing a poor image with a positive image;
- associating the negative image with its consequence.

Apps – the impact of technology

A good example is Mood Mint which works by 'forcing' you to select a happy face from a range of four faces, three of which are unhappy (Figure 21.1).

FIGURE 21.1   Mood Mint

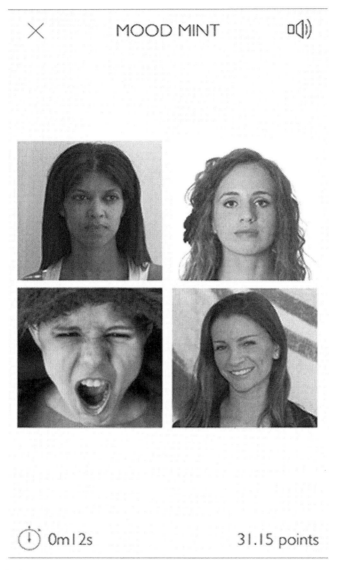

Image: Mood Mint

It is based on cognitive bias modification (CBM). If you focus on negative or threatening information, your brain (the amygdala) triggers the release of stress hormones and neurotransmitters. These are what cause the feelings of irritability, stress and anxiety.

Some people tend to focus on negative information. This negative bias can lead to high levels of stress, anxiety and depression. Mood Mint uses CBM to focus on more positive information (happy faces). The concept is well researched and well evidenced.

Usefully the app scores your responses depending on how often you select the correct happy face and how quickly you do this. This enables you to monitor progress. Just as usefully it is quick – sessions last 1–3 minutes – and it is compelling, which helps with purposeful practice.

Controlled distraction

By concentrating on something else, this technique allows the individual to be distracted from a negative situation. It is useful because it can be a quick intervention in many circumstances. It can sometimes be easier to concentrate on something else to take your mind off your anxiety rather than seeking to talk yourself out of it. Essentially this is controlled distraction. By attending to something that doesn't cause anxiety, you can regain control and refocus. Examples include:

- Mental tasks – eg doing a puzzle in your head, a sudoku, thinking of a poem or the lyrics to a song; imagining a relaxing scene – a beach, looking at pictures, listening to music you really like etc.

- Concentrating on your immediate surroundings – eg counting lamp-posts, adding up the items in your shopping basket etc.

- Bringing a pet to work – enabling you to focus on something which is not creating anxiety but demands enough attention for you to be distracted, even for a short while, from the source of the anxiety.

- Breaking routines – doing something differently so that you focus on maintaining the new routine.

What will I do tomorrow?

At the end of each day, identify one, two or three things that you are very confident you can accomplish the next day. The fewer the better – you need a virtual guarantee of success. The tasks must be achievable.

This operates by reinforcing/applying the old adage 'success breeds success'. Most people like the sense of winning and it banishes the sense of failure like nothing else. Once a more positive mindset is achieved you can take on more challenging tasks with the confidence that you can succeed with those too.

Anchoring

An anchor is a trigger which is, for you, strongly associated with a (positive) feeling. It's easy to identify negative anchors: have a row with someone important to you and you might forever associate that place with a negative feeling. The goal is to use these triggers and associate them with positive thoughts and feelings.

Where you become aware of your negative anchors and their cause, you can work to replace the negative ones with positive ones. That might be through giving the negative anchor a new positive meaning or by seeing a positive outcome from the initially negative event. The classic anchoring techniques relay on identifying something physically distinct in the environment. So an example might be:

- When travelling to work, identify a physical landmark with which you are familiar. When this enters your consciousness, this should trigger a script, ie a list of positive statements that you have prepared and which have a motivating effect on you.

- Similarly, when travelling back, the trigger could be used to end thinking about work and start a home/leisure/family script.

Think three positives

Most of us get through most days getting most things right. We can easily, if we reflected diligently, see that we have completed perhaps a hundred tasks perfectly well. Mostly, however, when we get to the end of the day and ask ourselves 'how did things go?' we will default to thinking about what went wrong. It's probably right to do that but if we repeatedly spend each day dwelling on what went wrong we can easily develop the sense that there is not a lot going right in our lives.

Consequently, a useful and highly effective activity is to write down at the end of each day (or some suitable time) a reminder of, say, three things that you have done well. This reminds you that you do get some things right and doing this repeatedly restores a sense of balance – 'I make mistakes but I mostly get it right'.

This is especially effective with young people. They are adept at seeing what went wrong before they see what went right. It is a useful parenting activity which, in a structured and systematic way, enables parents to provide positive feedback to their charges. The propensity for negative thought can often be attributed to lack of, or critically negative, comment from parents when their children are in their formative years.

Reframing negatives into positives

Inevitably there are times when we do get it wrong. If you find yourself thinking you didn't do something well enough or got something wrong, try identifying what might be the positive in the situation. It is very rare that you get everything wrong and there will be positive aspects even in failure.

Listen to sports coaches talking about their team after a defeat. Most will acknowledge the defeat but they will also identify what went well and will often identify the mistakes as opportunities for improvement. The important thing here is to understand that things do go wrong and that we do make mistakes – but very rarely is it fatal in any way. Instead give yourself credit for what you do, remember that you are not perfect and that you can do better next time. A good discipline is to take time out to consider:

- What kinds of thing always make me think negatively?
- What kinds of thing always make me think positively?
- What advice would you give to someone who consistently showed these negative thoughts?
- How could you identify the positives in these situations? (It can be useful to work with others to do this.)

The positive-thinking (attitude) ladder

Fiona Mackay Young has developed an interesting scale which she calls the attitude ladder. It represents 10 points on a positive-thinking scale from low to high positive thinking (see Figure 21.2).

It is a useful device for self-reflection and for use by coaches, mentors, managers etc who want their clients to understand realistically where they are in terms of thinking positively. This kind of diagnosis provides perspective for the individual as well as indicating what might be useful 'next steps' to be considered. It usefully combines self-awareness with goal setting. The ladder breaks a 'big goal' – attainment of a truly positive attitude – into smaller more achievable milestones.

The first question is – where do you fit right now? Think about the language that you or the individual is most likely to use in most circumstances. Does that affect performance, wellbeing and behaviour? It almost certainly will. When people say to themselves 'I can't' in any form, they are programming themselves for failure. The more often they think or say it, the more they believe it.

FIGURE 21.2 The positive-thinking ladder

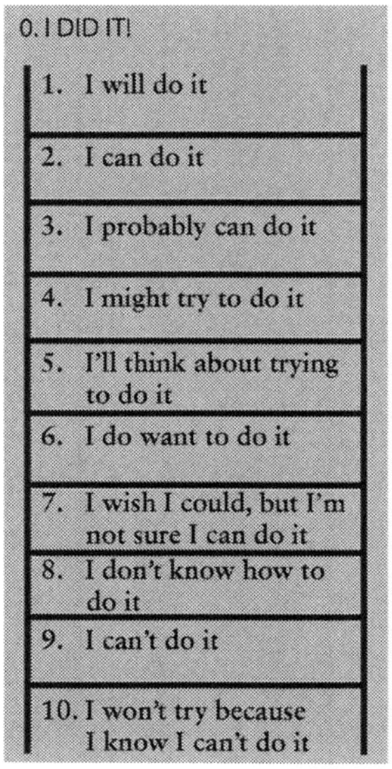

```
0. I DID IT!
1.  I will do it
2.  I can do it
3.  I probably can do it
4.  I might try to do it
5.  I'll think about trying
    to do it
6.  I do want to do it
7.  I wish I could, but I'm
    not sure I can do it
8.  I don't know how to
    do it
9.  I can't do it
10. I won't try because
    I know I can't do it
```

Using the mental toughness development tools and techniques described elsewhere in this book and in this chapter, and with the support of others, it is possible to make progress in developing a more positive mindset – and to monitor that using the ladder.

Mindfulness

We are introducing mindfulness here for completeness although it could equally have been introduced under later headings of visualization, attentional control and anxiety control.

Emerging in the 21st century as a powerful and popular approach to improving wellbeing, mindfulness has its roots in Buddhism as well as many other religions that have contemplation as one of their practices.

It is not intended here to write about how to go about this. There are many good books and videos which bring the practice of mindfulness to life. It clearly works and it is very valuable for dealing with many of life's challenges for very many people. We recommend Liz Hall's excellent *Mindful Coaching* (Kogan Page, 2103).

Liz has suggested that mindfulness supports the development of the 4 Cs very well. A popular definition of mindfulness is provided by Kabat-Zinn (1994) who defines it as paying attention in the present moment but in a non-judgemental way. Developing mindfulness means bringing attention to what we see and what we do with compassion and non-judgement. Without this our minds will naturally wander. This enables us to:

- Control our attention, focusing better and focusing longer. In turn this will impact on the control element of mental toughness.

- Attend to the present moment – whatever seems to distract us – a requirement for commitment.

- Manage difficult emotions, thoughts and feelings – this aligns with emotional control.

- Be compassionate to ourselves and to others – confidence is built on this.

- Drop evaluation and judgement – again this is important in developing the challenge element of mental toughness. This is how openness to learn can develop.

- Reframe positively – bring under control what you can control.

There is a great deal of synergy between this approach and both the concept and how mental toughness is developed in others.

Visualization

22

Although described here as a separate technique, there is a close relationship between visualization and other positive-thinking techniques.

Curiously, most of us don't have to learn how to visualize – we do it all the time. What we have to do is learn how to harness it for our benefit. The challenge lies in the fact that often when we consider a situation in our mind we will visualize it in a negative way. If asked to do a presentation we will imagine it going horribly wrong. We'll fluff our lines; we'll lose our place; we'll drop our notes; the audience will ask awkward questions that we fail to answer properly and so on.

Similarly, a student visualizing an examination will often imagine arriving in the exam room unprepared; they will look at the exam paper and not understand the questions; they imagine running out of time etc. Creating these negative pictures can change you emotionally and these have a negative effect on your mind and body that impact on the real performance when it arises.

But it can work the other way around. Creating positive pictures can have a positive impact on the mind and body. You can use your mental voice to increase self-belief in your ability to deal with change and deadlines; and to relax, you can use your imagination. Your imagination communicates with your mind at the deepest levels and visual imagery is far more potent than words alone. Psychologists will confirm that practising something in your head is as real to your mind as doing it in practice. The human mind doesn't discriminate between the two sets of experiences. Instead of telling yourself that you will be successful, you 'see' yourself being successful. Visualization is like watching a video of yourself.

Visualization is widely used in sports, particularly to support 'anchoring' behaviour. Consider penalty-takers in soccer. They will imagine taking penalties before they ever get to a live situation. If they have a picture in their mind of the ball sailing into the net and scoring a goal they will tend to function better when taking a real penalty. Moreover, if they see, in their mind's eye, a huge goalkeeper and a small goal, they will approach their task with less confidence than if they can imagine a large goal and a small goalkeeper. This is similarly true for golfers, place-kickers in rugby, athletes, tennis players etc. It's also true for just about everything we do which is moderately challenging.

To be effective with visualization:

- it should be grounded in real life using information from your experiences;
- focus on the positive feelings you are experiencing within your imagined scenario;
- any negative thoughts should be pushed away and replaced with positive thoughts or affirmations.

Visualization is believed to encourage activity in the right side of your brain – related to creativity and emotions. It leaves you free to focus on over-coming a fear, achieving insights about an emotional anxiety or focusing on a particular goal you want to pursue. Useful visualization exercises include 'imagine a pink elephant' (or any unusual depiction of a normal situation).

Exercise: Imagine a pink elephant

This exercise simply describes the capability to visualize. Imagine an elephant. Most elephants are uniformly grey. Then imagine it in a different, bright colour – say, pink. Develop that in your mind until it is a robust image. Then imagine an even more unlikely or outrageous addition – like adding big yellow spots, putting a hat on the elephant, giving it four tusks instead of two.

Visualizing success

One of the best places for us to rehearse a daunting task, especially an intellectual task, is inside our heads. You have at your disposal an environment that you can control, adjust and adapt at will. Athletes will often use visualization to imagine winning and particularly what it feels like to be a winner. If success breeds success you can start that in your head. Athletes will imagine stepping onto a podium having won a competition – and will be able to sense what that feels like.

Most of us at some time will be asked to do a presentation or address a group of people. It could be a formal presentation, a casual address, a wedding speech. Few people find these activities without challenge. However, you can imagine the presentation and even when you imagine something going wrong you can stop the 'tape in your head', rewind and imagine how you can do it better. You can be as difficult with yourself, asking the most awkward questions imaginable, knowing that you can envisage how you might respond smoothly and smartly.

Visualize yourself in the situation, behaving, reacting and looking as you would wish to do. Imagine yourself there. What does it mean to you? How do you react? How do others around you respond? How do you feel? What emotions are you experiencing?

Exercise: Visualization for a specific event

You have an important presentation coming up:

1 See yourself there. Fill in all the details that you know – the office, the people, right down to the coffee machine in the corner. The more realistic the visualization, the more effective it will be.

2 Imagine yourself there, looking confident, relaxed, in control, and aware of everything that is going on around you.

3 See yourself preparing your materials, greeting people, and asking them to take a seat.

4 As you stand up to begin your presentation, hold on to that feeling of mastery and calmness.

5 See yourself working through your materials, everything in order and according to plan, answering questions as they arise with confidence and authority.

6 Imagine the questions you might be asked. And imagine providing a ready response.

7 Visualize the engaged expressions on your colleague's faces as they lean forward slightly to take in everything you are saying.

Now try imagining and writing your own script.

Exercise: Creating a visualization of your future

The goal is to use the inside of your head to create a picture there of something you would like to achieve or be. When that is done, do two things: 1) see what that looks like; 2) imagine how you would feel when it is done. If that is something you wish to experience, this can become a driver. 'I liked how I would feel and I will go for it'.

1 Think of something you would lie to achieve – ideally something that is potentially within your control and relies only on you for attainment.

2 Anchor it at a specific point in time.

3 Contextualize the goal – what does the situation look like, how will you know what you have achieved, what is the evidence for your success, how might others be responding to your success and, most importantly, what does it feel like to have achieved that success?

4 Now, imagine you are 'a fly on the wall': visualize this from that perspective. What will others see?

5 This is what you should hold in your mind. Anchor it to situations in your present routines and visualize it when you come across that situation. It could be when you are out walking, getting ready for bed, taking a break or when meditating.

6 Keep adding to the visualization to make it feel more real.

Guided imagery

Guided imagery is extremely useful when in challenging situations which are creating stress and pressure and there is little you can do about it. The principle behind the use of guided imagery is that you can use your imagination to recreate the situation and enjoy a situation that is very relaxing. The more intensely you imagine the situation, the more relaxing the experience will be.

The situation can be real, for example, a particularly satisfying experience from your past. It can be imagined, based around a scenario you would like to experience but have not yet done so.

1 Make yourself comfortable. If a lying-down position would make you go to sleep, opt for a cross-legged position, or sit in a comfortable chair.

2 Use diaphragmatic deep breathing (see the relaxation section in Chapter 23) and close your eyes.

3   Once you are in a relaxed state, begin to envision yourself in the midst of the most relaxing environment you can imagine. For some, this would be floating in the cool, clear waters off a tropical beach, where you are waited on 'hand and foot'. For others, this might be sitting by a fire in a secluded snow cabin, deep in the woods, sipping hot cocoa and reading the latest prize-winning novel.

4   As you imagine your scene, seek to involve all your senses. Imagine what it looks like, are there any particular smells or sounds. What does it look like? Is there a special feeling emerging? Can you taste the scenario? The more detail you can develop the better.

Do this for as long as you need to feel relaxed. When you return, you'll feel more calm and refreshed. An example of a guided imagery scenario is shown in the box below.

Guided imagery – example scenario

Having made yourself comfortable, gradually allow your mind to enter a place that is quite special to you. This place can be real or imaginary: somewhere you have visited on holiday (a beach or woodland, or somewhere you like to visit); or somewhere from your dreams. Allow your mind to drift ... drift to a pleasant, peaceful place; a place that you know ... where you will always feel able to relax ... completely; a safe ... secure place ... where no one ... and nothing can ever bother you.

This is your place ... your safe place ... your haven. It could be outside ... a clearing in the woodland; a meadow in the countryside; a secluded beach. Or it may be a room ... a room you once had, or still have ... or a room you would like to have. It is a place where you feel free to let go ... completely ... your haven ... a haven of tranquillity ... unique and special to you.

Really experience this place ... notice first the light: is it bright, natural, dim ... where is the light coming from: is it sunlight, candlelight, lamplight. Notice also the temperature ... is it hot, warm, cool ... what is its source ... can you feel the warmth from the sun, a fire, can you feel a cool breeze. Be aware of the colours that surround you ... the shapes ... textures ... the familiar objects that make this place special.

Begin to see it in all its detail. You can just be there ... enjoying the sounds ... the smells ... the atmosphere ... with nobody wanting anything, nobody needing anything, no one demanding anything from you. This is your place ... your time ... relax.

Happy memories

This is a particular form of guided imagery, which makes use of the happy events in your past to enable a form of controlled distraction. You can effectively transport yourself, in your mind, to a time when things were going better.

Think of a time when you were happy or things went well. Develop it in your mind until you see in substantial detail and you sense how you felt at that time. Savour it.

The psychological context of confidence development

The worlds of confidence development and psychology have huge overlaps. It is the core business of many psychology professionals. The interventions briefly described in this chapter all have something in common. They are techniques that help us control our inner voices. As already mentioned, many of the techniques are drawn from the world of cognitive behavioural therapy, an approach developed by Aaron Beck. When dealing with his clients he noted that their internal thought processes were complicated and often deeply flawed. They were often more interested in what he thought about them than in dealing with the real problem. Basically he became aware that thinking impacts on feeling and feelings impact on thinking. It is easy therefore to get caught up in a serious downward spiral.

Our minds are undoubtedly cluttered with often unwanted thoughts. These negative thoughts often stop us achieving our full potential. It is clear that for many of us our own worst enemy is us. We are quick to point the finger of blame at the 'amorphous them' as the root of our troubles, but with a little insight we can begin to see it is perhaps us. Earlier in the book we talked about attribution errors. We are all naïve scientists, trying to make sense of a complex world. However, we can confidently say that our data analysis is deeply flawed. We try to deal with the world on the basis of what we think is happening, not what is really happening.

Thoughts are not the truth. They are a subjective representation of reality.

The important lesson in this chapter is to recognize that you can control what goes on in your brain. In fact I often say to our undergraduates that it's the only thing we can control. We can influence others, but no more than this. By 'thinking about thinking' we can first recognize the patterns and then tackle them. Basically we are talking to ourselves. We often know what we are going to say – it is after all just us talking to ourselves – but on occasion negative thoughts seem to pop up from nowhere. We need to find out where these are coming from and, more importantly, learn how to counter them.

It is unclear where these thoughts emerge from. Psychologists have very different perspectives. These range from the psychoanalytic tradition that often refers to the unconscious mind. This, by definition, is not easily accessible. It is a dark recess that may reveal itself through dreams and talking therapies. At the opposite end of the scale it can be argued that the thoughts occur due to inappropriate firing of neurones – a sort of faulty wiring.

Whatever the causes – which are beyond the remit of this book – it can be agreed that controlling your thoughts is a positive thing. Mentally tough individuals are better able to do this. Time and time again we find that mentally tough people are better able to face reality. They consistently adopt fewer avoidance strategies and tend to attack the problem straight on. Excitingly, we can now begin to explain this. Brain scans show that the reality-testing centres in the brains of tougher individuals are more active.

Positive psychology and mental toughness

A philosophy or school of thought that has gained much credibility in recent years is that of positive psychology. We have spent a lot of time trying to ascertain whether or not this is a competing or supportive model.

Positive psychology is most interested in happiness. The work is spearheaded by the excellent Professor Seligman. At first glance it would appear that happiness is not at the forefront of mental toughness research. However, it is there – just below the surface. Much of this book is devoted to examples of performance enhancement related to mental toughness. It is our core philosophy that mental toughness is about providing every individual with the opportunity to reach their full potential.

Seligman and the positive psychology school are right when they say that a great deal of psychology concentrates too much on the negatives of life. We tend to look for problems and then solutions. We do not really focus on the positives. In this chapter we show that this can be done, and should be done. However, many people are not in a position to count their blessings.

Much of the work we have done has been carried out in Hull. This once proud city now has an unemployment rate which is twice the national rate, and it suffers the social issues that go along with it. Most psychological models reflect the environment in which they developed. Ours is no different. We seek positive growth but make no apologies for identifying and trying to repair the holes that society leaves. Happiness is predicated on a secure foundation of resource, health and opportunity.

Wellbeing can be described in two ways. Firstly there is subjective wellbeing. This is about a state called happiness and will often have a material undertone. This is what the positive psychology school appears to focus on. It is often associated with ideas such as avoiding challenge and avoiding putting people at risk.

Alternatively there is psychological wellbeing. This is driven from older traditions of motivation and satisfaction as described by Maslow and Hertzberg. Here we are concerned with self-actualization and with being a fully functioning person accepting risk and meeting challenge. And understanding that hard work can produce reward and be its own reward. In addition, with any move forward the risk of failure cannot be far away.

Rather than use the term happiness we can use a related term – contentment. This approach is supported by an article in *The Sunday Times* by a head-hunter who described himself as possessing awesome power. He said that he often approached people who appeared to be perfectly happy in their roles. They earned a good salary (say £100,000 a year), had a good package and enjoyed status and authority. All he had to say was: 'I can get you double your present salary, a bigger office and a better car' and he could often create instant unhappiness. But nothing had actually changed for the individual. They were instantly dissatisfied with their situation. The same situation that 10 minutes before had provided 'happiness' now produced a state of 'unhappiness'. He pointed out that if they were truly content and in control of their lives this couldn't happen most of the time.

It's useful to take a philosophical perspective when looking at these concepts. A philosopher will say that happiness is not a proper goal for humans. Happiness is just an emotion, transitory feeling, not an adequate purpose for a life. They suggest that it is infantile to expect to feel happy. Your life's work should be something more enduring – like contentment or fulfilment of your potential or self-actualization. So if we construct a check list of the components which create lasting wellbeing we can compare and contrast the two ideologies as follows:

TABLE 22.1   Wellbeing components – alternative philosophies

Component	Contentment Self-actualization Hard-working culture	Happiness X-factor culture
Competence – compared to others	Self-confidence: – in abilities – in being able to express ideas	What you think will make you happy won't always make you happy
Growth	Commitment – determination to achieve	
Self-regulation	Control	
Self-acceptance	Confidence	Hedonic treadmil! – often running just to stand still
Positive relationships with others	Interpersonal confidence	
	These are all the components of mental toughness!!	

The upshot is that we think that you can't make people happier in any meaningful way, but perhaps you can make people more content. Contentment is just as aspirational.

Mental toughness is about opening doors to opportunity and contentment and then having the psychological equipment to go through them. Maslow's self-actualization in practice.

Anxiety control and relaxation

23

A physiotherapist's perspective

Introduction

This chapter will focus on relaxation as a valuable and effective approach to anxiety control. Anxiety control deals with those situations and moments when the individual is 'paralysed' by some event and finds that they can't do what is needed or doing it is utterly exhausting.

The underlying principle here is that psychological responses such as fear and worry have a physiological consequence – sweating, heart rate, muscle tension, breathing difficulty etc. Controlling those physiological responses can help us to manage the mental responses by 'reversing' the process.

Feelings of worry, fears, negative self-talk can impact on interpersonal confidence, life control, emotional control and how the individual sees challenge. The reason for this is well understood. It is part of the alarm system which our ancestors developed a long time ago to deal with danger. The alarm system works by producing adrenaline in response to the danger. This provides a boost to our energy in the short term and enables us to do what we need to, eg run away from a sabre-toothed tiger. Ultimately, and if stimulated too often, this overwhelms – seemingly, for the individual, for no apparent reason. The modern-day problem is that this is often the response to modern-day challenges – real and apparent. We don't switch it off. It impacts behaviour, wellbeing and performance if unchecked.

Anxiety control is about coping with that which you can't control. There are three broad approaches which work for most people:

- relaxation techniques;
- controlled breathing;
- controlled distraction – already discussed in Chapter 22.

Controlled breathing techniques are well understood and are easily available. The remainder of this chapter examines relaxation techniques.

The Laura Mitchell relaxation method

There are many physiotherapeutic approaches to relaxation. This chapter will firstly focus on the method widely used and taught by physiotherapists: the physiological relaxation technique described by Laura Mitchell (Mitchell, 1977, 1990). Her textbook has been reprinted five times and the latest edition was 1990. It is well-validated, safe and effective. It is the method of relaxation most commonly utilized by physiotherapists (Salt and Kerr, 1997) in the United Kingdom for the management of stress through physiological relaxation.

It is hoped this chapter will see a new audience benefiting from this approach to relaxation. Other techniques will also be described. These techniques all have their place as well; their main advantage is that they are quicker.

I was fortunate to meet the physiotherapist, Laura Mitchell, when I was an undergraduate student myself in the early 1980s. Laura was an inspiring teacher. Her approach was well received by those she taught and it has become my personal favourite approach to teaching a versatile method of relaxation to a variety of clients.

The first time I used the approach in a clinical setting, post-graduation, was with some of the first liver transplant patients in Leeds. Patients appreciated their traditional respiratory physiotherapeutic care being enhanced by the Laura Mitchell method of relaxation, reporting a positive response to their wellbeing, and welcomed learning a skill to make them feel less tense and less stressed. Although they were self-reported, the positive subjective comments made by patients, prior to the accepted present-day focus on evidence-based practice, have stayed with me as a clinician and now as a university lecturer of some long-standing.

Over the years I have successfully used the approach with patients with asthma, chronic pain and low back pain. I have utilized it widely in a sporting context with a variety of top-level athletes and particularly successfully in rugby league players as part of training and enhancement of wellbeing. I teach the approach to all my undergraduate honours degree students as a technique to add to their 'toolkit' in dealing with their own exam stress as well as being a skill for the students to practise and utilize with future clients. Physiotherapy, sport rehabilitation and psychology undergraduate students have benefited from an appreciation of learning the skill of the Laura Mitchell physiological approach to relaxation and incorporating it into their own lives and the lives of clients they deal with.

Mitchell (1977) stated that the technique brings about postural realignment by reversing stress-related posture, termed as 'the punching position'. This position is commonly adopted whilst sitting slouched working for long periods on a computer. The poor postural position tends to include a 'poking chin' posture of the head, a clenched jaw, rounded shoulders, bent elbows on crossed legs. The overall position is very 'flexed', often mimicking the foetal position of a growing baby in the womb. The punching position is thought to increase muscle tension and as a consequence influences the nervous and endocrine system. This releases epinephrine and norepinephrine, which if sustained, may enlarge adrenal and lymphatic glands, eventually resulting in physical illness and even acting as a contributing factor to death.

The brain does not understand the word 'relax'. 'Relax' conveys no definitive information to produce muscular change in body position. It needs a series of controlled instructions to muscle groups, first, to appreciate the positions that create tension, then secondly, to contrast this sensation with that felt in a position of ease. Exact, clear orders are required: that is what the human body is used to receiving and acting upon.

Learning the technique

There are six important factors that are key to successful mastery of the Laura Mitchell method of physiological relaxation:

1 The brain must be given a definite 'order' – a clear, descriptive word and action that it recognizes will produce work.

2 The 'order' Mitchell chose to give each joint will produce relaxation in the tense group of muscles if the client performs the movement *exactly* as indicated by the words. When instructed to 'pull your shoulders towards your feet', the action is 'pull' *not* 'drop'. Only an active voluntary activity will produce the reciprocal relaxation in the muscle group opposite to the 'working' muscle group.

3 When instructed to 'stop', it must mean just that. The client must stop moving the part. It is essential that the therapist does *not* try to substitute the word 'relax' for 'stop'. Clients understand 'stop moving', so utilize that instruction and correct any misunderstandings early in the mastery of this relaxation method.

4 Clients are instructed to be 'aware' of or to register the feeling of the new position, to focus on this new position of ease. It requires concentration and, like all skills, it requires repetitive practice. Often it is useful to give clients the analogy of learning to play an instrument or driving a car. Those skills require concentration and practice to acquire a consolidated skill. The Laura Mitchell method of physiological relaxation requires that same dedicated practice to become skilled at it and to reap the benefits from it.

5 The client must be reminded that they will be training themselves in both *joint* and *skin* consciousness and *not* muscle consciousness, as that is the way the human body works. There are *no* nerves that recognize muscle tension connecting with the brain. The client should be made aware of that so that they are educated to not waste time trying to feel it. The client will instead be focusing upon the millions of sensory messages that a conscious brain is constantly receiving from human joints and skin as muscles change their position.

6 It is important to train the conscious brain to identify sensations that have always been received but of which the client may not have been previously aware until they have been educated about them and instructed on how to focus upon them.

A systematic approach

It is vital to utilize a systematic approach to ensure effectiveness of the technique. The client is required to consider:

- if they are working with:
  - a reader as a partner;
  - or alone;
- the room;
- the starting positions;
- the order of the instructions;
- the use of additional skills:
  - diaphragmatic breathing;
  - visualization;
  - use of background music.

Working with a reader as a partner

If the client is working with a partner to read out the orders to them, there are some useful tips to enhance the effectiveness:

- use a clear but ordinary voice;
- select the partner carefully – it is essential the partner considers the technique to be as important as the client and has an understanding of the reasoning and principles behind it;
- avoid the temptation to add bits;
- follow the timing of the client;
- the partner should sit as far away as is practicable so as not to interfere with what the client is doing;
- as soon as the orders have been memorized, it is advisable to dispense with the use of a reader as a partner.

Working alone

If the client is confident with the principles of the approach he or she may prefer to work alone and to memorize the orders for each body part from the outset, or indeed to record them.

The room

It is recommended that the room used is at a comfortably warm temperature. The reason for this is that the human body loses heat as muscles relaxes. It is not practical to have a room with absolute silence as it would make it impractical to incorporate the approach into busy lifestyles.

The starting positions

The client may choose from three starting positions: A, B or C.

Position A

The client lies on his or her back on a mat or carpeted floor (Figure 23.1). If this position is comfortable for the client it is probably the best starting position to use. Ideally, the legs should be uncrossed and the hands resting either on the client's own tummy or thighs. One pillow should support the client's head. Some clients find it helpful to have additional pillows: one under the knees, one under each upper arm. Other clients may find them unnecessary.

FIGURE 23.1   Position A

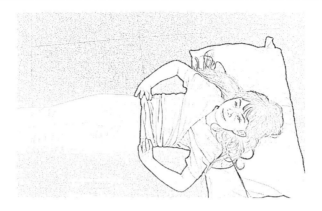

Position B

As an alternative to position A if it is not suitable, possibly due to either heart or breathing problems, the client can sit on a firm chair at a table (Figure 23.2). The client sits well back in the chair for good support for the thighs. It is essential that the feet are supported flat on the floor. Two pillows on the table is normally sufficient but as many pillows as the client wishes may be utilized to raise the height in order to position the arms and head comfortably.

FIGURE 23.2   Position B

Position C

An additional alternative position which clients with more severe respiratory problems may find useful is sitting upright in a supportive high-back chair with arms on the chair (Figure 23.3). This is often favoured by the elderly or infirm. Ideally the back of the chair should be high enough to rest the head against. The client is advised to sit well back in the chair so the back is supported and the feet resting on the floor. The forearms and the hands are supported by the arms of the chair, which ideally should be broad and long enough to support outstretched fingers.

FIGURE 23.3   Position C

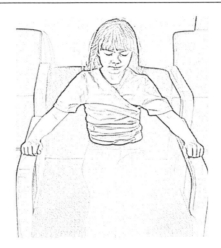

The order of the instructions

Orders to the arms

Shoulders

The order is 'Pull your shoulders down towards your feet'.

Elbows

The order is 'Elbows out and open' (Figure 23.4).

FIGURE 23.4   Shoulders

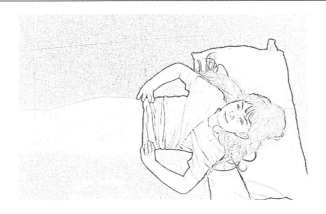

Hands

The order is 'Reach your fingers out long...' (Figures 23.5 to 23.7).

FIGURE 23.5   Hands (1)

FIGURE 23.6   Hands (2)

FIGURE 23.7   Hands (3)

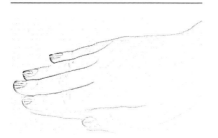

Orders to the legs
Hips
The order is 'Turn your hips outwards' (Figure 23.8).

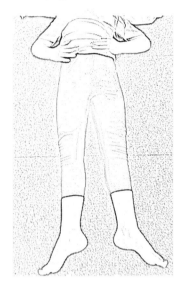

FIGURE 23.8
Hips

Feet and ankles
The order is 'Push your feet away from your face' (Figure 23.9).

FIGURE 23.9   Feet and ankles

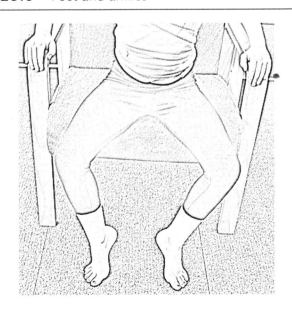

Orders to the body

The order is 'Push your body into the support'.

Orders to the head

The order is 'Push your head into the support'.

Orders to the face

The order is 'Drag your jaw downwards'. If the eyes remain open add the order 'close your eyes'.

Shortened version of the Laura Mitchell method

Upper limbs

Shoulders

- Order – pull your shoulders down towards your feet. Stop.

- Results – feel your shoulders are now further away from your ears. Your neck may feel more elongated.

Hands

- Order – reach out with your finger and thumb. Stop.

- Results – appreciate the stretch, elongation and increased space between your fingers during the movement and the heavy position of ease when resting back on the supporting surface.

Lower limbs

Hips

- Order – turn your hips outward. Stop.

- Results – feel your thighs roll outward and kneecaps facing outward from the body.

Feet

- Order – push your feet away from your face. Stop.

- Results – feel the new position of ease. Appreciate the heaviness.

Trunk/head

Trunk

- Order – push your back into the supporting surface. Stop.
- Results – feel the contact of your body on the support.

Head

- Order – push your head into the supporting surface. Stop.
- Results – feel the contact at your head on the supporting pillows.

Overview

- Appreciate the supporting surface under the head, back, arms, thighs, calves and heels.
- Appreciate the new supported position of ease.
- Focus on breathing control, on the passive component of breathing out and pause before you breathe in again.

Other relaxation techniques

Other relaxation strategies can also be extremely helpful and useful in managing stress, tension and anxiety. The relaxation techniques described below can be used anywhere and definitely become easier with practice. Ultimately they help you to cope more effectively with stressors and challenges. It is important that you put relaxation at the centre of your day and utilize the techniques that work for you! Some of the most popular relaxation techniques are outlined below.

Diaphragmatic breathing

Diaphragmatic breathing, sometimes known as stomach breathing, has a long history. More recently LauraMitchell (1977, 1990) included breathing techniques to complement the effectiveness of relaxation. Bell and Saltikov (2000) investigated the effectiveness of Mitchell's technique including diaphragmatic breathing compared with diaphragmatic breathing alone and lying supine (on the back). They found that diaphragmatic breathing with and without Mitchell's relaxation technique significantly reduced heart rate. Peddicord (1991) suggested that breathing techniques such as diaphragmatic breathing could be used alone for stress reduction and need not be incorporated into a more generalized relaxation technique to elicit the relaxation response.

Diaphragmatic breathing exerts its effects on the cardiovascular system in two ways. One mechanism is due to stimulation of the vagus nerve, resulting in parasympathetic dominance and therefore reduction in heart rate and stress. The second mechanism occurs during the inspiratory stage of diaphragmatic breathing, where increases in thoracic volume result in a flattened diaphragm. This causes an increase in the intra-abdominal pressure and compresses abdominal veins, increasing venous blood flow towards the heart. As a result the improved venous return increases stroke volume, causing a reduction in heart to maintain cardiac output at an appropriate level.

A quick guide to diaphragmatic breathing

When new to the technique, you should probably do it lying down. It is important that your head is fully supported and shoulders relaxed. You may find it comfortable to use two pillows: one under the shoulder blades and a second one in a 'butterfly' shape to cradle and support the curve of the neck. If it is more comfortable you may also use a pillow under your knees. This takes the stretch of the abdominal muscles.

Place a hand (in a light 'fist') at the end of the sternum (the mid-line bone that joins the ribs). Gently breathe in through your nose and out through the mouth. Focus on letting the air coming in around the lower ribs, feel your stomach rise gently against your fist. Breathe deeply and regularly.

After practice is quite easy to modify this technique to other positions so that it may be incorporated into every day. An alternative position is sitting with the shoulders relaxed and forearms supported on a couple of pillows to support the weight of the arms and enable the shoulders to relax.

Controlled breathing

Most of us only use between 10 and 20 per cent of our full breathing capacity. By learning to breathe properly you can begin to feel less fatigued, less overwhelmed by your thoughts and more able to cope with each new challenge. You will also become more optimistic as you learn to cope better:

- When done properly it can relieve anxiety, improve circulation, concentration and digestion and increase energy.
- It is bigger, stronger, deeper and more rhythmic than typical shallow breathes.

● Once you gain control of your breathing in a non-stressful environment, you can more readily call up your relaxation breathing during times of stress.

Breathing exercise

1 Take a deep breath. Exhale fully and completely.

2 Inhale again whilst mentally counting 1 to 4.

3 Hold your breath, and count from 1 to 4.

4 Slowly count from 1 to 8 while exhaling fully.

5 Repeat the sequence four times.

Directed relaxation

Directed relaxation (sometimes known as self-hypnosis or deep relaxation) is the process of directing yourself into a deep state of relaxation and suggestibility. Similar to classical hypnosis, this method allows you to 'programme' your unconscious mind with suggestions to help you experience fewer stress symptoms, sleep better, stop smoking, or achieve other goals or improvements in your lifestyle.

In this state of relaxation you are fully aware of what is going on, you have a focused frame of mind and are in complete control at all times. Directed relaxation increases our 'suggestibility'. Suggestions should be decided upon before you start. They should be short but visual suggestions are most effective – 'see' what you want to achieve. Alternatively you could embed the idea of being relaxed upon hearing or thinking a certain word.

Sarnoff Squeeze

The purpose of the Sarnoff Squeeze is to block the body's production of noradrenaline or epinephrine, the body's fear-producing chemicals in your system. This is a simple preventative tool against feeling nervous, ideally suited before delivering presentations:

1 Sit on a straight-backed chair, keeping your back straight, but not rigid.

2 Lean forward slightly while keeping your back straight.

3 Put your hands together in front of you with your fingertips pointing up and push.

4 Say 'sssss' as if you were a snake or a leak in your car tyre.

5 As you exhale while saying 'ssss', contract those muscles located right where your ribs begin to spread apart.

6 Be aware of the muscle tightness under your ribcage while you exhale. (This should feel like tightening a corset).

7 Relax the muscles at the end of your exhalation, and then inhale gently.

When you master the Sarnoff Squeeze, you will be able to tighten those muscles at will without having to sit in a chair and push your hands against each other.

Ear tap

To release tension in various parts of the body, tap the skin in front, above and behind the ear. This stimulates an area rich in acupressure points.

Smile and laugh

Strange as it may seem, smiling and laughing trigger chemicals in your body that make you feel better:

1 Take a moderate breath and smile as you exhale.

2 Feel the corners of your mouth go up and feel the relaxation in your forehead.

3 Repeat 10 times or until you can't help but chuckle.

The role of fitness

The evidence shows physical development and physical challenge can lead to psychological development. Originally demonstrated by a Canadian psychologist called Dienstbier, this was confirmed in some widely publicized work by Dr Peter Clough in 2005. Doing things which stretch you physically does have a positive impact on an individual's mental toughness. Furthermore, it seems that exercise and physical activity which gently stretches you appear to work best for most people. Big stretches can be counterproductive and can achieve the opposite effect.

However, it is also true that the more mentally tough you are the more likely you are to maintain exercise and to challenge yourself physically. To get yourself going you may need to use positive thinking, goal setting and visualization. For some this could be highly structured such as joining a gym or some form of classes eg yoga, swimming, running etc, or opting to do a sponsored 15-km walk. For others it can be less formal. Good examples include setting targets to walk to the summit of a hill or small mountain or run a half-marathon or clear the garden of weeds or dig over a patch of ground and replant it or even redecorate some or all of your home.

The essence here is to do something physical which requires some time and effort to complete and which you will find satisfying when completed. When achieved there is a double bonus: you have done something which develops your feeling of control (you can do it), commitment (you can set targets and achieve them), challenge (you can see challenges as opportunities) and confidence (you can persevere); and your mental toughness enables you to maintain fitness and health more easily. This significant factor is enabling you to deal with the stress and pressures of everyday life as well as developing your mental toughness.

The role of diet

There are two sets of consideration here. First, there is some evidence to show that eating a healthier, more balanced diet enables you to maintain the right weight and to achieve better physiological performance. Athletes demonstrate that all the time. It is also true that the more mentally tough you are the more likely you are to be disciplined about what you eat. There is scope for a 'virtuous circle' here. The opposite will also be true. We often see people respond to stress and pressure with comfort-eating which soon has its impact on the physical wellbeing of the individual.

Secondly, there is no such thing as a super-food or a particular nutrient which creates mental health and wellbeing. However, there is some evidence that combinations of some types of food can promote good mental health. These can be correlated with improved memory, better attentional control and better reasoning abilities – leading to better performance. These appear to include polyunsaturated fats (especially omega-3), minerals (such as zinc, magnesium and iron) and vitamins (vitamins B, C and E as well as folic acid).

Biofeedback

Biofeedback is a technique in which people are trained to improve their health by using signals from their own bodies. These techniques can be very effective, especially for those people who find it difficult to fully get to grips with the more standard approaches. For example, individuals who are particularly anxious often find it difficult to 'quieten their mind'. The negative thoughts just pop up. Biofeedback allows individuals to concentrate on something external to themselves and thus reduces the 'psychological intensity' of the relaxation programme. In many ways the Laura Mitchell method and biofeedback share a common core –that is, they rely on physiology to drive relaxation.

There are two 'classic' biofeedback approaches: galvanic skin response and monitoring brain activity. The most common form of this technological approach uses galvanic skin response (GSR). This refers to the ability of the skin to conduct electricity. A number of instruments are able to measure this. They pass a tiny electrical charge around the body and measure their speed of return. These simple machines can be very useful, especially when working away from the laboratory. The exact mechanism by which GSR works is unclear. McCleary (2007) carried out a review of 60 years of work on GSR and described three principal theories which purport to account for the phenomenon:

- muscular activity – GSR is the direct display of bio-electric changes in muscle;
- vascular changes – GSR is the electrical activity attendant on vasodilatation or vasoconstriction;
- secretory changes – GSR is the pre-secretory electrical activity of the sweat glands.

He reported that the third explanation was the most likely, but the evidence is not definitive.

A more modern approach is to monitor brain activity directly. Even 10 years ago this would have involved a massive and prohibitive cost. Recent advances in sensor technology allow this approach to be available to everyone.

AQR/Hull University make extensive use of this applied work, especially in their one-to-one sessions. Two different but related technologies are used. The first is Mindball. This system is basically a table with a small ball on it. Individuals move the ball by the 'power of their mind'. What this means in reality is that the more relaxed and focused they are the more they can move the ball. With Mindball you can set up a direct competition, allowing individuals to learn how to stay in the zone when under real and tangible pressure. We have recently started using headsets designed to work with computers rather than a physical device. These are much more cost effective and are a lot easier to transport and use. We have used these in professional sport, the classroom and for managers in industry.

The devices use complex formula to combine the various waves measured in the brain to produce simple, interpretable output. In general, they rely on four types of wave:

- alpha – awake, non-focused, relaxed;
- beta – alert, focused and problem-solving;
- theta – visual imagery and light sleep;
- delta – deep restful sleep.

It is the combination of alpha and beta states that produces the ideal performance state – *relaxed concentration*. The main advantage of using biofeedback is that it allows us to train more complex states. It's not simply about getting someone to relax or to get someone to concentrate. The end goal is to get them to do both at the same time!

Applying directed relaxation

This is a very effective technique but requires a degree of practice to be able to apply it properly and achieve the desired benefits. Basic directed relaxation is applied in five stages, as follows.

1. Preparation

Make sure you won't fall asleep.

Make sure you won't be disturbed and there are no unwelcome background noises.

It is important to write yourself a schedule of when you are going to practice.

Work out and memorize your suggestions.

2. Relaxation

Get your mind to slow down.

Relax your muscles, feel the tension drain out of you.

Progressive muscular relaxation is a good technique to adopt at this stage of self-hypnosis.

Don't rush.

3. Deepening procedures

Don't wait for this to happen, because if you do it won't. It will distract you.

This stage does take practice. Some will find this stage easier than others. Be patient.

Counting down from 100 or the 'swinging watch' techniques can help at this stage.

Don't count out loud.

4. Suggestion application

Suggestions should be worked out and memorized in advance.

Try to crystallize these suggestions into short phrases or a word, such as 'I am calm and relaxed'.

You could engage in a monologue but make sure you use 'I' rather than 'you'.

Image suggestion is most effective – see what you want to achieve.

5. Termination

Don't just open your eyes.

Think to yourself that you are going to be fully alert and awake after you count up to three.

When finished don't stand up suddenly. Periods of deep relaxation can lower blood pressure and any sudden movements may cause faintness or dizziness.

Attentional control

24

Understanding attentional control

If there is one factor that underpins people's ability to perform at their best, whatever their occupation, whatever the situation, it is their ability to focus and control their focus of attention effectively. Professor Aidan Moran from University College Dublin defines concentration as our capacity to direct our mental effort in the face of distractions. Attentional control is something which is well understood in sport where most of the important and valuable research has taken place. But it is just as important and valuable in almost every other activity in which people are engaged. Yet, it remains, until now, one of the most underdeveloped areas for application in the occupational and educational worlds.

For athletes the ability to focus (avoid distraction) is vital and many psychological interventions are aimed at allowing them to focus better and for longer. Typically, for example, in soccer many individuals and teams emerge as winners because they have managed to maintain concentration until the final whistle, the end of the game. Losers are often those whose concentration wavers as they tire.

Similarly penalty-takers in soccer or place-kickers in rugby are generally more successful if they can block out unwanted distractions such as the behaviour of opponents, the barracking of the crowd and even the (unhelpful) advice from teammates. They focus their attention, albeit for a short period of time, on the one thing that matters – a good contact between the boot and the ball. Exactly the same applies in work, in play and in education.

It is variously estimated that the average attention span of a young person in the UK at the start of the 21st century may be as short as 7–8 minutes. Curiously, the estimates 20 years earlier were in the order of 10–12 minutes. It is hypothesized that the advent of new technology and the speed at which anyone can access information may be a causal factor here.

However, a study at Exeter University several years ago confirmed what many instinctively understood. When you are interrupted whilst carrying out a piece of mental activity (studying, writing, thinking etc) or you break off to do something else, when you return to that activity, you do not return to it at the point you left it. You have to retrace your steps to some extent and often re-do what you have already done before making fresh progress with that mental activity. In fact each time you stop you run the risk of losing some of the mental work you have just done! Up to three minutes' worth in many cases

Given that mental activity is stressful in its own right, this simply adds another level of stressor to an already stress-laden activity. The suggestion therefore is that, if we can improve attention span, we can carry out activities that involve some mental component (including creative work) more effectively, more efficiently and much less stressfully.

In education this would apply to study, revision and essay/dissertation writing. In the workplace this would apply to carrying out intricate work, high quality work, report writing, preparing for important meetings and conferences, listening carefully, reading important documents etc. In each of these areas the ability to focus and to do so for as long as possible is a clear advantage and brings significant benefits.

Recent research in the USA shows that it is possible to improve attention span fairly easily to 45 minutes or more and in many cases to two hours. Achieving this simply makes most mental activity much easier to accomplish. It is suggested that there is a need for a (short) break between sustained periods of focus to provide some opportunity to 'refresh' the mind.

Attentional control and mental toughness

When we consider focus and mental toughness, it is a variable that is intricately linked to each of the main components of mental toughness. Mentally tough individuals can effectively focus their attention under pressure (challenge), refocus their attention in the face of distraction (control), allocate attention to relevant tasks to achieve success (confidence) and know what their attention should be directed to in line with goal intentions (commitment).

Indeed, research has highlighted that mentally tough individuals are aware of what to focus on, particularly when under pressure. For example, research by Stephen Bull and colleagues from the sport psychology support team for the England and Wales Cricket Board showed that the in-performance confidence of mentally tough individuals was underpinned by a controlled self-focus. That is, these individuals were able to focus on their own needs to ensure that effective performance was supported. Furthermore, these researchers showed that during-task concentration of the mentally tough is characterized by an awareness of the relevant information on which they must focus.

This chapter will initially look to scientific research and findings from sport and exercise psychology to highlight key skills and techniques necessary for optimal focus. In particular, how can we deal with attentional problems such as: not focusing on the right things, unable to maintain focus, and distractions? Importantly, it is worth noting that research consistently shows that individuals are not necessarily born with the ability to effectively focus, but that these skills are developed over time through experience and training.

Then the reader will be introduced to some very accessible and highly effective tools and techniques for improving attentional control.

Practice

Our ability to focus effectively improves with practice, but this is not necessarily a simple relationship. It appears that practising to concentrate may not always facilitate effective concentration. For example, research by Iain Greenlees and colleagues at Chichester University assessed the utility of a concentration exercise commonly used to improve individuals' ability to concentrate.

Male soccer players were randomly allocated to a 9-week training programme or to a control group. In the training programme, the soccer players completed a concentration grid exercise at least five times a week. This activity involves scanning a 10×10 block grid of two-digit numbers ranging from 00 to 99 whilst crossing out as many consecutive numbers in a sequence starting from 00 in one minute.

Although this task is commonly used to improve concentration, these researchers showed that training using the concentration grid did not improve ability to concentrate as assessed by various measures (eg speed and accuracy on a visual search task). This is one of the few studies that have tried to utilize the scientific method to establish the usefulness of concentration interventions. It is clear that the jury is still out.

So, how can practice help with focus? When we practise tasks, whether this is learning a sport skill, driving a car, or doing mental arithmetic, their attentional demands reduce. That is, the amount of attentional resources we have to allocate to them is less, and we can then allocate these to other things. Think about how hard it was to concentrate on all the steps involved in driving when you were first learning. Then, with practice, these skills became more automatic, and require less of our mental effort or focus.

Such changes have been observed in brain activation research. Research by Dan Landers and colleagues at Arizona State University showed that novice archers changed their brain activation patterns from the start to end of a 15-week training scheme. As these novices improved their skills through practice, so their brain activation patterns more closely resembled those of experienced archers. Specifically, the activation of their left hemisphere increased, which, the authors noted, reflected changes in attentional allocation. So, it seems that for us to improve our focus, we must practise those tasks that we are looking to perform.

But, does practice need to be physical or mental? It appears that both are effective. Physically practising something assists in the learning process, which leads to improved automaticity and improved attentional allocation. The focus moves from being on step-by-step components of a task (slow and effortful focus) to the outcome of the task (fast and effective focus).

As such, deliberate practice is essential if individuals are to be able to effectively focus their attention on relevant information whilst performing a task. Furthermore, increased expertise allows individuals to make quicker judgements and rely on 'gut-instinct' – an approach that is often effective and does not demand conscious focus.

Practice that more closely resembles the task being prepared for assists the individual in dealing with distractions in the environment and also in identifying relevant information to focus upon. However, mental practice can also help individuals develop skills and their concentration. Appropriate visualization can help identify what they need to be focusing on when it comes to perform. Visualizing performances or tasks can assist learning, and also provides a situation where control over distraction can be practised. Visualizing a task whilst under pressure from distractions (eg music or noise) can help develop the ability to focus in the face of such distractions.

Why do routines help?

Rituals and routines are as much part of everyday life as they are part of sport. And research consistently shows that effective pre- and during-task routines help improve concentration during tasks through drawing attention to task-relevant information and away from distractions.

Routines help us to stay organized before and during tasks, without which our attention is free to wander in the run-up to important events or during tasks. Identifying routines for effective task completion is an important skill of the mentally tough individual, as such routines are often highly personalized and specific to the task at hand. Routines become even more important when under pressure or when attentional focus has lapsed.

People often find it difficult to refocus their attention after being distracted or after a break. Developing effective refocusing routines can assist in refocusing attention onto relevant information. Such refocusing routines involve the individual identifying what they need to achieve in their next period of activity.

Effective routines involve imagery and 'focus-words' that prompt the individual to identify relevant information to focus upon, for which an appreciation of outcomes and goals is important.

The power of goals

Focusing on what you are trying to do, rather than on how you are trying to do it, can help keep attention focused on relevant information.

Research conducted at Edge Hill University by Dr David Marchant has shown consistently that when individuals focus their attention onto the outcome of a task they perform better than when they focus their attention onto the specific aspects and/or movements involved with that task. Such benefits have been observed for fine motor-skill control (eg dart throwing) as well as force production and endurance. It seems that when we focus our attention onto the step-by-step components of a task, our attentional resources are significantly taken up. This leads to slower processes and more opportunity for error. It can also result in fewer attentional resources free to process other vital information.

Focusing on the outcome of a task is associated with more effective attentional allocation, leaving attention free to process other information that will be vital to success. In a similar manner, it is difficult to focus our attention if we do not know what our goal is. Setting effective goals is critical to effectively focusing attention, as they influence where we will direct our attention whilst approaching and performing tasks. A goal sets us up for looking for specific information that will support our progress. If an individual starts a day with an effective goal in mind, his or her attention will be focused onto information to work on that task. However, without an effective goal, attention is free to wander as it is not set to seek specific information and ignore irrelevant information.

Minimizing distractions

During our daily life, we face many distractions. In sport and exercise psychology, these have often been discussed as being either internal (eg self-doubts or anxiety) or external (eg noise or visual distractions).

Managing distractions is critical to maintaining focus, in particular when life is full of many potential distractions. Research by Terry Orlick and John Partington from the universities of Ottowa and Carelton demonstrated that an ability to control and reduce distractibility was a critical characteristic of successful Canadian Olympic athletes. In particular, they identified that these athletes had strategies in place for remaining focused in the face of distraction, and for refocusing when things hadn't gone well. Success was linked to the ability to stay focused on the task at hand, and not to be distracted by unrelated information.

Two issues are important to consider here. First, efforts and plans should be put in place to reduce the opportunity for distraction. Remove distractions from your environment that divert from the task at hand, or remove yourself from distracting environments. Recognize what those distractions are.

Secondly, some distractions cannot be removed or are intrinsically linked to the task being carried out, so plan for potential distractions. Being aware of the distractions you will face will help you control them. Plan for how you will deal with them, how you will approach the task, and be organized in your approach to the task to be completed.

Finally, a key strategy for effective focus in the face of distractions is also to recognize when one has been distracted. Knowing what distracts you can help you control those distractions. For example, e-mail is a common distraction, but recognizing this allows individuals to develop strategies to control it. Using a personal journal can help identify when we have become distracted on tasks through regular reflection on task progress and experiences.

The use of technology

For many, technology provides many distractions. The internet and e-mail both support and detract from everyday work and tasks through constant availability of information. However, modern technology allows for many opportunities to develop concentration and focus. Many computer games require constant directed mental focus in the face of distractions, and as such can be used to develop an appreciation of prolonged effective focus in addition to distraction control. They may also provide an opportunity to reset focus after prolonged engagement with tasks attentionally demanding tasks.

Managing stress and fatigue

Research has consistently shown that stress leads to a narrowing of attentional focus. When we perceive that we are under pressure, we are likely to miss important information. Such pressures can be situational (eg performing an important task whilst under the scrutiny of others) or cumulative (eg generally stresses of daily life). For example, research conducted by Tracie Rogers and Dan Landers demonstrated that negative life events experienced by athletes induced a narrowing of attentional focus which put them at a higher risk of injury.

As such, it is important for us to realize that when individuals experience significant or enduring stressful events, their ability to focus effectively is reduced. Recognizing this and looking to manage and cope with stressors are therefore important skills in being able to focus. It is also necessary to recognize that attention is limited in terms of our ability to focus for extended periods of time.

Taking breaks in work allows for attentional resources to recover from fatigue. Forcing ourselves to work through fatigue decreases our ability to focus on relevant information and increases the chances of distraction.

The impact of health and fitness

Our ability to focus effectively is intrinsically linked to our physical health. In particular, research has shown that being physically fit and active can impact upon concentration in two significant ways. First, those individuals who are active enough that it impacts upon their fitness have been shown to exhibit beneficial effects on their ability to concentrate and control their attention. Secondly, individual sessions of physical activity have been shown to *immediately* improve our ability to focus and concentrate.

So, taking a physically active break is an effective technique of helping maintain appropriate focus throughout a prolonged task. And making sure we stay physically fit allows us to develop and maintain our attentional capacity throughout our lifespan.

Nine ways to enhance your focus

1 Practise, practise, practise!
2 Use routines – reduce the cognitive load.
3 Set clear and realistic goals – you need to know what you are doing and when you have finished!

4 Minimize distractions.

5 Control technology – don't let it control you!

6 Manage stress and fatigue – if you're stressed or tired you cannot concentrate for long.

7 Work to stay fit and healthy.

8 Take a break – with a degree of physical activity.

9 Utilize the tools and techniques described below on a regular basis.

Some simple tips, tools and techniques that work

One of the challenges for developing attentional control compared to many of the other techniques described elsewhere in this book is that they have to be learned. Other techniques can be taught. One of the best ways to learn something is to use experiential learning: do something, experience it and practise it until it becomes embedded.

The stork stand

Find a spot away from chairs and other hazardous objects. Begin by standing and putting all your weight on one leg. Raise your arms out to the sides at shoulder level, and gradually raise your free leg. Keep that leg just off the ground. Close your eyes and try to maintain your balance. For most people this becomes easier if they 'empty their mind'. That is, they don't concentrate on *not* falling over.

Number grid

A number grid is shown in Figure 24.1. Described earlier in the chapter, this is a 10 × 10 grid which contains, in random order, the 100 numbers from 0 to 99. Create a few of those with different random orders.

Set a start time. Mark off in sequence as many consecutive numbers as possible in 90 seconds starting with the number 0. Clearly the person who is able to concentrate on this task will achieve a higher score than one who is distracted. Plot repeated scores on a graph.

Repeated practice should produce better results.

FIGURE 24.1 Number grid

24	43	58	90	49	67	89	86	62	50
3	64	76	84	10	52	27	94	8	77
92	45	53	37	29	17	54	42	19	99
81	00	22	57	31	96	39	12	33	20
25	36	65	88	14	2	78	85	47	87
56	13	6	74	48	23	90	73	98	91
60	41	80	5	11	51	68	38	72	83
97	75	34	79	26	46	82	9	63	16
35	44	21	40	1	69	61	7	55	71
4	30	93	66	59	32	18	70	28	15

Stroop test

This consists typically of grids containing words which describe a colour. Each of the words is in a different colour. But only one or typically two of the words are in the same colour as that described by the word. You are provided with sight of the grid for a limited period time. The better your ability to focus the better your ability to identify correctly the words which are in the same colour they describe. There are many versions of this available on the internet, and there are now a number of apps which illustrate this very well. The Nintendo DS brain-training software contains a Stroop test amongst other attentional control exercises.

Computer games

Curiously, whilst new technology is often cited as a cause of reducing attentional control, many computer games are excellent at developing focus, particularly for long periods of time. Racing games and 'war games' commonly demand high levels of sustained concentration for the user to be effective. Consequently, with practice the user can often develop a heightened sense of attentional control.

The challenge lies in helping them to reflect on this. That is, to make them aware of what it feels like to focus at this level, to recall how they managed to achieve this and to consider how they might transfer this learning to other activities in their lives.

The internet is also a rich source of attentional control exercise. The website **www.luminosity.com** is a particularly good site to visit. Many exercises are free of charge but the best do require a small outlay.

Games

Many everyday games require a degree of concentration to 'beat' your opponent. Many card games require the ability to focus in order to recall which cards have been played and therefore which cards remain. Card games such as whist, bridge, rummy etc are good for developing attentional control.

One of the most successful games for developing attentional control is Bop-It (Figure 24.2). This is an electronic game which requires the player to follow four or five oral instructions quickly. If completed within an acceptable timeframe the game barks out the next instruction. The game continues until an instruction is either incorrectly carried out or the instruction is carried out too late. The game then calculates how many instructions have been correctly followed and provides this as the score.

FIGURE 24.2   The Bop-IT game

It is almost entirely about the ability to focus. The better one's attentional control the higher the score achieved. It is therefore possible to monitor progress in improving attentional control. Commonly players master the game (it is then possible to switch it into a more difficult mode) and learn what the focus experience feels like.

The challenge lies in helping people to reflect, making them aware of what it feels like to focus at this level, to recall how they managed to achieve this and to consider how they might transfer this learning to other activities in their lives. The game is particularly useful in large groups. It is extremely noisy and if several people play at the same time the potential for distraction is very significant. This challenges the players to focus amidst a wide range of distractions – and most do master this.

Interruptions and distractions

Obstacles and distractions are things you notice when you take your eye 'off the ball'. Learning to sustain attention – to concentrate – is extremely important. Learning to still or *park the mind* enhances concentration.

Attentional control is essentially about maintaining focus. Failure to do this can affect performance and wellbeing in three important and potentially damaging ways. It impacts on commitment, confidence in your abilities and emotional control.

Interruptions

It is one thing to learn how to avoid being distracted by interruptions but it is also useful to minimize the possibility of distraction. When carrying out important and valuable work, seek to do it in an environment free from interruption – and free from the prospect of interruption.

Distractions

Being distracted and losing focus can affect performance, behaviour and wellbeing significantly.

Exercise – minimizing unwanted interruptions

Think of situations where interruptions can cause problems for you and the ways in which you can minimize interruptions.

Conclusions

Briefly highlighted here are important considerations in understanding and developing effective focus. Ultimately, we must appreciate the limits of our ability to focus, but also how we can train and prepare ourselves to focus more effectively. This can range from simple tasks such as removing opportunities for distraction to a more effortful process of deliberate practice and routine development. However, without such efforts, our attention is free to wander. Focus is not a resource to switch on or off; it is always online.

Goal setting

25

How goal setting works

Goal setting is widely recognized as an effective means to motivate individuals to achieve some valuable or important purpose. In this context we are talking primarily about individuals developing the ability to set goals for themselves (and perhaps for others too). Goal setting theory suggests that establishing clear, measurable, achievable goals is an important step in the process of achieving those goals. As Goldstein (1994) stated: 'Goals provide a sense of direction and purpose'.

Much of the pioneering work on goal setting has been carried out by Dr Edwin Locke. He found amongst other things that well-constructed goal setting has the ability to act as a mechanism that motivates the individual towards the goal. Locke and Latham (2002) have found four mechanisms through which goal setting can impact on individual performance. Goals appear to motivate by:

- focusing attention on activities directly relevant to the goal (and away from activities which are not important for the achievement of the goal);
- serving as an energizer; interestingly Locke found that the more challenging and specific the goals are, the harder the individual will work towards their attainment;
- affecting commitment;
- activating cognitive abilities and strategies which allow people to cope with the prevailing situation.

Locke and Latham (*A Theory of Goal Setting and Task Performance*, 1990) originally confirmed the need to set specific and difficult goals and identified other factors which have been variously described as the five goals or moderators of goal setting. To motivate, goals must have:

1 Clarity: setting SMART goals. Clarity focuses the individual on the goal.

2 Challenge: identifying challenging goals which are perceived as difficult but achievable opportunities. Once again we can see potential connection with Maslow's contention that self-actualization is a powerful driver for many.

3 Commitment: how important is the ultimate goal? Self-efficacy – a belief in the ability to achieve the goals – is closely related to the concepts of control and confidence in abilities in mental toughness. The extent to which promises are made to self and to others is at the heart of commitment in mental toughness.

4 Feedback: particularly whilst on the journey to the goal. Feedback enables the sense of progress and provides the opportunity to flex or adapt as needed.

5 Task complexity: the more complex the task the more difficult it will be to achieve. This needs to be taken into account in both planning and execution. There is a risk that individuals can take on too much without giving themselves a realistic chance of achieving the task.

Ultimately, understanding how goal setting works and how it can be applied helps the individual to be more effective.

Our experience in the full spectrum of applications indicates to us that there are three aspects of goal setting which are important:

1 Setting clear, realistic achievable goals – where the SMART or SMARTER process is a good way of achieving this.

2 Dealing with big goals – how do you eat an elephant?

3 Balancing goals.

Aspects of goal setting

SMART(ER) goals

Setting goals gives meaning and direction as well as fuel and energy to achieve objectives. For goals to be effective they should be SMARTER: a seven-letter acronym which describes the key steps in effective goal setting (Table 25.1). It is often found in the abbreviated original format SMART which describes the first five steps. Either is effective.

Eating the elephant – dealing with big goals

Sometimes we find that we have to achieve something big or significant. Even if we have the time and resources to do it in relative comfort the goal can appear overwhelming. It can appear to be too big a stretch. The challenge is to take these significant goals and turn them into something which is realistic and achievable.

TABLE 25.1   SMARTER Goals

Specific	You must be able to define them clearly and concisely. The clearer the goal the more effective it is. 'I want to do well at school' is better replaced with 'I want to get 4 Grade A passes in my A level exams'. It is useful to be equally clear about the benefit (to you or others) of achieving the goal.
Measurable	You must know when you have achieved success and what success will look like. As Henry Ford is reported to have said: 'If it ain't measured, it doesn't get done'. Measures are usually unambiguous and tangible – they remain in sight.
Achievable	Sufficiently challenging but not impossible. Generally the evidence shows that most people make progress by 'gently' stretching themselves. If you overreach yourself this can diminish motivation and failure can be damaging if you are not minded to 'learn from your mistakes'.
Relevant	It should be relevant to the circumstances and have a real impact.
Time bound	There must be a deadline to work towards. To say 'I'll write that report soon' is very different to 'I will write that report by next Monday'.
Exciting	They should inspire enthusiasm and commitment. The benefits and impact should be assessed as worthwhile or valuable. The process (the way the goal is achieved) should also provide a source of inspiration or development, for example, the need to learn a new skill.
Reviewable	There must always be provision for reviewing and re-establishing targets to take account of changing circumstances.

> **Question:** How do you eat an elephant?
> **Answer:** A slice at a time.

The key to achieving big goals is to break the task down into smaller relevant tasks which, when completed, are clear steps towards the achievement of the big goal. Not unreasonably these intermediate tasks each have SMART goals attached which we commonly call 'milestones'.

A useful technique which works well is the 2–4–8 rule. This simply takes a big goal that has to be achieved at some time in the future (say 8 weeks) and work out what you would need to have achieved by the mid-point (4 weeks) if you are to be on track for the big goal. These milestones hopefully will now begin to appear to be more achievable.

Then you repeat the exercise for the mid-point. What do you have to have done by the new mid-point of this shorter period (2 weeks away) to be on track for the mid-point and the end goal? Tasks and goals which are achievable in a 2-week timeframe should in most cases be eminently achievable.

Breaking a large goal into smaller interim goals or milestones will generally make the process more achievable. So, to summarize the approach:

- Take a large goal or target, eg write a whole new course on leadership in 8 weeks.

- Work out what you must do by the end of the next 8 weeks if this is to be achieved.

- Work out what you must do by the end of 4 weeks if this is to be achieved.

- Work out what you must do by the end of 2 weeks if this is to be achieved.

- Work on what you must achieve in the next 2 weeks which should now be very accessible. The actions will typically be 'small actions which are more easily handled'.

Review progress every 4 weeks and roll the targets forward for the next 2, 4 and 8 weeks. Ask someone to monitor your review with you to ensure some form of discipline. At any point you can ask:

- Does the 2-week target appear achievable? Are you more confident that you can achieve this target? Do you feel more in control?

- What might stop you achieving each target – have you planned to deal with it? Are there lead times you need to take into account?

- How confident do you feel that you will now hit the big target?

- How can you explain this to others and gain their commitment?

A psychological perspective on goal setting

Goal setting allows an individual to navigate through a complex world. There are many, many forces acting in many directions. By identifying a path an individual can deal with these stressors more effectively. Locke *et al* (1981) suggest that goal setting works to improve performance in four distinct ways:

- it causes the individual to focus;

- it mobilizes effort;

- it enhances long-term persistence;

- it promotes new learning strategies.

Most of the research into goal setting has been focused on how to maximize the technique. Much less attention has been paid to the underpinning psychology. What we can say is:

- Goal setting works better for some people. Certain personalities are drawn to it; others find it limiting and stifling. Everyone can benefit – not everyone wants to.

- Goal setting reduces anxiety, by allowing an individual to deal more effectively with competing demands. Anxiety is usually a pre-cursor to poor performance.

- Nearly everybody puts things off. Goals help to alleviate this. The reasons for procrastination are many but they probably have their roots in some other complex psychology. This includes self-handicapping (giving yourself an excuse), fear of failure, low self-esteem and attribution distortions.

It is clear that an individual's wellbeing impacts on goal setting, and is in turn impacted upon. Setting appropriate goals is one of the key aspects of self-development. It forms the bedrock of coaching. By better understanding the mental toughness of individuals you can help them become more effective goal-setters. However, you must always bear in mind that poor goal setting is not necessarily a product of poor technique. Poor goal setting could be simply a symptom of a more deep-seated issue. Failure to resolve this will certainly impact on the goal-setting process.

Learning how to set goals more effectively and applying these approaches consistently should enhance one's sense of commitment and control. When asked, I can do it, and if pressed, I can make a promise and keep it.

Research using the MTQ48

26

Introduction

This chapter hopefully provides an accessible overview of some of the recent research using the MTQ48 questionnaire. The work mostly cited is in peer-reviewed journals – the bedrock of scientific investigations.

Since the development of the MTQ48 and the MTQ18 (short version), researchers have been more able to objectively measure and quantify mental toughness, and a steady stream of scientific research has been conducted using these questionnaires. The following chapter provides an overview of some of that research. These studies have contributed to a greater understanding of what mental toughness is, and how it develops. However, while the MTQ48 has been the most frequently used measure of mental toughness in published research, it is important to acknowledge that other questionnaires have been developed and used for research purposes.

Mental toughness and coping

A number of studies have used the MTQ48 to investigate relationships between mental toughness and the ways in which people cope with stress. In a systematic review of coping in sport, Nicholls and Polman (2007, p 18) suggested investigating the 'obvious' relationship between mental toughness and coping. Numerous researchers have previously reported the ability to cope effectively when under pressure as being a key component of mental toughness (Bull *et al*, 2005; Jones, Hanton and Connaughton, 2002).

In a large study employing 677 athletes from a variety of sports and different levels of performance, Nicholls *et al* (2008) found significant relationships between mental toughness and use of coping strategies. Consistent with expectations, mental toughness was found to be associated with more problem- or approach-coping strategies (ie reducing or eliminating the stressor) such as mental imagery, effort expenditure, thought control and logical analysis; but less use of avoidance-coping strategies such as distancing, mental distraction or resignation. This finding suggests mentally tough athletes prefer to tackle problems head-on by actively seeking solutions. However, Nicholls *et al* did not address how stressors were viewed by athletes or the effectiveness of coping strategies in relation to mental toughness.

Building on this work, Kaiseler, Polman and Nicholls (2009) used the MTQ48 and assessed stress appraisal, coping, and coping effectiveness in a study where 482 athletes reported how they coped with a self-selected intense stressor experienced within a two-week period. These researchers reported higher levels of mental toughness to be significantly related to experiencing less stress and more control. This finding was consistent with Nicholls *et al* (2008) as higher mental toughness was associated with more problem-focused coping strategies and less emotion-focused (ie to regulate emotional distress) coping strategies. The results were the first to offer support to the notion that mentally tough athletes cope more effectively. Mentally tough athletes reported greater coping effectiveness when using problem-focused as opposed to emotion-focused coping strategies.

Mental toughness, emotional control/reactivity and emotional intelligence

Numerous theorists have proposed emotional control to be an important part of being mentally tough (Clough, Earle and Sewell, 2002; Gucciardi, Gordon and Dimmock, 2008; Jones, Hanton and Connaughton, 2007). While research has found that mentally tough athletes use more problem-focused as opposed to emotion-focused coping strategies, this line of research did not rule out the possibility that participants with higher or lower levels of mental toughness experienced more or less intense emotions. Thus, the ability to remain relatively unaffected by competition or adversity (Clough *et al*, 2002) might relate to being less emotional rather than using specific coping strategies to maintain control.

To investigate links to emotionality, Crust (2009) had 112 regular sports participants complete the MTQ48 to measure mental toughness and the affect intensity measure (Larsen, 1984) as a measure of typical responses to emotion-provoking stimuli. Previous research (Larsen, Diener and Cropanzano, 1987) had shown individuals with high affect intensity tend to engage in more personalizing (ie absorbed in personal meaning), generalizing (ie blowing things out of proportion) and selective abstraction (ie focus on emotional aspects of events). No relationships were found between affect intensity, total mental toughness and the six sub-scales of the MTQ48. Thus, there was no evidence to suggest that being able to remain calm and in control under pressure reflects mentally tough athletes being less emotional. It appears that differences in coping strategies are more likely to explain different reactions of athletes with higher or lower mental toughness when facing challenging or pressure situations. This appears to be good news in terms of developing mental toughness as coping strategies can be learned.

Recent research has begun to look at the link between emotional intelligence and mental toughness (eg Nicholls *et al*, in Press). They showed a positive relationship between mental toughness and emotional intelligence, suggesting that mental toughness development might be an important, but currently absent, component of emotional intelligence training.

Mental toughness and performance/levels of achievement

Many sports psychologists have suggested or implied relationships between mental toughness and performance although few have objectively tested these relationships. For example, Jones, Hanton and Connaughton (2002, 2007) studied mental toughness by interviewing elite/super-elite athletes, and justify their approach on the basis that mental toughness should be related to successful outcomes. However, other psychologists have cautioned against solely focusing on the elite or super-elite as this can be restrictive and potentially misleading (Crust, 2008; Nicholls *et al*, 2009). While having high levels of mental toughness can be an advantage in sport, numerous other characteristics (ie physiological, anatomical factors etc) are likely to impact upon whether athletes are more or less successful.

During initial testing of the MTQ48, Clough *et al* (2002) tested differences in performance between participants with higher or lower levels of mental toughness on a cognitive planning task following manipulated feedback. Those with higher levels of mental toughness were found to perform consistently well regardless of the feedback, while participants with lower levels of mental toughness performed much worse following negative feedback. Crust and Clough (2005) used the MTQ48 and found some support for a significant, yet relatively small relationship between total mental toughness and performance in an isometric weight-holding task (pain tolerance). Additionally, the sub-scales of control and confidence, but not challenge and commitment were associated with greater endurance. This outcome is likely down to participants believing in themselves and being able to ignore or block out pain.

Using a relatively small sample (n = 107), Crust and Azadi (2010) found athletes of county standard and above reported significantly higher levels of mental toughness than did club or university athletes, although the differences were relatively small. In the business rather than the sport domain, researchers have recently evaluated mental toughness across different levels of management.

Not all studies have found differences in performance or standard to be related to mental toughness. In a study assessing the mental toughness of trainee football players in an English Premier League football academy (using the MTQ18), no significant differences were found between players who were retained by the club and released at the end of the competitive season (Crust, Nesti and Littlewood, 2010). However, it is possible that the rather simplistic research design in this study did not capture the complexities of studying mental toughness within such a dynamic environment; this is one area where interviews with key personnel might be useful. More recently, Nicholls *et al* (2009) tested for differences in mental toughness on the basis of achievement level, gender, age, experience and sport types. Specifically, analyses of a large sample of athletes (n = 677) representing international, national, county, club/university and beginner levels revealed no significant differences in mental toughness between different levels of performer.

On the basis of these findings, and others that have used alternative measures of mental toughness (eg Golby and Sheard, 2004), Nicholls *et al* (2009) concluded that differences in mental toughness between different levels of athletic achievement are minimal or subtle. Such findings might offer support to the proposal of Crust (2008) who suggested mental toughness might best be considered in relative (making the most of one's abilities) rather than absolute terms. Future mental toughness researchers should also give more attention to non-elite athletes and underrepresented samples such as athletes with disabilities. Assessing mental toughness in match officials might also provide a useful comparison with athletic samples.

Nicholls *et al* (2009) found men reported significantly higher levels of mental toughness than women in their sample, and that age and experience predicted higher levels of mental toughness. Gender has previously been little considered in mental toughness research and these findings suggest this aspect is in need of much greater attention by future researchers. More recently, Crust and Keegan (2010) also found gender differences in mental toughness with male athletes reporting significantly higher values. With mental toughness found to be related to age, these results appear to offer support to researchers who found experience was a crucial factor in the development of mental toughness (Connaughton *et al*, 2008).

Mental toughness and psychological skills

Although Clough *et al* (2002) and other researchers (Horsburgh *et al*, 2009; Kaiseler *et al*, 2009; Nicholls *et al*, 2008) consider mental toughness to be a personality trait, different views exist and some suggest it is a mindset (Sheard, 2010). Viewing mental toughness as a mindset suggests that changing the way individuals think through a process of psychological skills training could lead to improvements. Indeed, there is some evidence that mental toughness, or at least components of mental toughness, can be influenced through a systematic mental skills training intervention (Sheard and Golby, 2006; Gucciardi, Gordon and Dimmock, 2009a). In terms of developing mental toughness, other researchers who used qualitative methods (interviews) have proposed a more significant role for environmental influences such as upbringing or competitive rivalries with others (Bull *et al*, 2005).

Beyond the work concerning mental toughness and coping, little is known about the relationship between mental toughness and the use of psychological skills. On the basis of previously reported relationships between mental toughness and performance (Crust and Clough, 2005), the use of mental skills and performance (Gould, Dieffenbach and Moffett, 2002) and evidence to suggest mental skills training can influence mental toughness (Gucciardi *et al*, 2009b; Sheard and Golby, 2006), Crust and Azadi (2010) predicted a positive relationship between use of psychological strategies and mental toughness. Mental toughness (as measured by the MTQ48) and use of a number of psychological performance strategies as measured by the Test of Performance Strategies (TOPS) (Thomas, Murphy and Hardy, 1999) were found to be significantly related. Three performance strategies were found to be significantly and positively related to mental toughness in both practice and competition: relaxation strategies, self-talk and emotional control. The small to moderate correlations found by Crust and Azadi appear similar to those reported for mental toughness and coping (Nicholls *et al*, 2008). Perhaps most noteworthy were relationships between the subscales of the MTQ48 and the use of psychological strategies. Specifically, commitment was found to be the sub-scale most frequently related to use of psychological strategies, which the authors speculated could reflect being deeply committed to one's chosen sport and thus seeking out alternative ways of enhancing performance. Despite these findings, it should be noted that the results were based upon a relatively small sample, and that the TOPS inventory only measures frequency with which athletes use psychological strategies and not effectiveness.

Mental toughness and personality

Through studying mental toughness in identical and non-identical twins, Horsburgh *et al* (2009) found that mental toughness is influenced by both genetics and features of the environment, and as such behaves 'in the same manner as virtually every personality trait that has ever been investigated in behavioural genetic study' (p 104). In establishing significant correlations between the MTQ48 and the so-called 'big five' personality factors (extraversion, openness, agreeableness, conscientiousness and neuroticism) Horsburgh *et al* suggest that mental toughness is strongly influenced by genetics and as such may not be easy to modify. However, these researchers did contend that aspects of mental toughness that showed least hereditability (ie commitment or control) may be easier to strengthen. Horsburgh *et al* support Clough, Earle and Sewell's (2002) view of mentally tough individuals having lower anxiety levels, being sociable, outgoing and competitive.

An intriguing research study was carried out by Onley *et al* (2013), who investigated the relationship between the 'dark triad' of personality (Machiavellianism, narcissism and psychopathy) and toughness. They reported that there was a small positive correlation with narcissism but negative associations with psychopathy and Machiavellianism. These findings, taken in conjunction with the recent findings by Nicholls *et al* (in Press) relating to emotional intelligence, may go some way to dispel the very unfair stereotype that the more mentally tough are not people-orientated. The evidence might suggest that they may be better at dealing with others than the more sensitive.

Mental toughness and health

Much of the research looking at health and the MTQ48 has been carried out by a research team based at the University of Basle. Gerber *et al* (2012) reported that mental toughness mitigated the relationship between high stress and depressive symptoms. They also compared the mental toughness of adolescents and young adults with self-reported exercise. Participants with higher physical activity levels scored higher in most MTQ48 sub-scales. Interestingly, they concluded that acquiring a mindset of mental toughness might be one way that physical activity and exercise can impact an individual's mental health.

Brand *et al* (2012), using a sample of 284 adolescents, investigated sleep and mental toughness. Increased mental toughness was highly associated with favourable sleep, decreased perceived stress, favourable coping strategies, increased curiosity and optimism. Similar positive findings were also reported by Brand *et al* (2014) and Brand *et al* (in Press). Finally, Gerber *et al* (2013) carried out the first longitudinal study using the MTQ48. Their 10-month study prospectively examined the association between mental toughness and stress resilience in students. Baseline toughness levels predicted depressive symptoms and life satisfaction over time.

Mental toughness and education

The use of mental toughness in education is the area that has increased most since the first edition of the book. This area is explored in more detail in other chapters. However, in summary, mental toughness as measured by the MTQ48 has been found to relate to student performance and wellbeing in higher education (Crust *et al*, 2014; Stamp *et al*, 2015) and performance and behaviour in secondary school (St Clair-Thompson *et al*, in Press). Finally, in a recent review by McGeown, St Clair-Thompson and Clough (in Press) the case for the widespread utilization of the 4 Cs model within education has been made.

Other studies using the MTQ48/MTQ18

A number of other studies have used the MTQ48. As would be expected, positive psychological constructs such as optimism have been found to be significantly related to mental toughness (Nicholls *et al*, 2008). While investigating the relationships between mental toughness and sports injury rehabilitation, Levy *et al* (2006) found higher levels of mental toughness (as measured by the MTQ18) were significantly related to more positive threat appraisals, greater pain tolerance, and higher levels of attendance at clinic-based sessions. However, the relationship between mental toughness and injury rehabilitation needs to be further explored as the MTQ18 only provides an overview of total mental toughness.

Crust and Azadi (2009) assessed the leadership preferences of mentally tough athletes using the MTQ48, and the Leadership Scale for Sports (Chelladurai and Saleh, 1980). Higher levels of mental toughness were significantly and positively related to a preference for training and instructive behaviours. This result appears consistent with the view that mentally tough athletes focus on the task at hand (Gucciardi *et al*, 2008; Jones, *et al*, 2007). Marchant *et al* (2009) looked at mental toughness and how it related to managerial level. A total of 522 participants working in UK-based organizations completed demographic information and the Mental Toughness Questionnaire. The analysis revealed that mental toughness ratings were higher in more senior positions, and that mental toughness generally increased with age. This suggests that increased exposure to significant life events may have a positive developmental effect on mental toughness and would suggest that mental toughness can be developed through appropriate training programmes.

On the 'lighter' side, Veselka *et al* (2010) showed that both positive and negative humour styles do exist, and that these are differentially associated with mental toughness. Individuals exhibiting either affiliative or self-enhancing humour are also more likely to yield high scores on mental toughness, thereby demonstrating greater resistance to life's adversities.

The MTQ48 has also been used in the workplace. Marchant *et al* (2009) showed that more senior managers had higher levels of mental toughness. Godlewski and Kline (2012) found that, within the Canadian armed forces, higher levels of toughness were associated with lower turnover and better transitions. Zalewski and Krzywosz-Rynkiewicz (2014) reported on the impact of mental toughness on citizenship behaviour.

Finally, as reported elsewhere in this book, researchers are beginning to investigate the cognitive aspects of the mental toughness advantage. Dewhurst *et al* (2012) used the directed forgetting paradigm. Participants with high mental toughness showed better recall of a to-be-remembered list following instructions to forget the previous list. The findings suggest that mentally tough individuals have an enhanced ability to prevent unwanted information from interfering with current goals.

Conclusion

A significant amount of research has been produced using the MTQ48. The MTQ48 is at present the most frequently used measure of mental toughness in sports research and is equally applicable in other performance settings. The body of evidence from studies using the MTQ48 complements, rather than competes with, other perspectives and approaches to studying mental toughness. There are some limitations since at present the vast majority of studies employing the MTQ48 have simply examined the correlates of mental toughness. More experimental work is necessary to understand how thoughts, feelings and behaviours differ between individuals with higher or lower levels of mental toughness.

A summary – and thoughts about 'what's next?'

27

At the start of the book we described our work for the past 20 years as a journey. It remains just that in many ways. The application for mental toughness and MTQ48 widens all the time.

Writing this book has also been extremely valuable for us. The process has helped both of us to develop a comprehensive big picture of where we are and where new interests are emerging. Having done this, we have been pleasantly surprised by the amount of evidence emerging for mental toughness and its application both in academic research and in practical applications in the world we live in.

We will bring this chapter of the story to a conclusion by focusing on three themes: the big picture – a global perspective; a psychological perspective – how is this resonating with what is happening elsewhere in psychology; and – for the practitioner – what next?

A global perspective

We have now introduced mental toughness and MTQ48 to around 80 countries. Two questions regularly emerge: 'Is mental toughness more important now than ever before because life is more stressful now than ever before?' and 'Should everyone be mentally tough?' The answers are: yes, no and maybe.

It is unlikely that life has been more stressful over the past 50 years than in any time before then. Mortality rates and advances in health would support that. The working classes in industrial societies did not enjoy an easy life until the latter part of the 20th century. Life was challenging, difficult, threatening and yet somehow one had to survive. People did. To survive they developed some degree of mental toughness. There are different stressors these days but it is also likely that we have generally become less adept at dealing with crises, with stress and with challenge. Witness the response to the global recession.

Will life become more stressful? Probably. Will mental toughness become more important? Maybe it will. Related to this are issues previously treated as separate, and 'joining the dots' enables us to see a bigger picture. For example, the relationship between education and employment has often been a difficult one. Employers argue that education systems don't provide them with suitable people and the educationalist argues that employers don't value the education that is provided.

The common factors which are emerging are those of transition and employability. They are flip sides of the same coin. As discussed earlier in the book, we are seeing employers and educators beginning to engage with one another. Our work is frequently part of the common ground.

As for the mentally sensitive, from the macro-perspective a healthy society is one which contains a rich mix of different people, types, personalities etc. They all bring something to the party. At a micro-level, if we look at individuals there is evidence that the more mentally tough do get more out of life than the mentally sensitive (although the latter can and do lead happy and fulfilling lives).

A fuller response might be that there could be a case for shifting the mental toughness of the whole population a little to the right, which is not the same as saying that everyone should become mentally tough. If life generally is to be more challenging, then improving our general response to that should be beneficial.

'Do we know how that will shape up?' We have our ideas but it is important that we engage with practitioners and researchers out there and be guided by them. Already we see some evidence of the increasing importance of leadership at all levels of activity. And we mean *leadership*; we are not just talking about leaders. A classroom teacher must show leadership, employees at all levels can provide leadership which benefits them and others etc.

The psychological perspective – where does mental toughness fit into the rest of the picture?

Mental toughness is not, and never can be, a stand-alone concept. It is embedded in the beginnings of resilience research and is designed to be complementary to its research relatives. Self-efficacy, self-esteem, locus of control etc have a major role to play in understanding human behaviour.

In psychology a new model does not wipe away its predecessors. It builds on them and tries to add explanatory power. Our aim is to understand why people do what they do and how we can help them to do it better. Mental toughness has a 'new flavour', driven largely by its clear focus and applied origins.

From a research perspective two psychological drivers exist when developing our model, tools and techniques. First, there is the need to investigate the linkages with other psychological, sociological and cultural perspectives. Secondly, there is the need to continue to try and validate our approach and also to extend the validation process itself.

Looking at linkages, the two most high profile ones are arguably with positive psychology and emotional intelligence. The positive psychology movement is predicated on the notion that the psychology profession has concentrated too much on the negatives. Psychologists have tended to look for problems, then label them!

However, we feel that you can't ignore the negatives. Many people do have significant challenges to deal with. Our work does not deal with people with psychological illness and those dealing with life's major problems, but rather focuses on how they deal with everyday, but non-trivial, problems. Labelling this as 'not positive' depends on your perspective. We do not feel that stress, challenge and problem solving are necessarily a negative. Is stress bad? Chronic stressors are, but as long as people have the right tools, the challenge of earning a living, making a difference, feeding the family, is what gets them out of bed each day – often with a spring in their step. *Burn–out is terrible, but so is brown-out.* Brown-out is the feeling associated with slowly 'rusting away', stuck in a mundane rut.

Stress is both something that needs to be controlled and something that attracts people to it. Our approach is somewhat akin to the warning most of us got from our parent – you can't have any pudding unless you eat your vegetables. In our case the 'vegetables' are the everyday problems and challenges we all face. The 'pudding' is life's good bit – the things that drive wellbeing. By dealing with the problems, we can develop our coping skills in the same way that eating vegetables provides vitamins and other essential nutrients.

In our work we have focused more on contentment than happiness. Happiness is more transient and ephemeral in nature. It can be materialistic and acquisitive. Contentment is about self-actualization – facing risk and facing challenge. Problems cannot be ignored, but they can be the root of growth.

The second burgeoning link is between mental toughness and emotional intelligence ... and especially intelligent emotions. What we can say for certain is that, as has been discussed earlier, this link is not an obvious or straightforward one.

The practitioner's needs – product development

There are three things that practitioners need: good products, good training and support materials, especially case studies.

Products – the questionnaires

The MTQ48 was developed and launched in January 2003 and has served us very well. The design has stood the test of time and has proved popular. Like everyone and everything else it is now evolving to meet the needs of target populations.

Training for users

There are two core sets of programmes available. One is for those who wish to administer and use the questionnaires and is principally focused on assessment and feedback. The other is for those who wish to be involved in mental toughness development work. Both are supported with workbooks and materials. The programmes are now well developed and contain some excellent material which has been well received. They too will continue to evolve – particularly with the use of technology.

Development of support materials

This is possibly the most important area for development. Those engaged in the use of mental toughness, the concept or the measure, tend to look for two things:

1 Case studies and research – there is a huge volume of case studies and research papers (many published in peer-reviewed journals). AQR makes these routinely available through its website and its mental toughness LinkedIn group. There is a major commitment to:

   - structure, catalogue and organize the case study and research database;

   - develop processes which make the material more accessible;

   - encourage the development of case studies and research.

2 Support materials – this includes any form of materials which helps the practitioner explain or apply the model. However, for most this means access to interventions and exercises. As with case studies, there is a commitment now to:

   - catalogue over 100 exercises currently in use;

   - lead the development of new and engaging exercises and interventions;

   - support development groups, particularly those interested in specific applications. This is now an AQR-supported LinkedIn Mental Toughness Group.

What we currently have works well. Like the world we have described above, we can't and won't stand still; we can do it better still.

> It is not the strongest of the species that survives, or the most intelligent, but the one most responsive to change.
>
> Attributed to Charles Darwin

Ultimately, our presentation of mental toughness is emerging as a concept, an approach and a measure which achieve two goals which are not always seen as mutually compatible: helping individuals, groups and society to improve performance (by creating that wealth we need for growth); and at the same time indicating how wellbeing can be enhanced through the same approach.

REFERENCES

Ackerman, PL (2011) *Cognitive Fatigue: Multidisciplinary perspectives on current research and future applications*, American Psychological Association, Washington, DC

Averill, JR (1973) Personal control over aversive stimuli and its relationship to stress, *Psychological Bulletin*, **80**, pp 286–303

Bandura, A (1977) Self-efficacy: Towards a unifying theory of behavioural change, *Psychological Review*, **84**, pp 191–215

Bell, J and Saltikov, JA (2000) Mitchell's Relaxation Technique: Is it effective? *Physiotherapy*, **86**, pp 473–78, ed BS Bloom (1985) *Developing Talent in Young People*, Ballantine, New York

Blum, L (1980) Compassion, in *Explaining Emotions*, ed AM Rorty, University of California Press, Berkeley, CA

Boggiano, AL, Main, DS and Katz, PA (1988) Children's preference for challenge: The role of perceived competency and control, *Journal of Personality and Social Psychology*, **54**, pp 134–41

Borg, G (1978) Subjective aspects of physical and mental load, *Ergonomics*, **21** (3), pp 215–20

Borg, MG and Riding, G (1990) Occupational stress in British educational settings: A review, *Educational Psychology*, **10** (2), pp 103–26

Boyce, CJ, Wood, AM and Brown, DA (2010) The dark side of conscientiousness: Conscientious people experience greater drops in life satisfaction following unemployment, *Journal of Research in Personality*, **44**, pp 535–39

Brand, S, Gerber, M, Kalak, N, Kirov, R, Lemola, S, Clough, PJ, Pühse, U and Holsboer-Trachsler, E (2012) 'Sleep well, our tough heroes!' – In adolescence, greater mental toughness is related to better sleep schedules, *Behavioral Sleep Medicine*

Brand, S, Gerber, M, Kalak, N, Kirov, R, Lemola, S, Clough, PJ and Pühse, U (2014) Adolescents with greater mental toughness show higher sleep efficiency, more deep sleep and fewer awakenings after sleep onset, *Journal of Adolescent Health*, **54**, pp 109–13

Brand, S, Kalak, N, Gerber, M, Clough, PJ, Lemola, S, Pühse, U and Holsboer-Trachsler, E (in Press) During early and mid-adolescence, greater mental toughness is related to increased sleep quality and psychological functioning, *Journal of Health Psychology*

Brennan, S (1998) Mental toughness wins out, in *Christian Science Monitor*, ed DS Looney, **90**, Issue 173

Brewer, J and Davis, J (1995) Applied psychology of rugby league, *Sports Medicine*, **13**, pp 129–35

Brown, R (2004) The Psychological Performance Inventory: Is the mental toughness test tough enough?, *International Journal of Sport Psychology*, **35**, pp 91–108

Brown, P and Brown, V (2012) *Neuropsychology for Coaches: Understanding the basics*, Open University Press

Bull, S, Shambrook, C, James, W and Brooks, J (2005) Towards an understanding of mental toughness in elite English cricketers, *Journal of Applied Sport Psychology*, **17**, pp 209–27

Butler, RJ (1989) Psychological preparation of Olympic boxers, in *The Psychology of Sport: Theory and practice*, eds J Kremer and W Crawford, pp 78–84, UK British Psychological Association, Leicester

Butler, RJ and Hardy, L (1992) The performance profile: Theory and application, *The Sport Psychologist*, **6**, pp 253–64

Chelladurai, P and Saleh, S (1980) Dimensions of leader behavior in sports: Development of a leadership scale, *Journal of Sport Psychology*, **2**, pp 34–45

Clark, EH (1980) An analysis of occupational stress factors as perceived by public school teachers, *Dissertation Abstracts International*, **41**, p 10

Clough, PJ, Shepherd, J and Maughan, RJ (1989) Marathon finishers and pre-race drop-outs, *British Journal of Sports Medicine*, **23**, pp 97–101

Clough, PJ, Earle, K and Sewell, D (2002) Mental toughness: The concept and its measurement, in *Solutions in Sport Psychology*, ed I Cockerill, pp 32–43, Thomson, London

Clough, PJ, Newton, S, Bruen, P, Earle, F, Earle, K, Benuzzi, F, Gardini, S, Huber, A, Lui, F and Venneri, A (2010) Mental toughness and brain structure, Poster presented at the 16th Annual Meeting of the Organisation for Human Brain Mapping, 6–10 June, Barcelona

Clough, PJ and Strycharczyk, D (2012) Mental toughness and its role in the development of young people, in *Coaching in Education: Getting better results for students, educators and parents*, ed C Van Nieuwerburgh, Karnac, London

Cohen, J (1988) *Statistical Power Analysis for the Behavioural Sciences*, 2nd edn, Erlbaum, Hillsdale, NJ

Connaughton, D, Wadey, R, Hanton, S and Jones, G (2008) The development and maintenance of mental toughness: Perceptions of elite performers, *Journal of Sport Sciences*, **26**, pp 83–95

Coulter, T, Mallett, C and Gucciardi, D (2010) Understanding mental toughness in Australian soccer: Perceptions of players, parents and coaches, *Journal of Sports Sciences*, **28**, pp 699–716

Covey, SR (1989) *The Seven Habits of Highly Effective People*, Simon and Schuster, New York

Coyne, IJ, Clough, PJ, Alexander, T and Clemment, G (2006) Workplace bullying: the role of mental toughness, in *British Psychological Society, Division of Occupational Psychology, Annual Conference Book of Proceedings*, pp 107–10, BPS, London

Cox, RH (1998) *Sport psychology: Concepts and applications*, McGraw Hill, Boston

Crust, L and Clough, PJ (2005) Relationship between mental toughness and physical endurance, *Perceptual and Motor Skills*, **100**, pp 192–94

Crust, L (2008) A review and conceptual re–examination of mental toughness: Implications for future researchers, *Personality and Individual Differences*, **45**, pp 576–83

Crust, L (2009) The relationship between mental toughness and affect intensity, *Personality and Individual Differences*, **47**, pp 959–63

Crust, L and Azadi, K (2009) Leadership preferences of mentally tough athletes, *Personality and Individual Differences*, **47**, pp 326–30

Crust, L and Azadi, K (2010) Mental toughness and athletes' use of psychological strategies, *European Journal of Sport Science*, **10**, pp 43–51

Crust, L and Keegan, R (2010) Mental toughness and attitudes to risk-taking, *Personality and Individual Differences*, **49**, pp 164–68

Crust, L, Nesti, M and Littlewood, M (2010) A cross-sectional analysis of mental toughness in a professional football academy, *Athletic Insight Journal*, **2**, pp 165–74

Crust, L and Clough, PJ (2011) Developing mental toughness: From research to practice, *Journal of Sport Psychology in Action*, **2**, pp 21–32

Crust, L, Earle, K, Perry, JL, Earle, F, Clough, AE and Clough, PJ (2014) Mental toughness in higher education: Relationships with achievement and profession in first-year university sports students, *Personality and Individual Differences*, **69**, pp 87–91

Cummings, J and Bennett, V (2012) *Compassion in Practice*, www.commissioningboardnhs.uk

Curtis Management Group (1998) *Motivation Lombardi Style*, p 20, Celebrating Excellence Publishing, Lombard, IL

Curtis, K, Horton, K and Smith, P (2012) A grounded theory study on student nurses' socialisation in compassionate practice: Balancing to manage dissonance between professional ideals and practice, *Nurse Education Today*, **32** (7), pp 790–95

Csikszentimichalyi, M (1990) *Flow: The Psychology of Optimal Experience*, Harper and Row, New York

Dale, GA and Wrisberg, CA (1996) The use of a performance profiling technique in a team setting: Getting the athletes and coaches on the 'same page', *The Sport Psychologist*, **10**, pp 261–77

deCharms, R and Carpenter, V (1968) Measuring motivation in culturally disadvantaged school children, in *Research and Development Toward the Improvement of Education*, eds HJ Klausmeirer and GT O'Hearn, Educational Research Services, Madison, WI

Dewhurst, SA, Anderson, RJ, Cotter, G, Crust, L and Clough, PJ (2012) Identifying the cognitive basis of mental toughness: Evidence from the directed forgetting paradigm, *Personality and Individual Differences*, **53**, p 58

Dienstbier, RA (1989) Arousal and physiological toughness: Implications for mental and physical health, *Psychological Review*, **96** (1), pp 84–100

Drinkwater, K, Dagnall, N and Parker, A (2012) Reality testing, conspiracy theories, and paranormal beliefs, *Journal of Parapsychology*, **76**, pp 57–78

Duckworth, AL, Peterson, C, Matthews, MD and Kelly, DR (2007) Grit: Perseverance and passion for long-term goals, *Journal of Personality and Social Psychology*, **92**, pp 1087–91

Dweck, CL (2006) *Mindset: The new psychology of success*, Random House, NY

Dyer, JG and McGuinness, TM (1996) Resilience analysis of the concept, *Archives of Psychiatric Nursing*, vol X, no 5 (October), pp 276–82

Earle, F (2004) The construct of psychological fatigue: A psychometric and experimental analysis, unpublished PhD dissertation, University of Hull

Earle, K and Clough, PJ (2001) When the going gets tough: A study of the impact of mental toughness on perceived demands, *Journal of Sport Sciences*, **19**, p 61

Earle, F, Hockey, GRJ, Earle, K and Clough, PJ (in Press) Separating the effects of task load and task motivation on the effort–fatigue relationship, *Motivation and Emotion*

Easterbrook, J A (1959) The effect of emotion on cue utilization and the organisation of behaviour, *Psychological Review*, **66**, pp 183–201

Evers, WJ, Brouwers, A and Tomic, W (2006) A quasi-experimental study on management coaching effectiveness, *Consulting Psychology Journal: Practice and Research*, **58** (3), pp 174–82

Eysenck, HJ (1967) *The Biological Basis of Personality*, Thomas, Springfield, IL

Fazey, J and Hardy, L (1988) The Inverted-U Hypothesis: A catastrophe for sport psychology? *British Association of Sports Sciences Monograph*, no 1, The National Coaching Foundation, Leeds

Ferrari, JR and Tice, DM (2000) Procrastination as a self-handicap for men and women: A task-avoidance strategy in a laboratory setting, *Journal of Research in Personality*, **34**, pp 73–83

Frankenhaeuser, M (1971) Behavior and circulating catecholamines, *Brain Research*, **31** (August 20), pp 241–62

Funk, FC (1992) Hardiness: A review of theory and research, *Health Psychology*, **11** (5), pp 335–45

Goleman, DJ (1996) *Emotional Intelligence: Why it can matter more than IQ*, Bantam Books, New York

Gould, D, Dieffenbach, K and Moffett, A (2002) Psychological talent and its development in Olympic champions, *Journal of Applied Sport Psychology*, **14**, pp 177–210

Grant, AM (2009) *Workplace, Executive and Life Coaching: An annotated bibliography from the behavioural science and business literature*, Coaching Psychology Unit, University of Sydney, Australia

Green, LS, Grant, AM and Rynsaardt, J (2007) Evidence-based life coaching for senior high school students: Building hardiness and hope, *International Coaching Psychology Review*, **2** (1), pp 24–32

Galluci, NT (2008) *Sport psychology: Performance enhancement, performance inhibition, individuals and teams*, Psychology Press, New York

Gardner, H (1989) *Frames of Mind*, Basic, New York

Gerber, M, Kalak, N, Lemola, K, Clough, PJ, Pühse, U, Holsboer–Trachsler, E, Elliot, C and Brand, S (2012) Adolescents' exercise and physical activity are associated with mental toughness, *Mental Health and Physical Activity*, **5**, pp 35–42

Gerber, M, Kalak, N, Lemola, S, Clough, PJ, Perry, JL, Pühse, U, Elliot, C, Holsboer–Trachsler, E and Brand, S (2013) Are adolescents with high mental toughness levels more resilient against stress? *Stress and Health*, **29**, pp 164–71

Glaser, B and Strauss, A (1967) *The Discovery of Grounded Theory*, Aldine, Chicago, IL

Godlewski, R and Kline, T (2012) A model of voluntary turnover in male Canadian forces recruits, *Military Psychology*, 24, pp 251–69, 201

Golawski, A (2014) Parents' role in developing young people, in *Developing Mental Toughness in Young People*, eds D Strycharczyk and PJ Clough, Karnac, London

Golby, J, Sheard, M and Lavallee, D (2003) A cognitive behavioural analysis of mental toughness in national rugby league football teams, *Perceptual and Motor Skills*, 96, pp 455–62

Golby, J and Sheard, M (2004) Mental toughness and hardiness at different levels of rugby league, *Personality and Individual Differences*, 37, pp 933–42

Goleman, D J (1996) *Emotional Intelligence: Why it can matter more than IQ*, Bantam Books, New York

Goleman, D (1998) *The meditative mind: The varieties of meditative experience*, Tarcher, New York

Gucciardi, D, Gordon, S and Dimmock, J (2008) Towards an understanding of mental toughness in Australian football, *Journal of Applied Sport Psychology*, 20, pp 261–81

Gucciardi, D and Gordon, S (2009) Development and preliminary validation of the Cricket Mental Toughness Inventory (CMTI), *Journal of Sports Sciences*, 27, pp 1293–1310

Gucciardi, D, Gordon, S and Dimmock, JA (2009a) Development and preliminary validation of a mental toughness inventory for Australian football, *Psychology of Sport and Exercise*, 10, pp 201–09

Gucciardi, D, Gordon, S and Dimmock, JA (2009b) Evaluation of a mental toughness training programme for youth-aged Australian footballer: 1 A quantitative analysis, *Journal of Applied Sport Psychology*, 21, pp 307–23

Gustafsson, C and Fagerberg, I (2004) Reflection: the way to professional development? *Journal of Clinical Nursing*, 13, pp 271–80

Hackman, JR and Oldham, GR (1976) Motivation through the design of work: Test the theory, *Organisational Behaviour and Human Performance*, 16, pp 250–79

Hanin, YL (1980) *A Study of Anxiety in Sports*, Mouvement, Ithaca, NY

Hanin, YL (1986) *State and Trait Anxiety Research on Sports in the USSR*, Hemisphere, Washington, DC

Hanin, YL (1997) Emotions and athletic performance: Individual zones of optimal functioning, *European Yearbook of Sport Psychology*, 1, pp 29–72

Hardy, L, Parfitt, G and Pates, J (1994) Performance catastrophes in sport: A test of the hystereris hypothesis, *Journal of Sport Sciences*, 12, pp 327–34

Heider, F (1944) Social perception and phenomological causality, *Psychological Review*, 51, pp 358–74

Heider, F (1958) *The Psychology of Interpersonal Relations*, Wiley, New York

Herzberg, F (1966) *Work and the Nature of Man*, World Publishing, Cleveland

Hockey, GRJ (2013) *The Psychology of Fatigue: Work, effort and control*, Cambridge University Press

Holloway, SD (1988) Concepts of ability and effort in Japan and the United States, *Review of Educational Research*, 58 (3), pp 327–45

Horsburgh, V, Schermer, J, Veselka, L and Vernon, P (2009) A behavioral genetic study of mental toughness and personality, *Personality and Individual Differences*, **46**, pp 100–05

Hull, CL (1943) *Principles of Behaviour*, Appleton-Century-Crofts, New York

Hull, CL (1951) *Essentials of Behaviour*, Appleton-Century-Crofts, New York

Irwin, HJ (2004) Reality testing and the formation of paranormal beliefs: A constructive replication, *Journal of the Society for Psychical Research*, **68**, pp 43–152

Irwin, HJ, Dagnall, N and Drinkwater, K (2012) Paranormal beliefs and cognitive processes underlying the formation of delusions, *Australian Journal of Parapsychology*, **12**, pp 107–26

Jackson, SA (1992) Athletes in flow: A qualitative investigation of flow states in elite figure skaters, *Journal of Applied Sport Psychology*, **4**, pp 161–80

Jackson, SA (1995) Factors influencing the occurrence of flow state in elite athletes, *Journal of Applied Sport Psychology*, **7**, pp 138–66

Jackson, SA (1996) Toward a conceptual understanding of the flow experience in elite athletes, *Research Quarterly for Exercise and Sport*, **67**, pp 76–90

Jackson, R and Watkin, C (2004) The resilience inventory: Seven essential skills for overcoming life's obstacles and determining happiness, *Selection and Development Review*, **20** (6), pp 13–17

Jones, CM (1982) Mental toughness, *World Bowls*, pp 30–31

Jones, G (1993) The role of performance profiling in cognitive behaviour interventions in sport, *The Sport Psychologist*, **7**, pp 160–72

Jones, G and Hanton, S (1996) Interpretation of competitive anxiety symptoms and goal attainment expectancies, *Journal of Sport and Exercise Psychology*, **18**, pp 144–57

Jones, G and Hanton, S (2001) Pre-competitive feeling states and directional anxiety interpretations, *Journal of Sports Sciences*, **19**, pp 385–95

Jones, G, Hanton, S and Connaughton, D (2002) What is this thing called mental toughness? An investigation of elite sport performers, *Journal of Applied Sport Psychology*, **14**, pp 205–18

Jones, G, Hanton, S and Connaughton, D (2007) A framework of mental toughness in the world's best performers, *The Sport Psychologist*, **21**, pp 243–64

Kabat-Zinn, J (1994) *Wherever you go, there you are: Mindfulness mediation for everyday life*, Piatkus, London

Kaiseler, M, Polman, R and Nicholls, A (2009) Mental toughness, stress, stress appraisal, coping and coping effectiveness in sport, *Personality and Individual Differences*, **47**, pp 728–33

Karasek, RA (1979) Job demands, job decision latitude, and mental strain: Implications for job redesign, *Administrative Science Quarterly*, **24**, pp 288–308

Kobasa, SC (1979) Stressful life events, personality, and health: An inquiry into hardiness, *Journal of Personality and Social Psychology*, **37** (1), pp 1–11

Kobasa, SC, Maddi, SR and Kahn, S (1982) Hardiness and health: A prospective study, *Journal of Personality and Social Psychology*, **42**, pp 168–77

Larsen, R (1984) Theory and measurement of affect intensity as an individual difference characteristic, *Dissertation Abstracts International*, **5**, 2297B (University microfilms No 84–22112)

Larsen, R, Diener, E and Cropanzano, R (1987) Cognitive operations associated with individual differences in affect intensity, *Journal of Personality and Social Psychology*, **53**, pp 767–74

Lazarus, RS (1966) *Psychological Stress and the Coping Process*, McGraw–Hill, New York

Lazarus, RS (1993) Coping theory and research: Past, present, and future, *Psychosomatic Medicine*, **55**, pp 234–47

Levy, A, Polman, R, Clough, P, Marchant, D and Earle, K (2006) Mental toughness as a determinant of beliefs, pain, and adherence in sport injury rehabilitation, *Journal of Sports Rehabilitation*, **15**, pp 246–54

Locke, EA (1968) Towards a theory of task motivation and incentives, *Organisational Behaviour and Human Performance*, **3**, pp 157–89

Locke, EA, Shaw, KN, Saari, LM and Latham, GP (1981) Goal setting and task performance (1969–1980), *Psychological Bulletin*, **96**, pp 125–52

Locke, E A and Latham, G P (1990) *A Theory of Goal Setting and Task Performance*, Prentice Hall, Englewood Cliffs, NJ

Locke, EA and Latham, GP (2002) Building a practically useful theory of goal setting and task motivation: A 35-year odyssey, *American Psychologist*, **57**, pp 701–17

Loehr, JE (1982) *Athletic Excellence: Mental toughness training for sport*, pp 58–70, Forum Publishing Company

Loehr, JE (1986) *Mental Toughness Training for Sports: Achieving athletic excellence*, Stephen Greene Press, Lexington, MA

Loehr, JE (1995) *The New Toughness Training for Sports*, Plume Publishers, New York

McCleary, RA (2007) The nature of galvanic skin response, *Psychological Bulletin*, **47** (2), pp 97–117

McClelland, DC (1962) Business drive and national achievement, *Harvard Business Review*, July–August, pp 99–112

McCrae, RR and Costa, PT, Jr (1987) Validation of the five–factor model of personality across instruments and observers, *Journal of Personality and Social Psychology*, **52**, pp 81–90

McGeown, S, St Clair-Thompson, H and Clough, PJ (in Press) The study of non–cognitive attributes in education: Proposing the mental toughness framework, *Educational Review*

Maddi, SR (2004) Hardiness: An operationalization of existential courage, *Journal of Humanistic Psychology*, **44** (3), pp 279–98

Maddi, SR, Hoover, M and Kobasa, SC (1982) Alienation and exploratory behaviour, *Journal of Personality and Social Psychology*, May, **42** (5), pp 884–90

Maddi, SR and Khoshaba, DM (2001) *Personal views survey* (3rd edn rev), The Hardiness Institute, Newport Beach, CA

Marchant, D, Polman, R, Clough, P, Jackson, J, Levy, A and Nicholls, A (2009) Mental toughness: Managerial and age differences, *Journal of Managerial Psychology*, **24**, pp 428–37

Martens, R, Burton, D, Vealey, RS, Bump, LA and Smith, DE (1990) The Competitive State Anxiety Inventory-2 (CSAI-2), in *Competitive Anxiety in*

Sport, eds R Martens, RS Vealey and D Burton, pp 117–90, Human Kinetics, Champaign, IL

Martin, AJ and Marsh, HW (2006) Academic resilience and its psychological and educational correlates: A construct validity approach, *Psychology in the School*, **43**, pp 267–81

Martin, AJ and Marsh, HW (2008) Workplace and academic buoyancy: Psychometric assessment and construct validity amongst school personnel and students, *Journal of Psychoeducational Assessment*, **26**, pp 169–84

Maslach, C (1976) Burned-out, *Human Behavior*, **5** (9), pp 16–22

Maslow, A (1943) A Theory of Human Motivation, *Psychological Review*, **50**, pp 370–96

Mento, AJ, Steele, RP and Karren, RJ (1987) A meta–analytic study of the effects of goal setting on task performance: 1966–1984, *Organizational Behaviour and Human Decision Processes*, **39**, pp 52–83

Middleton, SC, Marsh, HW, Martin, AJ, Richards, GE, Savis, J, Perry, C and Brown, R (2004) The Psychological Performance Inventory: Is the mental toughness test tough enough? *International Journal of Sport Psychology*, **35**, pp 91–108

Mitchell, L (1977) *Simple Relaxation: The Mitchell method for easing tension*, Butler and Tanner, London

Mitchell, L (1990) *Simple Relaxation: The Mitchell method for easing tension*, new edn, John Murray, London

Moss, GE (1973) *Illness, immunity, and social interaction*, Wiley, New York

Murray, HA (1938) *Explorations in Personality*, Oxford University Press, New York

Neff, KD (2003) Self-compassion: An alternative conceptualisation of a healthy attitude toward oneself, *Self and Identity*, **2**, pp 85–102

Nesti, M (2010) *Psychology in Football*, Routledge, London

Nesti, M (2004) *Existential Psychology and Sport: Theory and application*, Routledge, London

Nicholls, A and Polman, R (2007) Coping in sport: A systematic review, *Journal of Sport Sciences*, **25**, pp 11–31

Nicholls, A, Polman, R, Levy, A and Backhouse, S (2008) Mental toughness, optimism, and coping among athletes, *Personality and Individual Differences*, **44**, pp 1182–92

Nicholls, A, Polman, R, Levy, A and Backhouse, S (2009) Mental toughness in sport: Achievement level, gender, age, experience, and sport type differences, *Personality and Individual Differences*, **47**, pp 73–75

Nicholls, AR, Perry, JL, Jones, L, Sanctuary, C, Carson, F and Clough, PJ (in Press) The mediating role of mental toughness in sport, *Journal of Sports Medicine and Physical Fitness*

Onley, M, Veselka, L, Shermer, JA and Vernon, PA (2013) Survival of the scheming: A generically informed link between the dark triad and mental toughness, *Twin Research and Human Genetics*, **16**, pp 1087–93

Pask, EJ (2003) Moral agency in nursing: Seeing value in the work and believing that I make a difference, *Nursing Ethics*, **10**, pp 165– 74

Peddicord, K (1991) Strategies for promoting stress reduction and relaxation, *Nursing Clinics in North America*, **26**, pp 867–74

Perry, JL, Clough, PJ, Crust, L, Earle, K and Nicholls, AR (2013) Factorial validity of the Mental Toughness Questionnaire48, *Personality and Individual Differences*, **54**, pp 587–92

Perry, JL (2014) Sport and its role in developing young people, in *Developing Mental Toughness in Young People*, eds D Strycharczyk and PJ Clough, Karnac, London

Peterson, C and Barrett, LC (1987) Explanatory style and academic performance among university freshmen, *Journal of Personality and Social Psychology*, **53**, pp 603–07

Putwain, DW, Nicholson, LJ, Connors, L and Woods, K (2013) Resilient children are less test anxious and perform better in tests at the end of primary schooling, *Learning and Individual Differences*, **28**, pp 41–46

Rhodewalt, F and Agustsdottir, S (1984) On the relationship of hardiness to the Type A behavior pattern: Perception of life events versus coping with life events, *Journal of Research in Personality*, **18**, pp 212–23

Rotter, J B (1966) Generalised expectancies for internal versus external control of reinforcement, *Psychological Monographs: General and Applied*, **80** (1), all of no 609

Rutter, M (1985) Resilience in the face of adversity: Protective factors and resistance in psychiatric disorder, *British Journal of Psychiatry*, **147** (1,) pp 598–611

St Clair-Thompson, H, Bugler, M, Robinson, J, Clough, PJ, McGeown, S and Perry, JL (in Press) Mental toughness in education: Exploring relationships with attainment, attendance, behaviour and peer relationships, *Educational Psychology: An International Journal of Experimental Educational Psychology*

Salt, VL and Kerr, KM (1997) Mitchell's simple physiological relaxation and Jacobson's progressive relaxation techniques: A comparison, *Physiotherapy*, **83** (4), pp 200–07

Sappington, AA (1990) The independent manipulation of intellectually and emotionally based beliefs, *Journal of Research in Personality*, **24**, pp 487–509

Schwarz, RS (1975) Another look at immunologic surveillance, *New England Journal of Medicine*, **293**, pp 181–84

Selye, H (1936) A syndrome produced by diverse agents, *Nature*, **138** (32), pp 112–31

Selye, H (1950) *Stress*, Acta, Montreal

Selye, H (1976) *The stress of life*, 2nd edn, McGraw-Hill, New York

Selye, H (1983) The stress concept: Past, present, and future, in *Stress research*, ed CL Cooper, pp 1–20, John Wiley & Sons, New York

Seligman, MEP and Groves, D (1970) Non–transient learned helplessness, *Psychonomic Science*, **19**, pp 191–92

Seligman, MEP, Maier, SF and Solomon, RL (1971) Consequences of unpredictable and uncontrollable trauma, in *Aversive conditioning and Learning*, ed FR Brush, Academic Press, New York

Seligman, MEP (1972) Learned helplessness, *Annual Review of Medicine*, **23**, pp 407–12

Seligman, MEP (1975) *Helplessness*, Freeman, San Francisco, CA

Seligman, MEP and Beagley, G (1975) Learned helplessness in the rat, *Journal of Comparative and Physiological Psychology*, **88**, pp 534–41

Sheard, M (2010) *Mental Toughness: The mindset behind sporting achievement*, Routledge, London, UK

Sheard, M and Golby, J (2006) Effect of psychological skills training program on swimming performance and positive psychological development, *International Journal of Sport and Exercise Psychology*, **2**, pp 7–24

Spence, G and Grant, AM (2007) Professional and peer life coaching and the enhancement of goal striving and well-being: An exploratory study, *Journal of Positive Psychology*, **2** (3), pp 185–94

Spence, JT and Helmreich, RL (1983) Achievement-related motives and behaviours, in *Achievement and Achievement Motives: Psychological and sociological approaches*, ed JT Spence, pp 7–74, WH Freeman, San Francisco, CA

Spielberger, CD (1983) *Manual for the State Trait Anxiety Inventory*, Consulting Psychologists Press Inc, Palo Alto, CA

Stamp, E, Crust, L, Perry, JL, Swann, C, Clough, PJ and Marchant, D (2015) Relationships between mental toughness and psychological wellbeing in undergraduate students, *Personality and Individual Differences*, **75**, pp 170–74

Strycharczyk, D and Elvin, C (2014) *Developing Resilient Organisations*, Karnac, London

Tenenbaum, G (1984) A note on the measurement and relationships of physiological and psychological components of anxiety, *International Journal of Sport Psychology*, **15**, pp 88–97

Thelwell, R, Such, B, Weston, N, Such, J and Greenlees, I (2010) Developing mental toughness: Perceptions of elite female gymnasts, *International Journal of Sport and Exercise Psychology*, **8**, pp 170–88

Thomas, P, Murphy, S and Hardy, L (1999) Test of performance strategies: Development and preliminary validation of a comprehensive measure of athletes' psychological skills, *Journal of Sports Sciences*, **17**, pp 697–711

Tough, P (2014) *How Children Succeed*, Arrow, London

van der Cingel, M (2009) Compassion and professional care: Exploring the domain, *Nursing Philosophy*, **10**, pp 124–36

van Yperen, N (2009) Why some make it and others do not: Identifying psychological factors that predict career success in professional adult soccer, *The Sport Psychologist*, **23**, pp 317–29

Veselka, L, Schermer, JA, Martin, RA and Vernon, PL (2010) Laughter and resiliency: A behavioural genetic study of humour styles and mental toughness, *Twin Research and Human Genetics*, **13**, pp 442–49

Weiner, B (1972) *Theories of Motivation: From mechanics to cognition*, Markham, Chicago

Weiss, JM, Glazer, HI, Pohorecky, LA, Brick, J and Miller, NB (1975) Effects of chronic exposure to stressors on avoidance–escape behavior and on brain norepinephrine, *Psychosomatic Medicine*, **37**, pp 153–60

Westman, M (1990) The relationship between stress and performance: The moderating effect of hardiness, *Human Performance*, **3**, pp 141–55

Whitmore, J (2002) *Coaching for Performance*, 3rd edn, Nicholas Brealey, London

Wickens, CD (1986) The effects of control dynamics on performance, in *Handbook of perception and performance*, eds KR Boff, L Kaufman, and JP Thomas, vol II, pp 39–1/39–60, Wiley and Sons, New York

Williams, RM (1988) The US open character test: Good strokes help, but the most individualistic of sports is ultimately a mental game, *Psychology Today*, **22**, pp 60–62

Williams, JM and Krane, V (1993) Psychological characteristics of peak performance in *Applied Sport Psychology*, ed JM Williams, 2nd edn, pp 137–47, Mayfield, Palo Alto, CA

Wiseman, R (2003) *The Luck Factor*, Random House, London

Yerkes, RM and Dodson, JD (1908) The relationship of strength of stimulus to rapidity of habit formation, *Journal of Comparative Neurology and Psychology*, **18**, pp 459–82

Yorke, M (2004) *Employability in Higher Education: what it is – what it is not*, Higher Education Academy/ESECT

Zalewski, AM and Krzywosz-Rynkiewicz, B (2014) Personality and profiles of citizenship behaviour among young people, *Personality and Individual Differences*, 60, S38

INDEX

Page numbers in *italic* indicate figures or tables.